Daily Learning Drills

Grade 2

An imprint of Carson-Dellosa Publishing LLC
Greensboro, North Carolina

Brighter Child®
An imprint of Carson-Dellosa Publishing LLC
P.O. Box 35665
Greensboro, NC 27425 USA

ISBN 978-1-4838-0085-1

01-034147784

Table of Contents

Name _____

Food for Gregory

Print Gregory's food in ABC order. Then draw each meal on the plate.

Breakfast

tin can   juice
eggs   ham

Eggs ham
ham
juice

Lunch

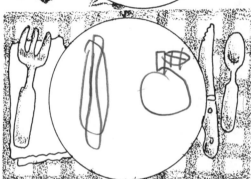

milk   rubber boot
hot dog   apple

Hot dog appel

Dinner

shoe   fish
carrots   bread

fish carrots
bread

Draw what you ate yesterday for breakfast, lunch and dinner on these plates.

Breakfast   **Lunch**   **Dinner**

Name _____

Which Part Shall I Play?

Grace loves to act out stories. Read the list of characters. Then write them in alphabetical order.

Joan of Arc
Anansi
Peter Pan
Juliet
Captain Hook
Hiawatha
Wendy
Romeo
Mowgli
Aladdin

1. Joan of Arc
2. Anansi
3. Hiawatha
4. Mowgli
5. Aladdin
6. Juliet
7. Romeo
8. Peter Pan
9. _____
10. _____

Name _____

Which Way?

Read the words in the Word Bank. Write them in alphabetical order on the lines.

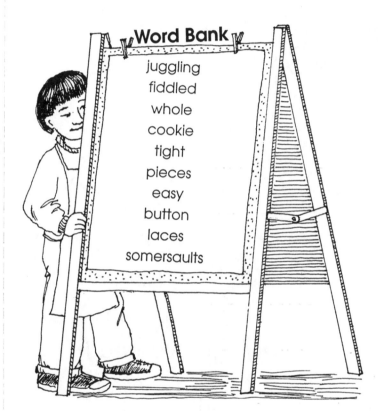

Word Bank

juggling
fiddled
whole
cookie
tight
pieces
easy
button
laces
somersaults

1. _____

2. _____

3. _____

4. _____

5. _____

6. _____

7. _____

8. _____

9. _____

10. _____

Write the missing lowercase letters in alphabetical order.

___ ___ c ___ ___ ___ ___ h ___ ___ k ___ ___

___ o ___ ___ ___ ___ ___ u ___ ___ x ___ ___

ABC Potion

Name _____

Write the words in alphabetical order.

1. always
2. baron
3. control
4. drink
5. flashes
6. _____
7. _____
8. _____
9. _____
10. _____
11. _____
12. _____
13. _____
14. _____
15. _____

point
scientist
world
lightning
hard
baron
flashed
monster
rumbled
control
ketchup
overhead
drink
thunder
always

Name _____

Crazy Creatures

Draw a line to each letter in ABC order to finish this dot-to-dot picture.

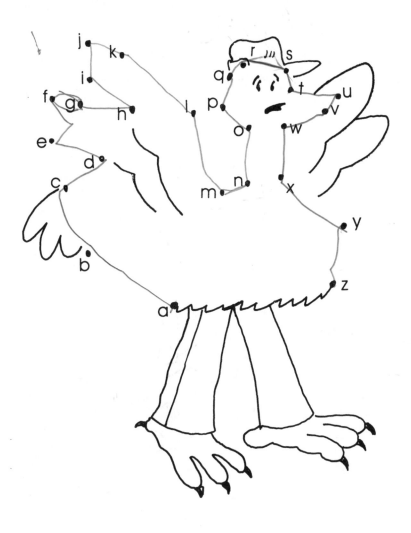

Now color and add details to the picture. Then write all the consonants in order on these lines.

1. _____   5. _____   9. _____   13. _____   17. _____   21. _____

2. _____   6. _____   10. _____   14. _____   18. _____

3. _____   7. _____   11. _____   15. _____   19. _____

4. _____   8. _____   12. _____   16. _____   20. _____

Name _____

Alphabet Soup

Nan Cook has a special way of making alphabet soup. She mixes two boxes of soup together. Then she adds two secret ingredients — mystery and fun. After the soup is cooked, a strange thing happens. All the vowels rise to the top of the pot.

Write the consonant that can be used in both the front and back of each vowel or pair of vowels to make a word. One is done for you.

peep   _ a _

_ o _   _ a _

_ o _   _ o _   _ ee _

_ oo _   _ i _   _ u _

_ o _   _ u _   _ i _   _ o _

_ o _   _ u _   _ u _

_ i _   _ oo _   _ e _

_ ee _   _ a _

_ i _

Name

Stretch and Grow

Goofy Gladys got new glasses. The glasses had springs on them which stretched words out and then added another vowel to each one.

Add a vowel to each word below to see what words Gladys saw through her glasses.

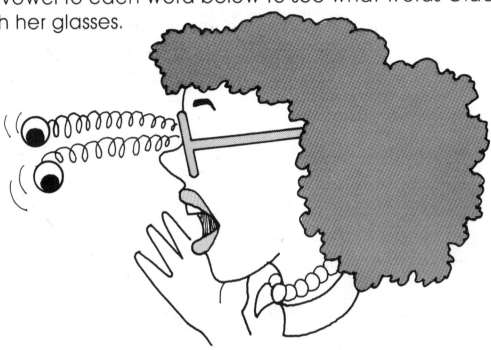

1. pal   pa __ l

2. fed   fe __ d

3. chin   ch __ in

4. ran   ra __ n

5. cat   c __ at

6. Jon   jo __ n

7. shut   sh __ ut

8. bran   bra __ n

9. lid   l __ id

10. hat   h __ at

11. bad   b __ ad

12. flat   fl __ at

13. bit   b __ it

14. pin   p __ in

15. men   me __ n

Name _____

Motorcycle Maze

Help Ralph move through the maze to the Mountain View Inn by tracing over the path in which all of the words have two syllables.

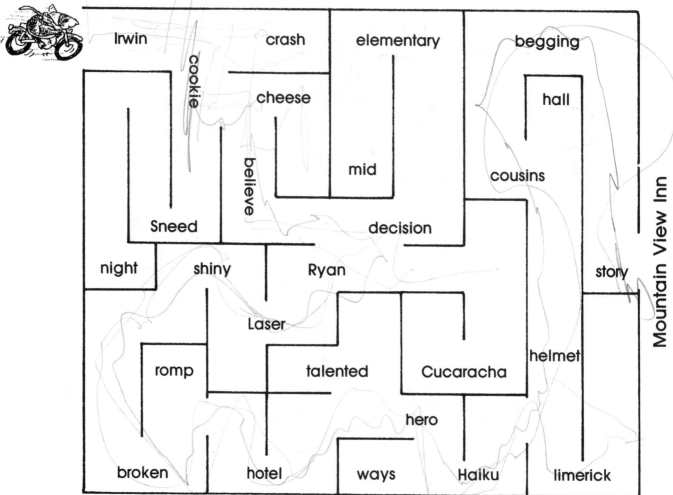

Now write the words from the correct path in alphabetical order on the lines below.

1. _____   8. _____
2. _____   9. _____
3. _____   10. _____
4. _____   11. _____
5. _____   12. _____
6. _____   13. _____
7. _____   14. _____

Name _____

Trick or Treat Syllables

Think about how many syllables are in each word in the Word Bank. Then write each word on the correct jack-o'-lantern.

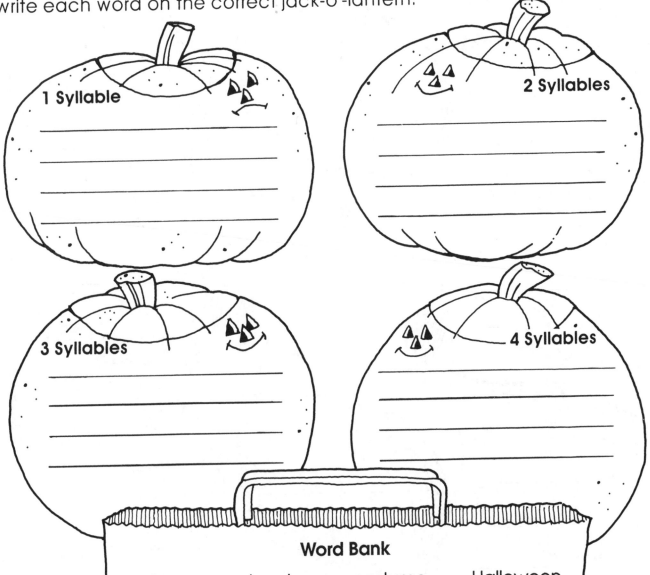

1 Syllable

2 Syllables

3 Syllables

4 Syllables

Word Bank

voice	elevator	costume	Halloween
clothes	pirate	faraway	anybody
masks	spooky	princess	apartment
invited	ghost	escalator	evaporate

All Together Now

Name _____

Match a word in the Word Bank with a word on a feather to make a compound word. Then write it on the line.

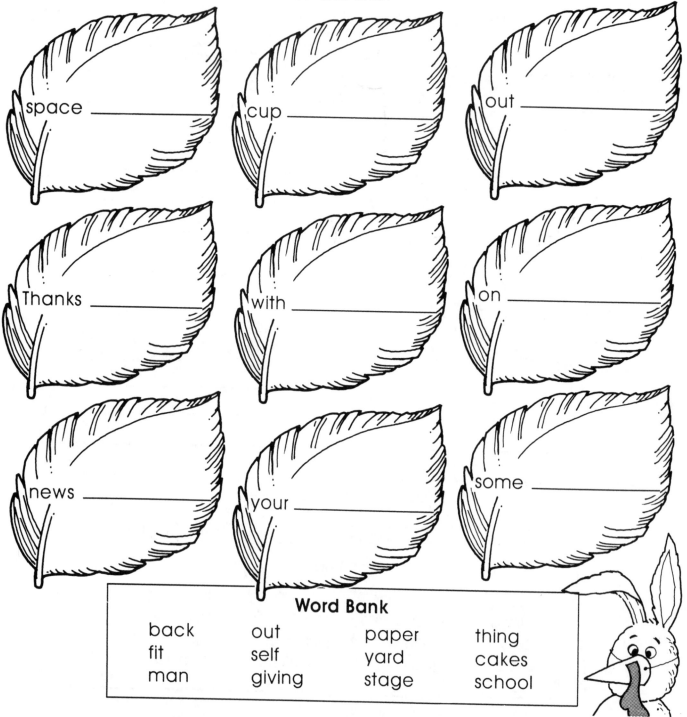

space _____

cup _____

out _____

Thanks _____

with _____

on _____

news _____

your _____

some _____

Word Bank

back	out	paper	thing
fit	self	yard	cakes
man	giving	stage	school

Name _____

Word Magic

Maggie Magician announced, "One plus one equals one!" The audience giggled. So Maggie put two words into a hat and waved her magic wand. When she reached into the hat, Maggie pulled out one word and a picture. "See," said Maggie, "I was right!"

Look at each picture below. Use the Word Bank to help write a compound word for each.

_____

_____

_____

_____

_____

_____

_____

_____

_____

_____

_____

Word Bank

ball	door	rain
basket	ear	shirt
bell	fish	shoe
book	foot	star
bow	lace	stool
box	light	sun
cake	mail	tail
cup	phone	worm

_____

_____

Name _____

Compound Your Effort

Read each word. Find the word in the Word Bank that goes with it to make a compound word. Cross it out. Then write the compound word on the line.

1. coat _____
2. snow _____
3. home _____
4. waste _____
5. tip _____

6. chalk _____
7. note _____
8. grass _____
9. school _____
10. with _____

Look at the words in the Word Bank you did not use. Use those words to make your own compound words.

1. _____
2. _____
3. _____
4. _____
5. _____

Word Bank			
board	room	thing	side
writing	book	hopper	toe
bag	ball	class	where
work	out	basket	

Name _____

Mystery Word Mix-Up

Put on your detective hat! How many words can you make using only the letters in the words:

N a t e   t h e   G r e a t

1. _____
2. _____
3. _____
4. _____
5. _____
6. _____
7. _____
8. _____
9. _____
10. _____
11. _____

12. _____
13. _____
14. _____
15. _____
16. _____
17. _____
18. _____
19. _____
20. _____
21. _____
22. _____

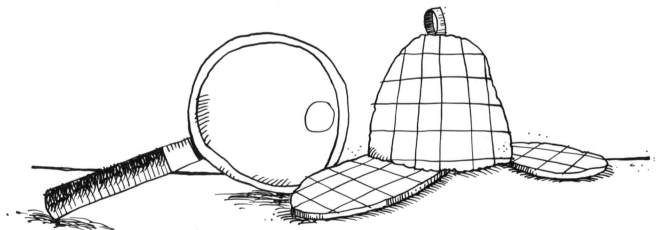

Name _____

Flower Fun

Find words in the Word Bank that are synonyms for the words in the leaves.
Write them on the leaves.

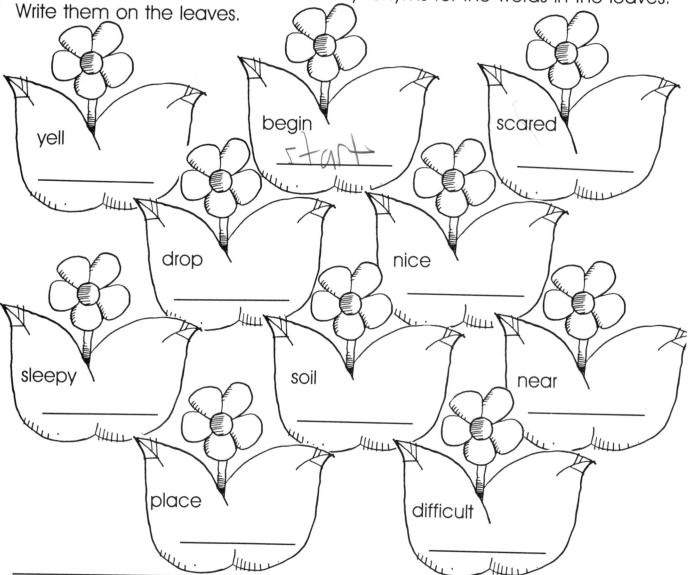

yell

begin
start

scared

drop

nice

sleepy

soil

near

place

difficult

Word Bank

pick	start	easy	sky
kind	rain	afraid	fall
close	hard	scream	awake
put	whisper	dirt	tired

14

Where?

Name _____

Read each word on the left. Find its synonym in the Word Bank and write it on the line.

1. below _____

2. drummed _____

3. hear _____

4. scrambled _____

5. over _____

6. close _____

7. slipped _____

8. woods _____

9. spring _____

10. cleaned _____

11. sturdy _____

12. paths _____

13. perhaps _____

14. house _____

15. evening _____

Word Bank

above

listen

shut

maybe

beneath

forest

leap

tapped

home

hurried

strong

sunset

trails

washed

slid

Name _____

Who's Afraid?

Help Frog and Toad escape from the snake. Read the two words in each space. If the words are antonyms, color the space green. Do not color the other spaces.

Toad's House

Name _____

Should We Wake Them?

Read the words on each of the pillows. Find a word in the Word Bank that means the opposite and write it on the line.

sold	off	first
_____	_____	_____

hated	warm	front
_____	_____	_____

remembered	small	to
_____	_____	_____

yours	everybody	early
_____	_____	_____

Word Bank

bought	on	all	tiny
nobody	big	last	late
ahead	mine	from	cool
forgotten	loved	back	

Name _____

Flying Free Like an Eagle

Read the beginning of each sentence. Draw a line to the words on the feather that best complete each sentence.

1. The strong stallion fought like...

2. The bolt of lightning lit the sky like...

3. The wild horses roamed the hills as free as...

4. The thunder roared like...

5. The running herd crossed the land like...

6. The stallion's eyes were as cold as...

7. The hills were as dark as...

8. The rising sun was like...

the wind.

a wave rolling to shore.

a match being lit on a dark night.

a panther's coat.

a mighty warrior.

an arching rainbow.

an ice-covered pond.

an angry lion.

Name _____

Rain, Rain Go Away!

Read the naming parts in the tent.

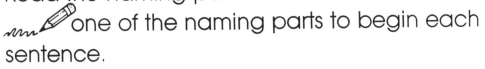 one of the naming parts to begin each sentence.

Rain
Black clouds
A big wind
The campfire
Todd and Clint
The old green tent

1. _____ went camping.

2. _____ was hard to set up.

3. _____ blew the trees.

4. _____ filled the sky.

5. _____ ran off the tent.

6. _____ went out.

Daily Learning Drills Grade 2

Name _____

It Takes Many Colors

Read the words in the Word Bank. If the word means one, write it on the paint jar. If the word means more than one, write it on the paintbrushes.

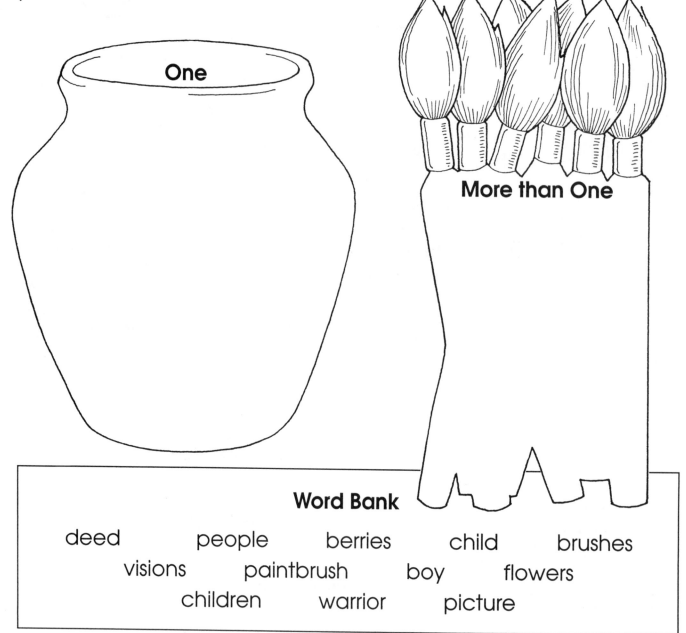

One

More than One

Word Bank

deed   people   berries   child   brushes

visions   paintbrush   boy   flowers

children   warrior   picture

Name _____

Fun Around the Campfire

Word Bank

beat	sang	told
danced	sat	wore

✏ a verb in each sentence below. Use the word bank to help you.

1. The boys and girls _____ around the campfire.

2. They _____ songs.

3. Brian _____ a drum.

4. Jerry and Helen _____ Indian costumes.

5. They _____ around the campfire.

6. The teacher _____ stories.

Name _____

It's Time 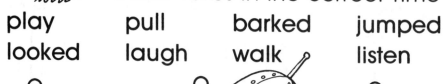 these verbs in the correct Time Machine.

play   pull   barked   jumped   danced
looked   laugh   walk   listen   lived

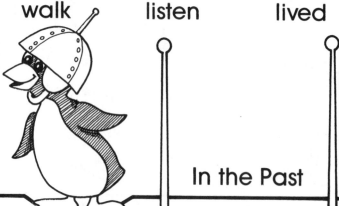

Now   In the Past

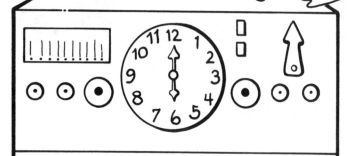
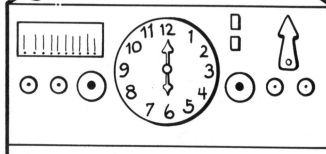

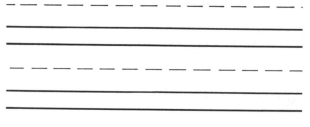

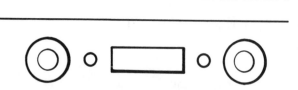
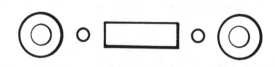

Name _____

I Was. Were You?

Use "was" and "were" to tell about something that happened in the past. Use "was" to tell about one person or thing. Use "were" to tell about more than one person or thing. Always use "were" with the word "you."

"was" or "were" in each sentence below.

1. Lois _____ in the second grade last year.

2. She _____ eight years old.

3. Carmen and Judy _____ friends.

4. They _____ on the same soccer team.

5. I _____ on the team, too.

6. You _____ too young to play.

Name _____

Playing in the Summer Sun

Look at the picture. Read the sentence. Circle the missing word. Then write it on the line.

It is _____
_____ .

rain   **raining**

He can _____
the boat. _____

row   **rowing**

The kite is _____
_____ .

fly   **flying**

He is _____
_____ .

swing   **swinging**

He is _____
_____ .

pick   **picking**

Name _____

An Owlish Activity
Write the words where they belong.

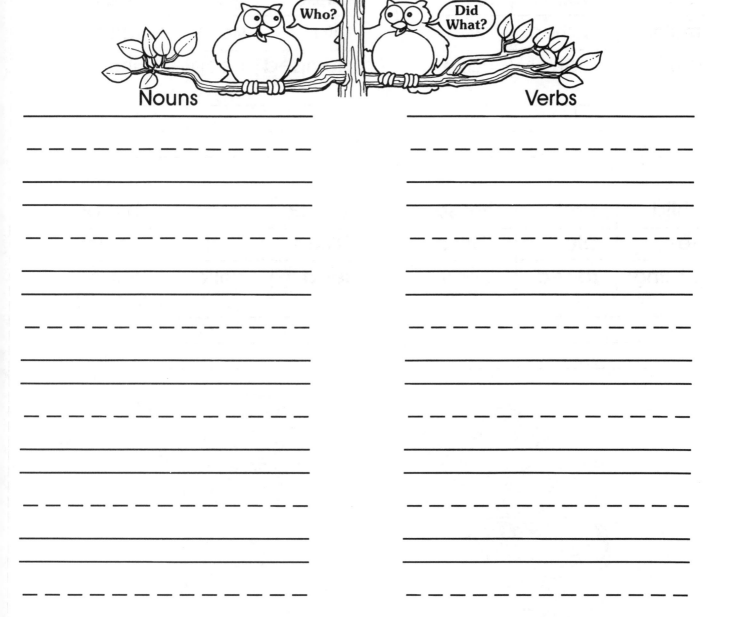

Word Bank

| bite | school | children | skip | donkey | house |
| jump | lunchbox | kitten | write | hop | run |

Nouns

Verbs

Flip Fun! Draw a picture of one of the nouns.

Name _____

Tic-Tac-Toe

Circle all of the naming words (nouns).
Put an **X** on all of the doing words (verbs).
Under each game, write the **X** words that scored a tic-tac-toe.

boy	well	fell
mother	wished	ladder
ran	man	cake

_____

_____

_____

fished	water	book
told	stone	lamp
pumped	people	shoe

_____

_____

_____

child	sent	house
tree	ate	China
Chang	raced	body

_____

_____

_____

paper	bear	bridge
Tikki	table	flower
read	yelled	jump

_____

_____

_____

Name _____

Picking Pronouns

LANGUAGE ARTS

> The words *he, she, it,* and *they* can be used in place of a noun.

Read the sentence pairs. Write the correct pronoun in each blank.

1. John won first place.
   _____ got a blue ribbon.

2. Janet and Gail rode on a bus.
   _____ went to visit their grandmother.

3. Sarah had a birthday party.
   _____ invited six friends to the party.

4. The kitten likes to play.
   _____ likes to tug on shoelaces.

5. Ed is seven years old.
   _____ is in the second grade.

Name _____

Marvelous Me!

You are a very special person!

Draw hair and eyes on the body below to make it look like you. Then use the describing words listed in the box to label your beautiful body parts. Be sure to label each part with a describing word that begins with the same letter. Write a story about how each part of your body is special.

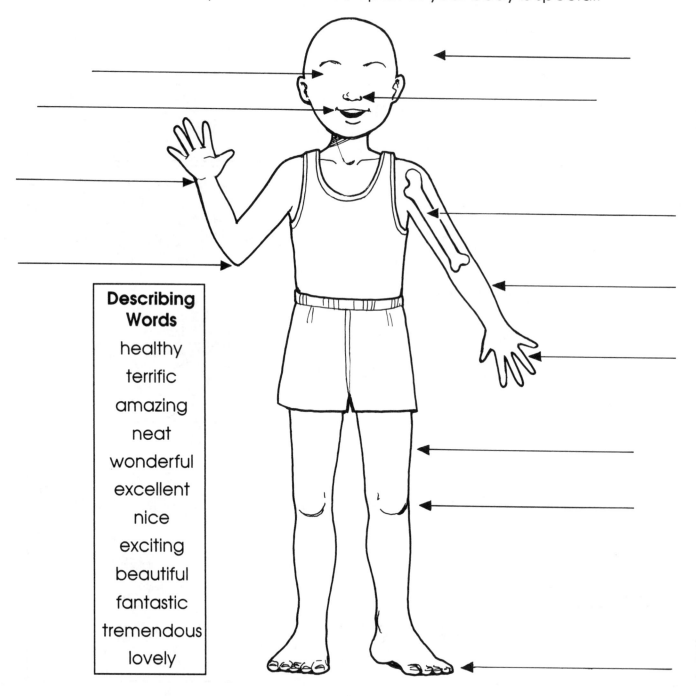

Describing Words

healthy

terrific

amazing

neat

wonderful

excellent

nice

exciting

beautiful

fantastic

tremendous

lovely

Name _____

Add the Adjectives

Read each sentence. Write a describing word on each line. Draw a picture to match each sentence.

High Mountain

The _____ flag waved over the _____ building.

A _____ lion searched for food in the _____ jungle.

We saw _____ fish in the _____ aquarium.

Her _____ car was parked by the _____ van.

The _____ dog barked and chased the _____ truck.

The _____ building was filled with _____ packages.

Wordy Treats

Name _____

Write the word from the Word Bank on the correct trick or treat bag. If the word **names** a person, place or thing, write it on the bag marked **Nouns**. If the word **describes** something, write it on the bag marked **Adjectives**.

Nouns

1. _____
2. _____
3. _____
4. _____
5. _____
6. _____
7. _____
8. _____
9. _____

Adjectives

1. _____
2. _____
3. _____
4. _____
5. _____
6. _____
7. _____
8. _____
9. _____

Word Bank

costumes	elevator	pirate	fifth
ghosts	spooky	robot	bossy
party	squeaky	scary	stairs
special	wings	high	crown
	heavy	silly	

Name _____

Summer Camp

A telling sentence begins with a capital letter and ends with a period. Write each telling sentence correctly on the lines.

1. everyone goes to breakfast at 6:30 each morning

_____

2. only three people can ride in one canoe

_____

3. each person must help clean the cabins

_____

4. older campers should help younger campers

_____

5. all lights are out by 9:00 each night

_____

6. everyone should write home at least once a week

_____

Daily Learning Drills Grade 2

Tell-a-vision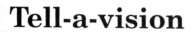

Name _____

Look at each TV picture. Write a telling sentence about each program.

_____

_____

_____

_____

_____

_____

_____

_____

_____

_____

_____

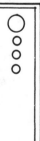

Name _____

Telephone Talk

An asking sentence is called a question. A question begins with a capital letter and ends with a question mark.

these questions correctly.

1. how old are you

_____

_ _ _ _ _ _ _ _ _ _ _ _ _ _

_____

2. are you in second grade

_____

_ _ _ _ _ _ _ _ _ _ _ _ _ _

_____

3. who is your teacher

_____

_ _ _ _ _ _ _ _ _ _ _ _ _ _

_____

4. did you read that book

_____

_ _ _ _ _ _ _ _ _ _ _ _ _ _

_____

5. where do you live

_____

_ _ _ _ _ _ _ _ _ _ _ _ _ _

_____

Name _____

Asking Questions

Look at the picture. Write **five** asking sentences about the picture.

_____

_____

_____

_____

_____

Name _____

That Doesn't Make Sense!

A sentence must make sense. Read each sentence. Put an **X** on the **two** words which do not belong. Write the corrected sentence on the lines below.

My neighbor is orange having a yard very sale.

1. _____

_____

She is snow selling lots of old things phone.

2. _____

_____

A man until is buying five candle old books.

3. _____

_____

My brother is buying an salt old checkers it game.

4. _____

_____

Two ladies pull are buying an old touch toy chest.

5. _____

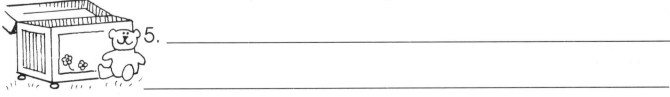

_____

Name _____

Flight to Fun

Would you like to fly away for a fun trip? Write words about a trip on the plane. Use the words to write five sentences about the trip.

1. _____

2. _____

3. _____

4. _____

5. _____

Name _____

About Me

That Go?

Sente correctly. Be sure to put **STAP** ods and exclamation h y belong.

ffy spoke the words very quietly

STAP Uffy _____

_____

2. buster said that the pilgrims sailed on a ship named the mayflower

_____

_____

3. francine said, "i will not play the part of a turkey "

_____

_____

4. arthur thought about turkeys while he and d w did dishes

_____

_____

5. arthur worried about finding a turkey

_____

_____

6. everyone looked at the audience and said, "happy thanksgiving "

_____

_____

Name _____

Punctuation Magic

Write the sentences correctly. Be sure to put capital letters, periods and question marks where they belong.

1. mrs paris talked to richard, alex, matthew and emily about the trip to the museum

_____

_____

_____

2. the children read a story about a king who was greedy

_____

_____

3. everyone but richard drew a picture about the story

_____

_____

4. why was drake sick

_____

_____

5. mrs gates asked matthew to take homework to drake

_____

_____

6. did richard's wish make drake sick

_____

_____

Name _____

An Excellent Exercise

The words *a* and *an* help point out a noun. Use *a* before a word that begins with a consonant. Use *an* before a word that begins with a vowel or a vowel sound.

1. Our class visited _____ farm.

2. We could only stay _____ hour.

3. A man let us pick eggs out of _____ nest.

4. We saw _____ egg that was cracked.

5. We watched _____ lady milk a cow.

6. We got to eat _____ ice cream cone.

Name _____

Add an Apostrophe

Add **'s** to a noun to show who or what **owns** something.

 the correct word under each picture.

The ____ nose is big.
clown   clowns   clown's

This is ____ coat.
Bettys   Betty's   Betty

I know ____ brother.
Burt's   Burt   Burts

The ____ hat is pretty.
girls   girl   girl's

That is the ____ ball.
kitten's   kitten   kittens

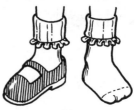

My ____ shoe is missing.
sisters   sister   sister's

The ____ coach is Mr. Hall.
teams   team's   team

The ____ cover is torn.
book's   books   book

Name _____

Fish for Plurals

Write the words on the fish in the correct tank.

| kites | mitten | star | cats | chick | matches | foxes | lunch |

One

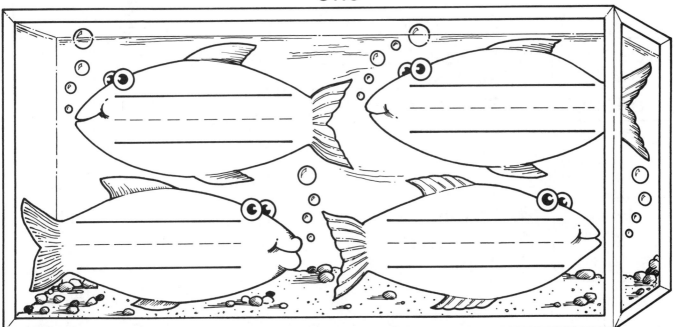

More Than One (Plural)

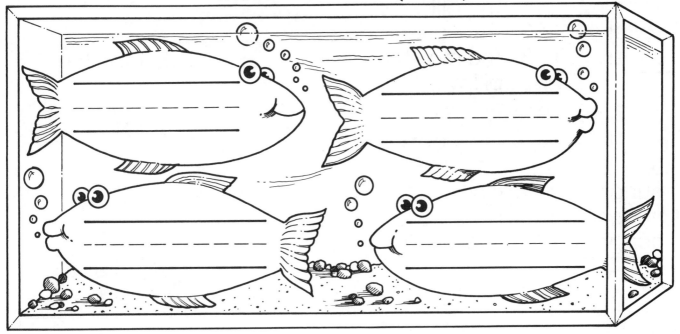

Name _____

Who Is Hungrier?

Use the pictures to help you complete each sentence with the correct word.

Sludge **Fang** **Big Hex**

sleepy sleepier sleepiest

1. Fang is _____ than Big Hex.
2. Big Hex is _____.
3. Sludge is the _____ of all.

 Rosamond **Annie**   **Eric**

dirty dirtier dirtiest

1. Rosamond's shirt is the _____ of all.
2. Eric's shirt is _____ than Annie's.
3. Annie's shirt is _____.

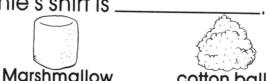

Marshmallow **cotton ball** **pillow**

soft softer softest

1. The pillow is _____.
2. The cotton ball is the _____.
3. The marshmallow is _____ than the pillow.

Nate **Finley** **Pip**

hungry hungrier hungriest

1. Pip is _____ than Nate.
2. Nate is _____.
3. Finley is the _____.

Name _____

Is It a World Record?

Read each sentence. Choose the correct word and write it on the line.

big

bigger

biggest

1. The town made the _____ snowball on record.

2. Emmett made a _____ snowball.

3. Sara helped him make it even _____ .

fast

faster

fastest

1. The snowball started to roll very _____ .

2. It was the _____ rolling snowball anyone had ever seen.

3. It rolled _____ than they could run.

white

whiter

whitest

1. As the snowball rolled closer, Mr. Wetzel's face became even _____ .

2. After it snowed all night, the town was the _____ it had ever been.

3. Mr. Wetzel's face turned _____ when he saw the snowball rolling toward his candy store.

Name _____

Can I, or Can't I?

Read each sentence. Write **can** or **can't** on the line.

_____
- - - - - - - - - - -

1. The day is warm so I _____ wear my mittens.

_____
- - - - - - - - - - -

2. It is snowing so I _____ wear my snowsuit.

_____
- - - - - - - - - - -

3. My boots are too big so I _____ wear them.

_____
- - - - - - - - - - -

4. My hat is too little so I _____ wear it.

_____
- - - - - - - - - - -

5. It snowed so I _____ make a snowman.

_____
- - - - - - - - - - -

6. The shade will not open so I _____ see if it has snowed.

Bunny Bunch

Name _____

There are ten bunnies in this family. Each one is special.

Read the clues and fill in the blank with the word that rhymes and makes sense.

1. I like to hop
   and drink _____ .

2. I can run fast,
   but still I am always _____ .

3. I like to run and jump,
   but sometimes I fall and get a _____ .

4. I like to help Mom and Pop
   by scrubbing the floor with a _____ .

5. After I feed the cat,
   I take out my baseball and _____ .

6. I like to go on a hike
   or ride my _____ .

7. I like to dig in the sand
   and play the drums in a _____ .

8. I like to play with a toy car
   while I eat a candy _____ .

9. I can walk in the fog
   and also chop a _____ .

10. I can fly my kite
    but not during the _____ .

band
bar
bat
bike
bump
cast
daylight
far
fat
fog
hand
last
like
log
mop
night
pop
pump
stop
top

Name _____

Loosey Goosey

Find the names of the birds at the bottom of the page that will rhyme with the words given. For example: Loose goose

narrow _____   bobbin _____

hairy _____   dark _____

men _____   pinch _____

pork _____   muffin _____

love _____   beagle _____

pleasant _____   frail _____

perky _____   hull _____

soon _____   lay _____

luck _____   howl _____

darling _____

dove
stork
canary
wren
robin
jay

starling
sparrow
pheasant
eagle
turkey
owl
gull

quail
loon
puffin
duck
lark
finch

Name _____

Do You Know a Boa?

Print a rhyming word under each word on the boa's body. Slither down from the head to the tail. Sssssssssssss.

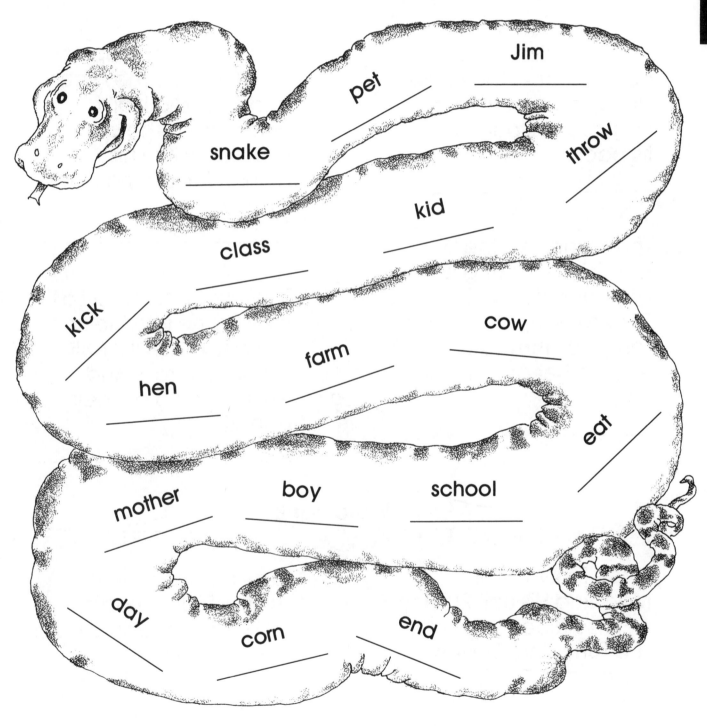

Name _____

What an Act!

Read about each act. Read the titles in the Word Bank. Write the best title for each act.

1. The lady climbed on the horse's back. The horse galloped around the ring as she stood up on its back.

   _____

2. Four seals stood up on their flippers. They spun and tossed a ball to each other. The biggest seal threw it to his trainer, Mac, who threw it back.

   _____

3. The trainer led the five bears into the ring. Each bear had its own bike. They rode up and down ramps as they raced each other around the ring.

   _____

4. The clowns tumbled as they came into the ring. They did forward rolls, backward rolls and even walked on their hands.

   _____

Word Bank

Three Brown Bears
Mac and His Ball-Playing Seals
A Horse Rider
The Tumbling Clowns

Mac and His Seals
The Bike-Riding Bears
Lady on a Galloping Horse
The Lazy Clowns

Name _____

High-Flying Acts

Read each sentence. Look at the underlined words. Write **who, what, when, where or why** to show what the underlined words tell.

1. Clifford and Emily Elizabeth spent the day <u>at the circus</u>. _____

2. The biggest elephant couldn't lead the parade <u>because he had a cold</u>. _____

3. <u>The circus owner</u> was afraid there would not be a show. _____

4. Clifford shot <u>a tent pole</u> at the hot air balloon. _____

5. Clifford caught the diver <u>before he landed in the empty tank</u>. _____

6. The clowns needed help <u>because some had quit</u>. _____

7. Clifford liked <u>the cotton candy</u>. _____

8. The poster said there would be a circus <u>today</u>. _____

9. The human cannon ball landed <u>on top of a haystack</u>. _____

10. The lions and tigers didn't listen to <u>the lion tamer</u>. _____

Name _____

Donuts, Anyone?

Write who, what, when, where or why to show what the underlined words in each sentence tell you.

1. The Pee Wee Scouts went to <u>Mrs. Peter's house</u> on Tuesday. _____

2. <u>The Scouts</u> turned in the money they had received for selling the boxes of donuts. _____

3. Roger and Rachel sold the most <u>boxes of donuts.</u> _____

4. Sonny's mother sold many boxes <u>at work.</u> _____

5. Rachel sold the donuts to <u>her relatives.</u> _____

6. Rachel was angry at Molly <u>because she was making fun of her relatives.</u> _____

7. Sonny and Rachel would win badges <u>because they sold the most boxes of donuts.</u> _____

8. If people eat <u>a lot of donuts,</u> they might get fat. _____

9. Everyone was happy that they had earned enough money to go to camp <u>in two weeks.</u> _____

10. The scout meeting started <u>after three o'clock.</u> _____

It's a Surprise!

Name _____

Read the clues. Find the answers in the Word Bank.

1. You need snow to do this. You can go fast or slow. You can turn corners. You need a pair of something to do this. What is it?

_____

2. This can be soft or hard. It can be made of paper or metal. You need it when you want to buy something. What is it?

_____

3. It is a place where you can buy sweet treats to eat. Many of the treats that can be bought there have to be baked in an oven. What is it?

_____

4. In larger cities these come out every day. It can have a few pages or many pages. It tells you what is happening in the world. What is it?

_____

5. It can be large or small. It smells very good. It is green. It is very special and people like to decorate it at one time of the year. What is it?

_____

6. It needs gas. It is very big. Its driver stops a lot at people's houses to pick up things. What is it?

_____

Word Bank

book	magazine	newspaper	garbage truck
coins	paper bag	holly plant	Christmas tree
money	gas station	candy store	snowballing
skiing	sledding	bakery	

Name _____

Reflect on the Riddles

Read each riddle. Find the answer in the Word Bank and write it on the line.

1. There are two of me. We can blink. We can see. We can wink. We can weep.

   What are we?_____

2. There is one of me. I can sing. I can form words. I can eat. I can even blow a big bubble. I can eat ice cream, too.

   What am I?_____

3. There is one of me. If I tickle, I will sneeze. I like to sniff flowers. I like the whiff of hot dogs, also.

   What am I?_____

4. We need to bend and stretch. We need rest. We need to work and we need to play. We are all different.

   What are we?_____

5. I can be almost any color. I can be long or short. I can be curled and I can be spiked.

   What am I?_____

6. We can change. We can be happy or sad. We can be worried or excited. We can even be scared.

   What are we?_____

7. I cover a lot. I keep muscles, bones, and blood inside your body. I let you know if it is hot or cold. I tell you if something is wet or dry.

   What am I?_____

8. We all have feelings. We all have bodies. We all like to do many of the same things. But, we also are all very different.

   Who are we?_____

Word Bank

bodies	eyes
people	feelings
hair	mouth
nose	skin

Name _____

It's a Fact!

Read each sentence. If it states a fact, write the word **fact** on the line. If it states an opinion, write the word **opinion** on the line.

1. An opera is a play that is sung.   _____

2. Many operas are terribly boring.   _____

3. Opera stars wear costumes on stage.   _____

4. People who have trunks filled with jewels are
   robbers.   _____

5. In many cities people dial 911 for emergency
   help.   _____

6. It is fun to check the mailbox every day.   _____

7. Seventy is a very old age.   _____

8. Second and third grade are about the same. _____

9. Many operas are recorded on records.   _____

10. It is all right to snoop in other people's things if you
    have a reason.   _____

Is This for Real?

Name _____

Read each sentence. If it tells something that could really happen, draw a pumpkin on the line.

1. Spiders spin cobwebs.   _____

2. Robots are people.   _____

3. Cats have nine lives.   _____

4. Bats hang upside down.   _____

5. Ghosts haunt houses.   _____

6. There really are spooks.   _____

7. A mask can hide your face.   _____

8. Boys and girls can run in high heels.   _____

9. Owls have wings.   _____

10. Witches ride on brooms.   _____

11. Some people buy costumes.   _____

12. Pirates sail on ships.   _____

Name _____

Elephant Dressing

Mrs. Marsh's kids need your help dressing. First color all of the elephants' skin gray. Then follow the directions to color their clothes.

Mollie   Jason   Gary   Megan   Robbie   Lisa

1. Color Robbie's pants brown and his shirt yellow. His shoes are brown.

2. Color Mollie's dress pink polka dots. Put a pink bow in her hair. Her shoes are black.

3. Color Lisa's dress blue, green and purple stripes. Her bow and shoes are purple.

4. Color Jason's jeans blue and his shirt red. His shoes are red.

5. Color Gary's pants orange. His shirt is orange and white stripes. His shoes are black.

6. Color Megan's dress red with pink flowers. Her shoes are red.

Name _____

Top or Bottom?

Read and follow the directions.

1. Paste the dog in the middle of the bottom shelf.
2. Paste the cat on the right side of the bear.
3. Paste the rabbit on the left side of the top shelf.
4. Paste the elephant on the shelf below the rabbit.
5. Paste the frog on the left side of the bottom shelf.
6. Paste the horse on the middle shelf below the cat.
7. Paste the giraffe on the middle shelf above the dog.
8. Paste the turtle on the right side of the bottom shelf.

Cut _ _ _ _ _ _ _ _ _ _ _ _ _ _ _ _ _

Where Is It?

LANGUAGE ARTS

Name _____

Follow the directions. **Hint:** Read through all of the directions before starting.

1. Draw a brown mound in the middle of the box.
2. Draw a red car on top of the mound.
3. Draw apartments behind and to the left of the mound.
4. Draw a bird nest, with four blue eggs inside, on top of the car.
5. Draw three yellow birds flying away from the nest.
6. Draw two tin cans at the bottom of the mound.
7. Put an **X** on one of the tin cans.
8. Draw you and your friend looking at the car.

Name _____

I'll Try Another Way

Help the little mole find his way to Percy's hut. Read and follow the directions. Write each word that tells what blocks his path as he looks for the loose floorboard. Then draw a line to show where the mole traveled.

					brick	
			rock			
	pipe					
				puddle of water		
			log			floor-board

Go right 1 space, then down 1 space. There is a _____ .

Go left 1 space, down 3 spaces,

then right 2 spaces. There is a _____ .

Go up 1 space, right 1 space, then up 1. There is a _____ .

Go left 1 space, up 2, then right 3 spaces. There is a _____ .

Go down 1 space, right 2 spaces,

down 2, then left 2 spaces. There is a _____ .

Go down 1 space, then right 1 space. Hooray! It's the _____ .

What Do I Do First?

Name _____

Look at the pictures. Number them in the correct order. Then read and number the sentences in the correct order.

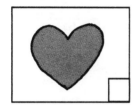 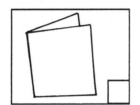 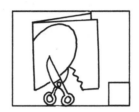 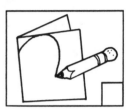

___ Cut along the line.
___ Fold a piece of paper in half.
___ Draw one half of a heart on the paper.
___ Open the heart.

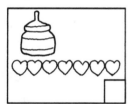 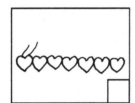 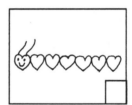 

___ Draw two antennas on the first heart.
___ Paste the hearts in a line.
___ Then draw two eyes and a mouth on the first heart.
___ Cut out seven small hearts.
What did you make? _____

 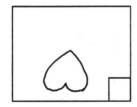 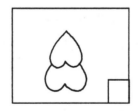 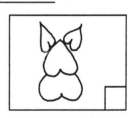

___ Draw two eyes and a nose. Paste a cotton ball on the big heart.
___ Paste a big heart upside down on a piece of paper.
___ Glue a smaller heart upside down on top of the big heart.
___ Paste two long skinny hearts upside down on the smaller heart.
What did you make? _____

Name _____

Terrific Toast

Lionel said he made the best toast in the world! Number the sentences to show the best order to make terrific toast. The first two are done.

____ Close the jar of jam.

____ Close the package of bread.

____ Push down on the toaster button.

____ Put butter on the hot toast.

____ Place the plate of toast on the table and enjoy.

_2_ Open the package of bread.

_1_ Plug in the toaster.

____ Put the toast on a plate.

____ Take out two slices of bread.

____ Place the two slices of bread in the toaster.

____ Open the jar of jam.

____ Wait for the toast to pop up.

____ Put jam on the toast.

____ Take the toast out of the toaster.

What do you like to put on your toast? _____

_____

What is your favorite flavor of jam? _____

Name _____

What's What?

Write the words from the Word Bank in the correct category.

Living	Non-Living
1. _____	1. _____
2. _____	2. _____
3. _____	3. _____
4. _____	4. _____
5. _____	5. _____
6. _____	6. _____

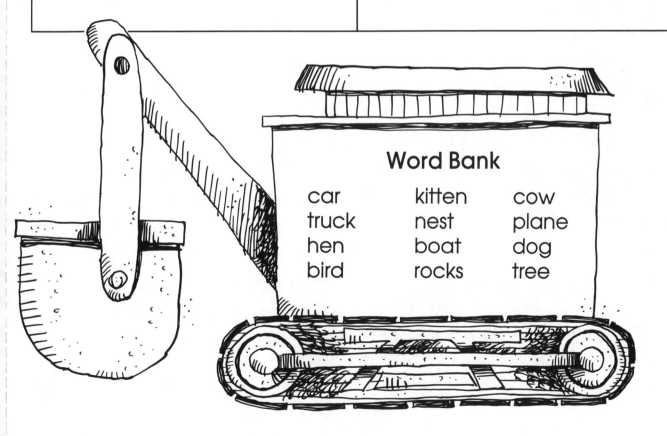

Word Bank

car	kitten	cow
truck	nest	plane
hen	boat	dog
bird	rocks	tree

Name _____

Tidying Up

Write the words from the Word Bank in the correct category.

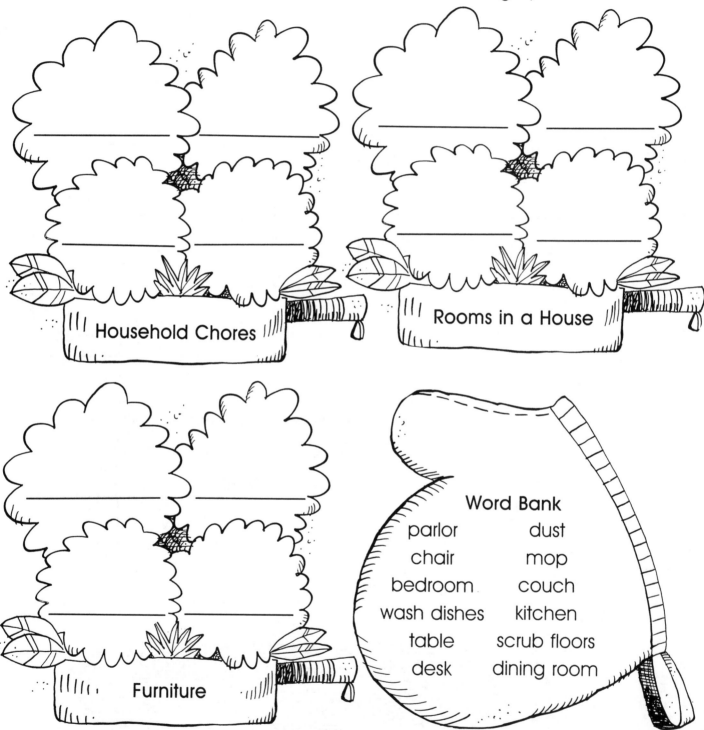

Household Chores

Rooms in a House

Furniture

Word Bank

parlor   dust

chair   mop

bedroom   couch

wash dishes   kitchen

table   scrub floors

desk   dining room

Name _____

Cookie Jar

Read the categories on the jars. Cut and paste the cookies in the correct jar.

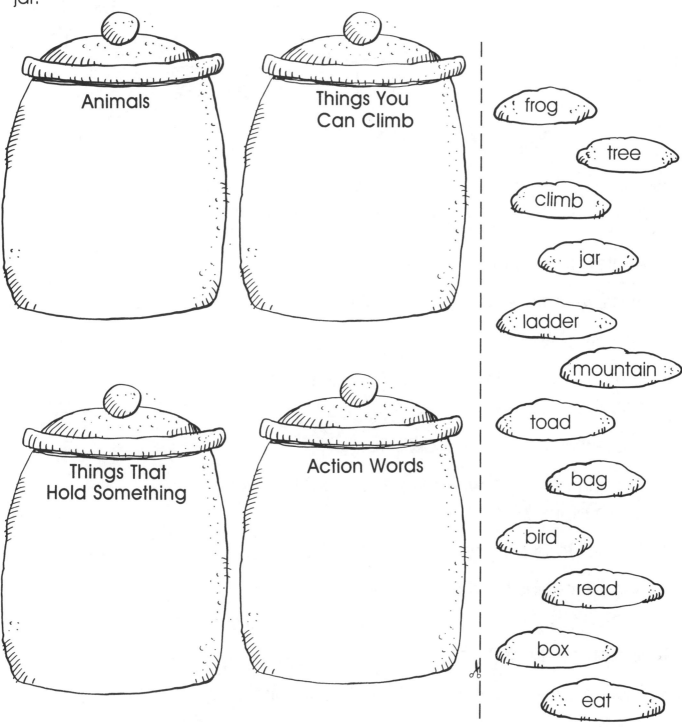

Animals

Things You Can Climb

Things That Hold Something

Action Words

frog

tree

climb

jar

ladder

mountain

toad

bag

bird

read

box

eat

Name _____

Sense-ational!

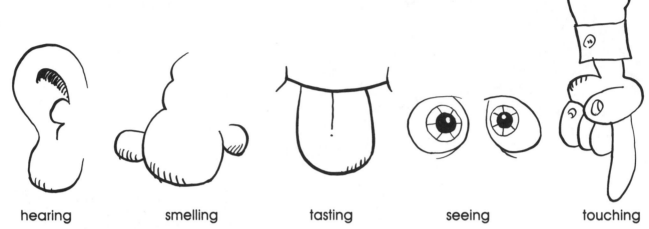

| hearing | smelling | tasting | seeing | touching |

Read each sentence. Then write which sense would be used for each one.

1. Andrew found page 64 in his reading book. _____

2. Andrew heard Sharon giggling at him. _____

3. Andrew poked Nicky. _____

4. Sharon was listening when Andrew asked Nicky about his freckles. _____

5. Andrew liked to count Nicky's freckles. _____

6. The number of freckles you get depends on how much of the juice you drink. _____

7. The bell rang and the students lined up. _____

8. Andrew couldn't find any freckles on Sharon's face. _____

9. Sharon ate bugs. _____

10. Miss Kelly told Andrew that it was time for his reading group. _____

Name _____

What's Going On?

Look at the pictures. Find the sentence in the Word Bank that explains each one. Write it on the lines.

_____

_____

_____

_____

_____

_____

_____

_____

Word Bank

The team was treated to hot dogs after their win.

They won the big Thanksgiving game.

Coach Swamp made them practice hard.

The team had lost every game.

Name _____

Just Rolling Along!

Help Emmett roll the snowball down the hill. Read the clues. Then find the words in the Word Bank and write them in the correct spaces. **Hint:** The last letter of each answer is the first letter of the next answer.

1. Boasting

2. Very, very good

3. Many moving cars and trucks

4. A little cold

5. Paid attention

6. Twice an amount

7. Comes after seventh

8. One of two equal parts

9. Very well-known

10. Not crooked

Word Bank

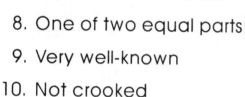

listened   half

bragging   great

cool   double

famous   traffic

eighth   straight

Name _____

A-maze-ing

Draw a line through the maze in the order of the clues to help baby bird find his way back to his nest.

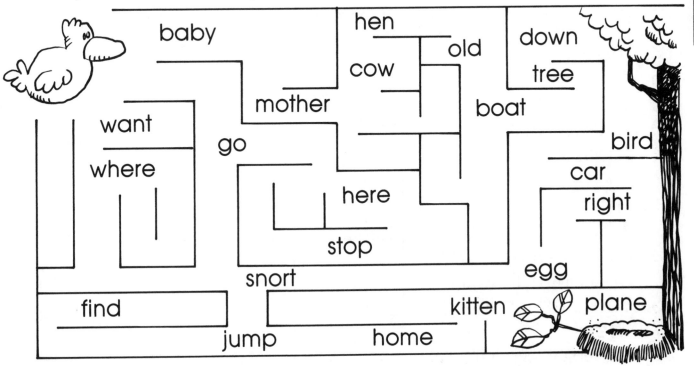

Clues

1. A very young child
2. Opposite of father
3. A large farm animal
4. A bird that lives on a farm
5. Opposite of new
6. Something that can float
7. A very large plant
8. Opposite of up
9. An animal that can fly

10. Something you can drive
11. Opposite of left
12. A bird hatches out of it
13. A sound
14. To leap
15. Your house
16. A baby cat
17. A machine that flies

Name _____

Circus Sights

Find the answers to the puzzle in the Word Bank.

Across
1. To save from danger
4. The last act
6. A silly person
8. Your mistake
10. To give an order
11. A poster

Down
2. A large weapon
3. A show with clowns and animal acts
5. You dress up in these
7. Great
9. A person who trains animals
11. A trick

Word Bank

cannon	costumes	command	trainer
grand	circus	rescue	clown
fault	stunt	sign	finale

Name _____

Hidden Mystery

Read the clues. Find the matching words in the Word Bank and write them on the lines. Then find each two-letter mystery word by circling the letters that are the same in each set of matching words. Write each mystery word on a magnifying glass.

1. Something you put on a hot dog _____
2. Outside part of bread _____
3. Dance or sing to . . . _____
4. Someone who might be guilty _____

The hidden mystery word is

1. Words you can sing _____
2. Not weak _____
3. A small rock _____
4. A round fastener _____

The hidden mystery word is

1. A note asking you to a party _____
2. Start _____
3. The meal you eat at night _____
4. A part of a fish _____

The hidden mystery word is

Word Bank			
strong	dinner	fin	stone
invitation	begin	crust	song
button	music	mustard	suspect

Daily Learning Drills Grade 2

Name _____

We're Just Hopping!

Find and circle the words in the puzzle.

Look → and ↓ .

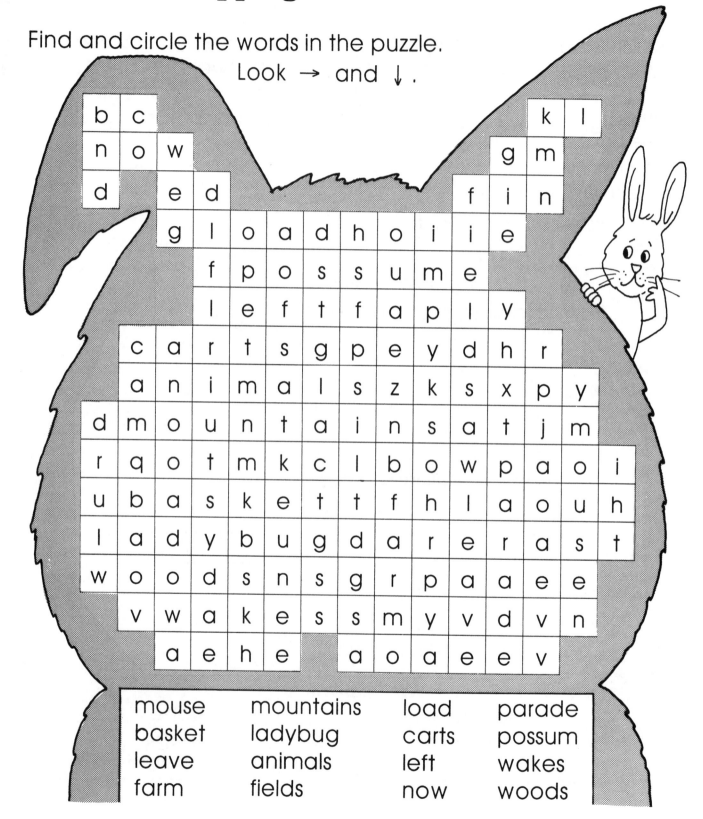

mouse	mountains	load	parade
basket	ladybug	carts	possum
leave	animals	left	wakes
farm	fields	now	woods

Name _____

Lazy One Liners

Use your laziest imagination to finish these lazy lines. An example would be, "The lion was so lazy that. . .he made his mate roar for him." Choose three of your best one liners and illustrate them on another paper.

1. The doctor was so lazy that _____
2. The baker was so lazy that _____
3. The teacher was so lazy that _____
4. The fireman was so lazy that _____
5. The dentist was so lazy that _____
6. The truck driver was so lazy that _____
7. The vet was so lazy that _____
8. The plumber was so lazy that _____
9. The house builder was so lazy that _____
10. The principal was so lazy that _____
11. The astronaut was so lazy that _____
12. The football player was so lazy that _____
13. The zookeeper was so lazy that _____
14. The TV repairman was so lazy that _____
15. The traffic cop was so lazy that _____

Name _____

A Story for the People

Look carefully at the picture on the buckskin. Write a story on the lines to tell what is happening in the picture.

_ _

_____

_ _

_____

_ _

_____

_ _

_____

_ _

_____

_ _

_____

Name _____

Using Descriptive Language

Stories are always more exciting when you can picture them happening in your mind. Descriptive words help make the story imaginable. Use these categories to think of words that describe a walk along the beach. Pretend you are barefoot walking close to the water. With a partner, write three words in each area. Then, use all the words in a story.

What I smell:

1. _____
2. _____
3. _____

What I taste:

1. _____
2. _____
3. _____

What I hear:

1. _____
2. _____
3. _____

What I see:

1. _____
2. _____
3. _____

What I feel on my feet:

1. _____
2. _____
3. _____

My Walk Along the Beach

_____
_____
_____
_____
_____
_____
_____
_____

Name _____

Writing Haiku Poetry

Haiku poetry is originally from the country of Japan. It is a very simple form of poetry and does not have to rhyme.

Example

The polar bear cubs
learn to swim and dive for fish
in the cold, blue sea.

Poem Pattern

5 syllables
7 syllables
5 syllables

Write your own haiku poem by yourself or with a partner. Give it a title and illustrate it.

_____
Title

By a Beary Special Poet _____
Name

Ready to Mail

Read the envelope Tilly addressed to Mr. Bunny.

tilly mole
102 garden road
forest maine 25136

mr bunny
523 sweet potato lane
forest maine 25136

Address the envelope correctly. Be sure to use capital letters, periods and commas where they belong.

Draw and color a stamp on the envelope.

Name _____

Write, Please

Read the thank you letter Louis wrote to his Uncle McAllister.

october 5   1990

> dear uncle mcallister
>
> thank you for the tadpole   i named him alphonse   he likes to eat cheeseburgers   this is the best gift you ever sent me
>
> thank you again
>
> love
>
> louis

Write the letter correctly. Be sure to use capital letters, periods and commas where they belong.

_____

_____

_____

_____

_____

_____

_____

_____

_____

_____

Name _____

Which Book?

Read the questions. Write which book you would use to find the answer.

| Dictionary | Encyclopedia | Telephone Book |

1. What makes rain? _____

2. What does purify mean? _____

3. When does the waterworks plant allow visitors? _____

4. Where would you find glaciers? _____

5. What is a water cycle? _____

6. What are impurities? _____

7. Where is your town's waterworks located? _____

8. What chemicals are put into the water on its way to the storage tank? _____

9. How do you pronounce the word evaporation? _____

10. What time does the waterworks open? _____

11. How do you pronounce the word reservoir? _____

12. How are clouds formed? _____

MATH

Name _____

Let's Get Cooking!

Read each phrase.

If you would need a **dictionary** to find the information, color the space **yellow**.

If you would need an **encyclopedia** to find the information, color the space **white**.

If you would need a **cookbook** to find the information, color the space **brown**.

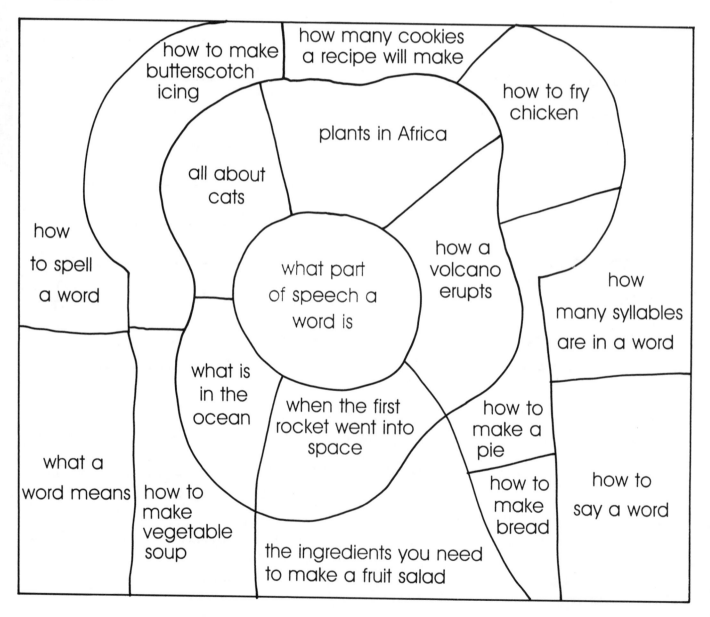

Name _____

Pottery Patterns

Before beginning a project, an artist who makes pottery must think about how the piece will be used, what type of clay to use, and what color and patterns to use.

This talented artist does something special with all the pottery he makes. Here are some examples of his pottery.

The pottery here is not his. Something is different.

Circle the pottery below that the talented artist might have made.

What is special about his pottery? _____

MATH

Name _____

Dressing the Part

People who act in plays are called actors and actresses. For each play, costumes are chosen that make the characters in the story seem more realistic.

Below is the inside of a costume closet.

Pretend that you want to act in some silly plays. Look at the titles of each play below. Write the names of the two costumes you would combine to fit the main character of each play.

1. "The Strong, Flying Ape" _____ _____

2. "The Invisible Man on His Horse" _____ _____

3. "The Cat Who Squeaked" _____ _____

4. "Her Royal Highness Barks up the Wrong Tree"

   _____ _____

5. "Flying Animal-like Man Saves Building from Fire" _____

   _____

Name _____

Everyone Is Welcome

Cut out the pictures of the people at the bottom of the page. Read the clues carefully. Paste the people where they belong at the table.

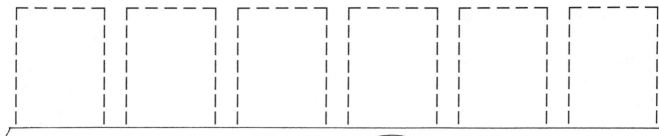

1. Robert already has his hamburger.

2. Kioko will pass the plate of hamburgers to the others at the table.

3. Mike asks Teresa to please pass the pitcher of lemonade so that he may fill his glass.

4. Pablo likes sitting between his friends Kioko and Teresa.

5. Sue likes hot dogs better than hamburgers.

Cut —

Pablo   Kioko   Robert   Sue   Mike   Teresa

Name _____

Comparing the Seasons

Each of the four seasons (winter, spring, summer, autumn) has certain characteristics. Choose two of the seasons and write their names on the lines above each shape below. Then, complete the other lines with words that describe the season. In the center area, write words that describe both seasons. This is called a Venn diagram.

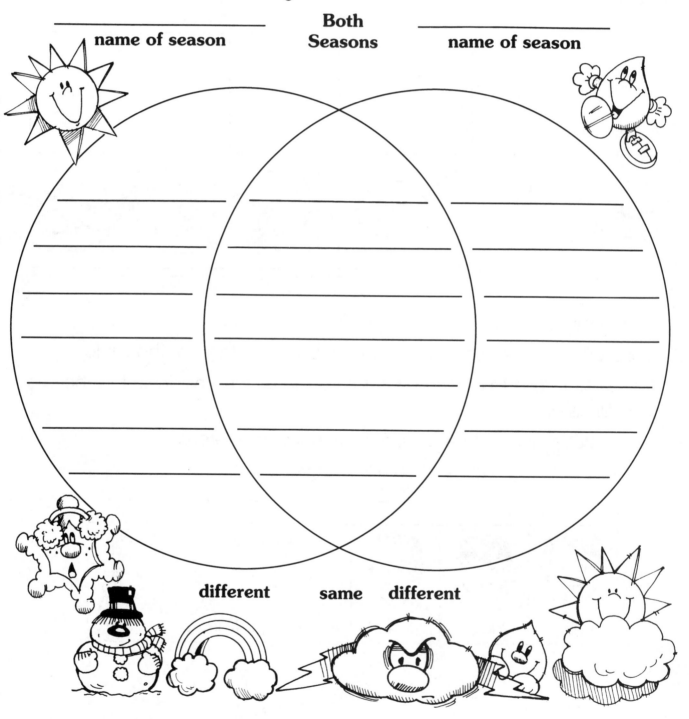

_____ **Both** _____
name of season **Seasons** **name of season**

different   **same**   **different**

Name _____

Just Napping

Count. Write the correct number of cats in the box on each cat bed.

Plump Piglets

Name _____

Pigs like to eat corn. These little pigs just ate lunch.

Read the clues to find out how many ears of corn each pig ate. Write the number on the line below each pig.

Who ate the most and was really piggy? _____

Who ate the least? _____

Name _____

Unpack the Teddy Bears

Cut out the bears at the bottom of the page. Paste them where they belong in numbered order.

Daily Learning Drills Grade 2

Name _____

Air Bear Addition

Help Buddy off the ground. Solve the problems. Then color the clouds with sums of 9 to find the right path.

$$\begin{array}{r} 5 \\ +5 \\ \hline \end{array}$$

$$\begin{array}{r} 7 \\ +4 \\ \hline \end{array}$$

$$\begin{array}{r} 3 \\ +7 \\ \hline \end{array}$$

$$\begin{array}{r} 4 \\ +4 \\ \hline \end{array}$$

$$\begin{array}{r} 6 \\ +3 \\ \hline \end{array}$$

$$\begin{array}{r} 8 \\ +1 \\ \hline \end{array}$$

$$\begin{array}{r} 6 \\ +4 \\ \hline \end{array}$$

$$\begin{array}{r} 2 \\ +7 \\ \hline \end{array}$$

$$\begin{array}{r} 2 \\ +5 \\ \hline \end{array}$$

$$\begin{array}{r} 10 \\ +1 \\ \hline \end{array}$$

$$\begin{array}{r} 5 \\ +4 \\ \hline \end{array}$$

$$\begin{array}{r} 6 \\ +5 \\ \hline \end{array}$$

$$\begin{array}{r} 3 \\ +4 \\ \hline \end{array}$$

$$\begin{array}{r} 3 \\ +2 \\ \hline \end{array}$$

$$\begin{array}{r} 4 \\ +5 \\ \hline \end{array}$$

$$\begin{array}{r} 2 \\ +5 \\ \hline \end{array}$$

$$\begin{array}{r} 0 \\ +9 \\ \hline \end{array}$$

$$\begin{array}{r} 9 \\ +0 \\ \hline \end{array}$$

$$\begin{array}{r} 2 \\ +6 \\ \hline \end{array}$$

$$\begin{array}{r} 8 \\ +2 \\ \hline \end{array}$$

$$\begin{array}{r} 3 \\ +6 \\ \hline \end{array}$$

Name _____

Math-Minded Mermaids

Each mermaid sits upon her own special rock.

Look at the number on each shell. Then look → and ↓ in the number boxes. Circle each pair of numbers that can be added together to equal the number in the shell the mermaid is holding.

12

7	5	3	6
9	6	8	6
3	9	1	8
10	2	11	4

9

1	9	6	3
8	0	4	7
5	9	5	2
3	2	7	5

11

10	7	8	3
5	4	4	8
6	3	6	5
2	9	3	8

10

3	7	9	1
10	5	5	9
0	8	6	4
8	2	3	7

MATH

Daily Learning Drills Grade 2

Name _____

Domino Math

Write the number that tells how many dots are on the greater side of each domino. Then, "count on" to find the sum of both sides.

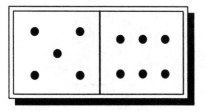

_____

sum _____

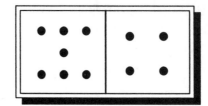

_____

sum _____

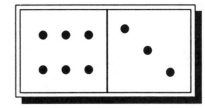

_____

sum _____

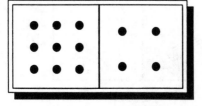

_____

sum _____

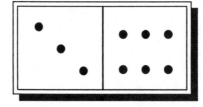

_____

sum _____

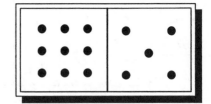

_____

sum _____

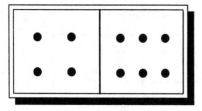

_____

sum _____

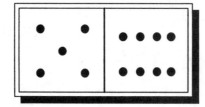

_____

sum _____

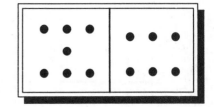

_____

sum _____

Name _____

Ride the Rapids

Write each problem on the life jacket with the correct answer.

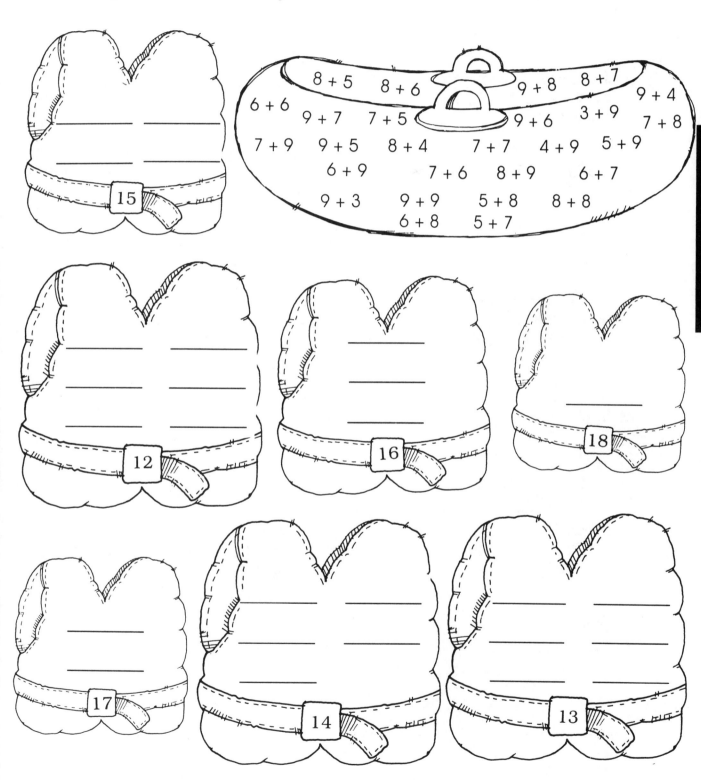

8 + 5   8 + 6   9 + 8   8 + 7
6 + 6   9 + 4
    9 + 7   7 + 5   9 + 6   3 + 9
                                    7 + 8
7 + 9   9 + 5   8 + 4   7 + 7   4 + 9   5 + 9
    6 + 9   7 + 6   8 + 9   6 + 7

9 + 3   9 + 9   5 + 8   8 + 8
    6 + 8   5 + 7

15

12

16

18

17

14

13

MATH

Name _____

Story Problems

The key words **in all** tell you to add. Circle the key words **in all** and solve the problems.

1. Jack has 4 white shirts and 2 yellow shirts. How many shirts does Jack have in all?

   4 ⊕ 2 = _____

2. Joan has 4 pink blouses and 6 red ones. How many blouses does Joan have in all?

   4 ◯ 6 = _____

3. Mack has 3 pairs of summer pants and 8 pairs of winter pants. How many pairs of pants does Mack have in all?

   3 ◯ 8 = _____

4. Betsy has 2 black skirts and 7 blue skirts. In all, how many skirts does Betsy have?

   2 ◯ 7 = _____

5. Willis has 5 knit hats and 5 cloth hats. How many hats does Willis have in all?

   5 ◯ 5 = _____

Name _____

Additional Story Problems

Circle the addition key words **in all** and solve the problems.

1. On the block where Cindy lives there are 7 brick houses and 5 stone houses. How many houses are there in all?

$$7 + 5 = \underline{\hspace{2cm}}$$

2. One block from Cindy's house there are 7 white houses and 4 gray houses. How many houses are there in all?

3. Near Cindy's house there are 3 grocery stores and 5 discount stores. How many stores are there in all?

4. Children live in 8 of the two-story houses, and children live in 2 of the one-story houses. How many houses in all have children living in them?

5. In Cindy's neighborhood 4 students are in high school and 9 are in elementary school. In all, how many children are in school?

Name _____

Problems in the Park

Circle the addition key words **in all** and solve the problems.

1. At the park there are 3 baseball games and 6 basketball games being played. How many games are being played in all?

3+6 = 9

2. In the park 9 mothers are pushing their babies in strollers, and 8 are carrying their babies in baskets. How many mothers in all have their babies with them in the park?

3. On one team there are 6 boys and 3 girls. How many team members are there in all?

4. At one time there were 8 men and 4 boys pitching horseshoes. In all, how many people were pitching horseshoes?

5. While playing basketball, 4 of the players were wearing gym shoes and 6 were not. How many basketball players were there in all?

Name _____

Solving Stories

Write a number sentence to solve each problem.

1. Brad ate five slices of pizza. Todd ate three. How many slices of pizza did both boys eat?

2. Sam scored four points for the team. Dave scored eight points. How many points did Sam and Dave score?

3. Missy bought six dresses. Dot bought two. How many dresses did they buy in all?

4. Three bears are having a picnic. Two more bears join the fun. How many bears are having a picnic now?

5. Matt has a barn. In the barn are four horses, three cows and five pigs. How many animals are in the barn?

MATH

Name _____

Daisy Subtraction

Work problems.
Use code to color.

2—green	7—orange	10—pink
3—blue	8—red	11—red
4—yellow	9—purple	12—purple

Name _____

Pick a Picnic

Subtract. Write each answer. Then draw a line to show where three answers are the same in a row.

12 – 9 =	11 – 2 =	9 – 8 =
8 – 6 =	7 – 4 =	7 – 5 =
7 – 3 =	10 – 1 =	11 – 8 =

10 – 7 =	12 – 3 =	11 – 2 =
12 – 7 =	9 – 0 =	8 – 5 =
11 – 4 =	9 – 2 =	12 – 5 =

10 – 4 =	8 – 3 =	8 – 4 =
12 – 4 =	12 – 8 =	8 – 2 =
11 – 7 =	10 – 3 =	11 – 3 =

9 – 7 =	11 – 9 =	10 – 2 =
11 – 5 =	9 – 3 =	12 – 6 =
8 – 1 =	12 – 7 =	9 – 5 =

7 – 7 =	11 – 6 =	9 – 1 =
10 – 3 =	9 – 4 =	10 – 0 =
8 – 8 =	10 – 5 =	12 – 4 =

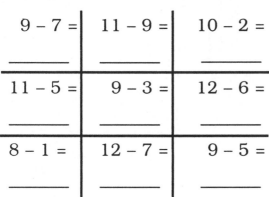

Daily Learning Drills Grade 2

MATH

Name _____

Connect the Facts

Subtract. Write the answer.

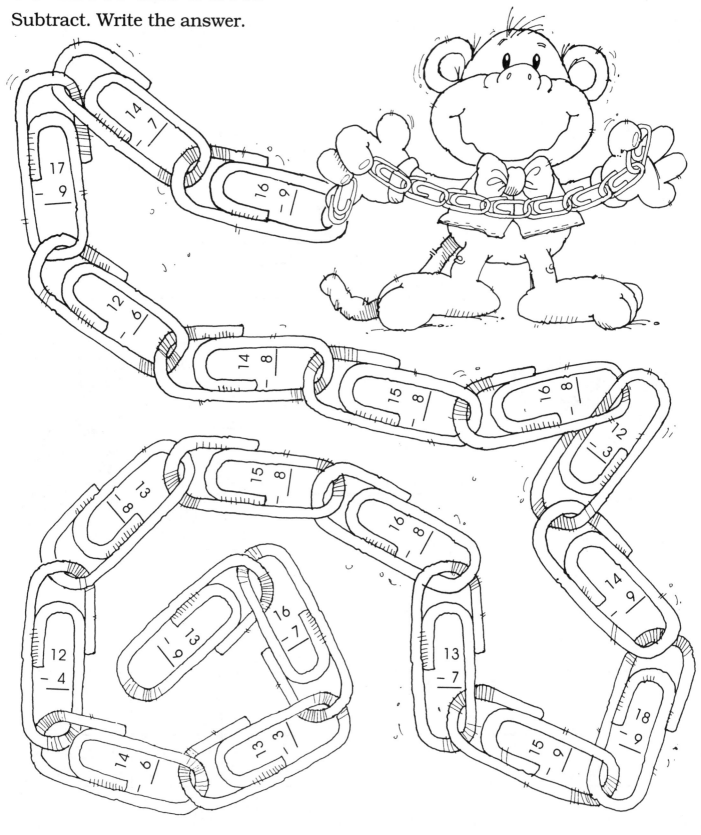

Name _____

How Many Animals Are Left?

The key word **left** tells you to subtract. Circle the key word **left** and solve the problems.

1. Bill had 10 kittens, but 4 of them ran away. How many kittens does he have left?

   10 — 4 = _____

2. There were 12 rabbits eating clover. Dogs chased 3 of them away. How many rabbits were left?

3. Bill saw 11 birds eating from the bird feeders in his back yard. A cat scared 7 of them away. How many birds were left at the feeders?

4. There were 14 frogs on the bank of the pond. Then 9 of them hopped into the water. How many frogs were left on the bank?

5. Bill counted 15 robins in his yard. Then 8 of the robins flew away. How many robins were left in the yard?

MATH

Name _____

Maggy at School

Circle the subtraction key word **left** and solve the problems.

1. In Maggy's classroom there are 12 girls. One day 4 of the girls went home with the flu. How many girls were left in school that day?

2. Maggy is in 10 different clubs. This week 5 of them will not meet. How many of Maggy's clubs are left to meet this week?

3. Maggy had 16 crayons. She broke 9 of them. How many crayons does Maggy have left?

4. There are 13 boys in Maggy's classroom. One morning 8 of the boys went to the gym. How many were left in the classroom?

5. One day 4 of the 13 boys were called in from the playground. How many of the boys were left on the playground?

Name _____

A Hidden Message

Add or subtract. Use the code to find out your new motto!

Code:	9	18	6	15	13	12	16	11	8	7	14	17
	H	Y	D	E	V	T	S	O	A	M	N	I

9
+ 8

16	14	8	6
- 7	- 6	+ 5	+ 9

14	9
- 7	+ 9

17	15	9	13	8
- 8	- 7	+ 5	- 7	+ 8

4	6
+ 7	+ 8

12	17	6	15
- 5	- 9	+ 6	- 6

Name _____

All Aboard!

Add or subtract. Match the related facts.

5 + 9 = <u>14</u>   •   • 6 + 9 = ___

8 + 7 = ___   •   • 14 − 9 = <u>5</u>

15 − 9 = ___   •   • 15 − 7 = ___

17 − 8 = ___   •   • 14 − 7 = ___

7 + 7 = ___   •   • 9 + 8 = ___

Add or subtract. Color spaces with answers greater than 12 brown.
Color the rest green.

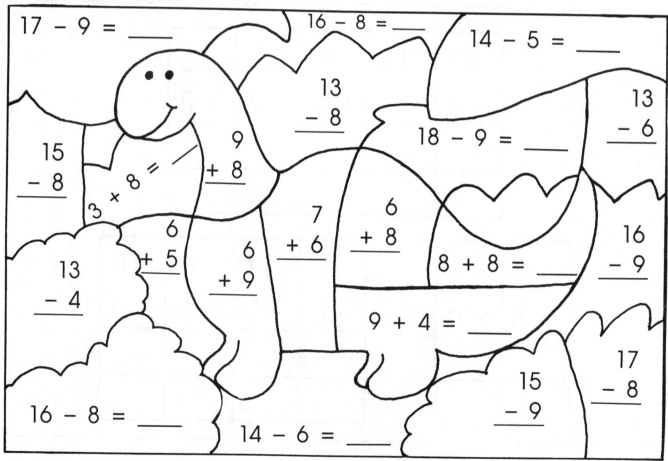

Name _____

Add or Subtract?

The key words **in all** tell you to add. The key word **left** tells you to subtract.
Circle the key words and solve the problems.

1. The pet store has 3 large dogs
   and 5 small dogs. How many
   dogs are there in all?

   3 ⊕ 5 = _____

2. The pet store had 9 parrots and
   then sold 4 of them. How many
   parrots does the pet store have
   left?

   9 ◯ 4 = _____

3. The pet store gave Linda's class 2
   adult gerbils and 9 young ones.
   How many gerbils did Linda's
   class get in all?

   2 ◯ 9 = _____

4. At the pet store 3 of the 8 myna
   birds were sold. How many myna
   birds are left in the pet store?

   8 ◯ 3 = _____

5. The monkey at the pet store has 5
   rubber toys and 4 wooden toys.
   How many toys does it have in
   all?

   5 ◯ 4 = _____

MATH

Name _____

Training with Facts

Use the numbers on each train to write the fact families.

$\underline{8}$ + $\underline{6}$ = $\underline{14}$

$\underline{6}$ + $\underline{8}$ = $\underline{14}$

$\underline{14}$ − $\underline{8}$ = $\underline{6}$

$\underline{14}$ − $\underline{6}$ = $\underline{8}$

___ + ___ = ___

___ + ___ = ___

___ − ___ = ___

___ − ___ = ___

___ + ___ = ___

___ + ___ = ___

___ − ___ = ___

___ − ___ = ___

___ + ___ = ___

___ + ___ = ___

___ − ___ = ___

___ − ___ = ___

Name _____

Adding Strategies

When adding three numbers, add two numbers first, then add the third to that sum. To decide which two numbers to add first, try one of these strategies.

Look for doubles.

$$
\begin{array}{r}
8 \\
3 \\
+\ 3 \\
\hline
14
\end{array}
\quad
\begin{array}{r}
4 \\
4 \\
+\ 5 \\
\hline
13
\end{array}
\quad
\begin{array}{r}
2 \\
9 \\
+\ 2 \\
\hline
13
\end{array}
$$

8 > 3 3 > 6 → 14

4 4 > 8 + 5 > 6 → 13

2 9 > 4 + 2 → 13

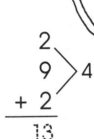

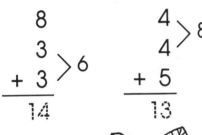

Look for a ten.

$$
\begin{array}{r}
7 \\
3 \\
+\ 4 \\
\hline
14
\end{array}
\quad
\begin{array}{r}
8 \\
4 \\
+\ 6 \\
\hline
18
\end{array}
\quad
\begin{array}{r}
1 \\
5 \\
+\ 9 \\
\hline
15
\end{array}
$$

7 > 10, 8 4 + 6 > 10, 1 5 > 10 + 9

Try these. Look for a 10 or doubles.

$$
\begin{array}{r}
5 \\
5 \\
+\ 4 \\
\hline
\end{array}
\quad
\begin{array}{r}
2 \\
6 \\
+\ 8 \\
\hline
\end{array}
\quad
\begin{array}{r}
7 \\
1 \\
+\ 7 \\
\hline
\end{array}
\quad
\begin{array}{r}
3 \\
7 \\
+\ 4 \\
\hline
\end{array}
\quad
\begin{array}{r}
6 \\
2 \\
+\ 6 \\
\hline
\end{array}
$$

$$
\begin{array}{r}
7 \\
6 \\
+\ 6 \\
\hline
\end{array}
\quad
\begin{array}{r}
7 \\
8 \\
+\ 3 \\
\hline
\end{array}
\quad
\begin{array}{r}
6 \\
7 \\
+\ 4 \\
\hline
\end{array}
\quad
\begin{array}{r}
5 \\
5 \\
+\ 3 \\
\hline
\end{array}
$$

MATH

Name _____

Sum Ice Cream

Add. If the sum is 11 or more, color the cone brown. If the sum is less than 11, color the cone yellow.

Name _____

Path Problems

Add. Show the detective the correct path. Color the path with sums of 13.

$6 + 4 + 3$

$6 + 5 + 5$

$\begin{array}{r} 9 \\ 1 \\ + 5 \\ \hline \end{array}$

$\begin{array}{r} 7 \\ 3 \\ + 3 \\ \hline \end{array}$

$\begin{array}{r} 8 \\ 3 \\ + 1 \\ \hline \end{array}$

$8 + 4 + 2$

$4 + 4 + 5$

$\begin{array}{r} 5 \\ 6 \\ + 4 \\ \hline \end{array}$

$\begin{array}{r} 9 \\ 8 \\ + 1 \\ \hline \end{array}$

$\begin{array}{r} 5 \\ 3 \\ + 5 \\ \hline \end{array}$

$\begin{array}{r} 4 \\ 6 \\ + 4 \\ \hline \end{array}$

$2 + 9 + 2$

$2 + 8 + 7$

Name _____

Something's Missing

In the forest, 13 animals have a picnic. Skunk brings 8 sandwiches. How many sandwiches should Raccoon bring so that each animal can have one?

$$8 + \underline{\ ?\ } = 13$$

What number added to 8 equals 13?

To find the missing addend, find the difference of 13 and 8. That is, subtract the given addend (8) from the sum (13).

$$13 - 8 = \underline{\ 5\ }$$

Since 13 − 8 = 5, then 8 + $\underline{\ 5\ }$ = 13.

Raccoon should bring $\underline{\ 5\ }$ sandwiches.

Try these. Find the missing addends.

$$\underline{\quad} + 6 = 15 \qquad\qquad \underline{\quad} + 7 = 13$$

$$9 + \underline{\quad} = 14 \qquad\qquad 8 + \underline{\quad} = 14$$

$$\underline{\quad} + 8 = 16 \qquad\qquad 9 + \underline{\quad} = 18$$

Name _____

Food Fun

The table below tells what each animal brought to the picnic.
Fill in the missing numbers.

Animal	Vegetables	Fruits	Total
Skunk	8	6	14
Raccoon	9		17
Squirrel		8	15
Rabbit	6		13
Owl	7		16
Deer		9	18

Write the name of the animal that answers each question.

1. Who brought the same number of vegetables as fruits?

   _____

2. Who brought two more fruits than vegetables? _____

3. Who brought two more vegetables than fruits? _____

4. Which two animals brought one more fruit than vegetables?

   _____ and _____

5. Which two animals brought the most vegetables?

   _____ and _____

6. Which two animals brought the most fruit? _____ and

   _____

7. Which animal brought the least vegetables? _____

8. Which animal brought the least fruit? _____

9. Who brought more fruit, Skunk and Squirrel, or Raccoon and

   Rabbit? _____

Name _____

Circus Fun

Add. Remember to add the ones first.

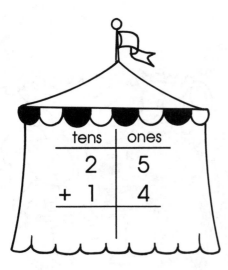

tens	ones
2	5
+ 1	4

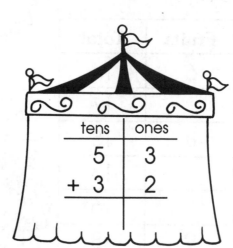

tens	ones
5	3
+ 3	2

tens	ones
7	1
+ 2	8

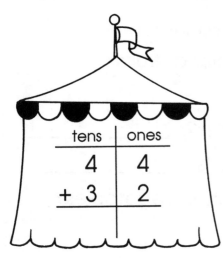

tens	ones
4	4
+ 3	2

tens	ones
5	1
+ 3	7

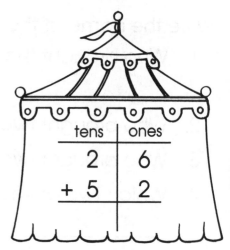

tens	ones
2	6
+ 5	2

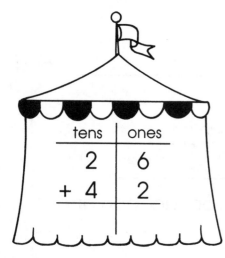

tens	ones
2	6
+ 4	2

tens	ones
3	7
+ 5	1

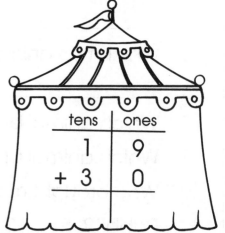

tens	ones
1	9
+ 3	0

Name _____

Nutty Addition

Sam Squirrel and his friend Wendy were gathering acorns. When they got 10 acorns, they put them in a bucket. The picture shows how many acorns Sam and Wendy each gathered. Write the number that tells how many.

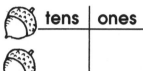

tens	ones

_____

tens	ones

_____

How many acorns did Sam and Wendy gather in all? To find out:

1. | Put numbers on ten's and one's table. |

tens	ones
3	6
+ 2	7

2. | Add ones first. |

tens	ones
1	
3	6
+ 2	7
	3

Ring 10.
Regroup 13 ones as 1 ten 3 ones.

3. | Add tens. |

tens	ones
1	
3	6
+ 2	7
6	3

Sam and Wendy gathered ___63___ in all.

Try this. Add. Regroup as needed.

tens	▼ ones
3	8
+ 4	6

tens	▼ ones
5	4
+ 2	7

tens	▼ ones
4	9
+ 1	3

tens	▼ ones
2	6
+ 1	7

Daily Learning Drills Grade 2

Name _____

Keep On Truckin'

Write each sum. Connect the sums of 83 to make a road for the truck.

17 + 66	58 + 25	42 + 19	38 + 25
26 + 57	17 + 75	48 + 26	28 + 38	65 + 29
58 + 37	64 + 19	48 + 35	65 + 16	37 + 39
39 + 59	59 + 27	55 + 28	39 + 44	

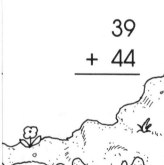

Name _____

Just Like Magic

Add. Write each answer.

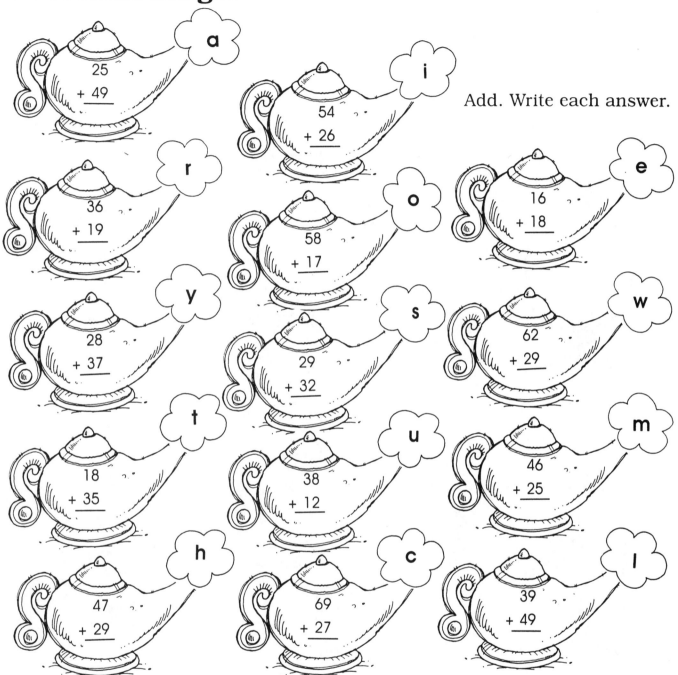

$$\begin{array}{r} 25 \\ + 49 \\ \hline \end{array}$$ **a**

$$\begin{array}{r} 54 \\ + 26 \\ \hline \end{array}$$ **i**

$$\begin{array}{r} 36 \\ + 19 \\ \hline \end{array}$$ **r**

$$\begin{array}{r} 58 \\ + 17 \\ \hline \end{array}$$ **o**

$$\begin{array}{r} 16 \\ + 18 \\ \hline \end{array}$$ **e**

$$\begin{array}{r} 28 \\ + 37 \\ \hline \end{array}$$ **y**

$$\begin{array}{r} 29 \\ + 32 \\ \hline \end{array}$$ **s**

$$\begin{array}{r} 62 \\ + 29 \\ \hline \end{array}$$ **w**

$$\begin{array}{r} 18 \\ + 35 \\ \hline \end{array}$$ **t**

$$\begin{array}{r} 38 \\ + 12 \\ \hline \end{array}$$ **u**

$$\begin{array}{r} 46 \\ + 25 \\ \hline \end{array}$$ **m**

$$\begin{array}{r} 47 \\ + 29 \\ \hline \end{array}$$ **h**

$$\begin{array}{r} 69 \\ + 27 \\ \hline \end{array}$$ **c**

$$\begin{array}{r} 39 \\ + 49 \\ \hline \end{array}$$ **l**

Use the answers and the letter on each lamp to solve the code.

___ ___ ___   ___ ___ ___   ___ ___ ___ ___
71 74 65   74 88 88   65 75 50 55

___ ___ ___ ___ ___ ___   ___ ___ ___ ___   ___ ___ ___ ___ !
91 80 61 76 34 61   96 75 71 34   53 55 50 34

Name _____

Squirrelly Fun

Add. Regroup as needed. Match the squirrels to their trees.

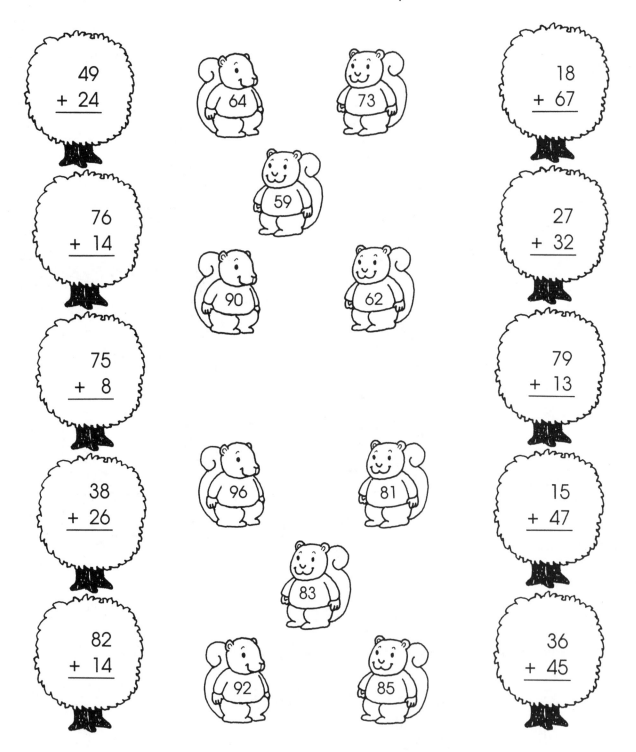

Name _____

Fishy Business

Write the numbers and subtract.

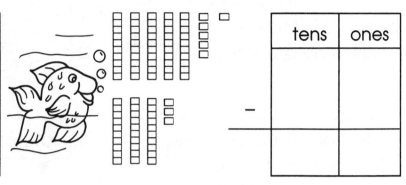

tens	ones
4	2
2	1

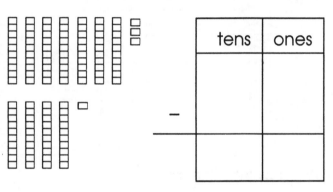

tens	ones

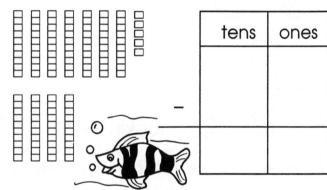

tens	ones

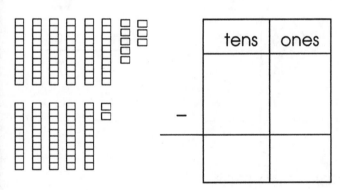

tens	ones

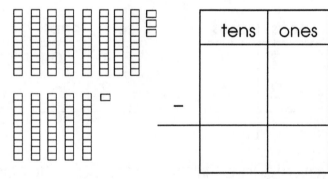

tens	ones

tens	ones

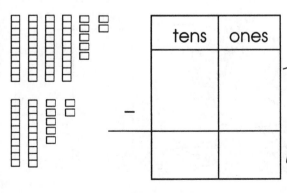

tens	ones

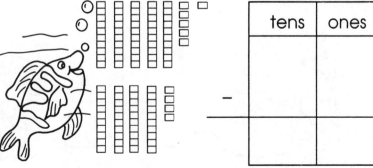

tens	ones

Daily Learning Drills Grade 2

MATH

Name _____

Cookie Mania

There are 46 cookies.
Bill eats 22 cookies.
How many are left?

$$\begin{array}{r} 46 \\ -\ 22 \\ \hline \end{array}$$

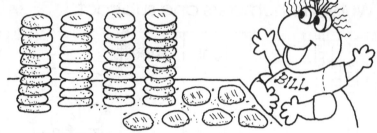

1.	Put numbers on ten's and one's table.

tens	ones
4	6
− 2	2

2.	Subtract ones.

tens	ones
4	6
− 2	2
	4

3.	Subtract tens.

tens	ones
4	6
− 2	2
2	4

There are __24__ cookies left.

Try these. Subtract the ones first. Then subtract the tens.

tens	ones
7	8
− 2	5

tens	ones
5	9
− 3	6

tens	ones
8	3
− 6	1

tens	ones
6	7
− 4	3

Rewrite in column form. Subtract ones, then tens.

97 − 14 = ____

tens	ones
−	

54 − 30 = ____

tens	ones
−	

Name _____

Prehistoric Problems

Work problems. Use color code. **25**—blue, **31**—yellow,
57—green, **14**—orange, **21**—brown, **11**—red

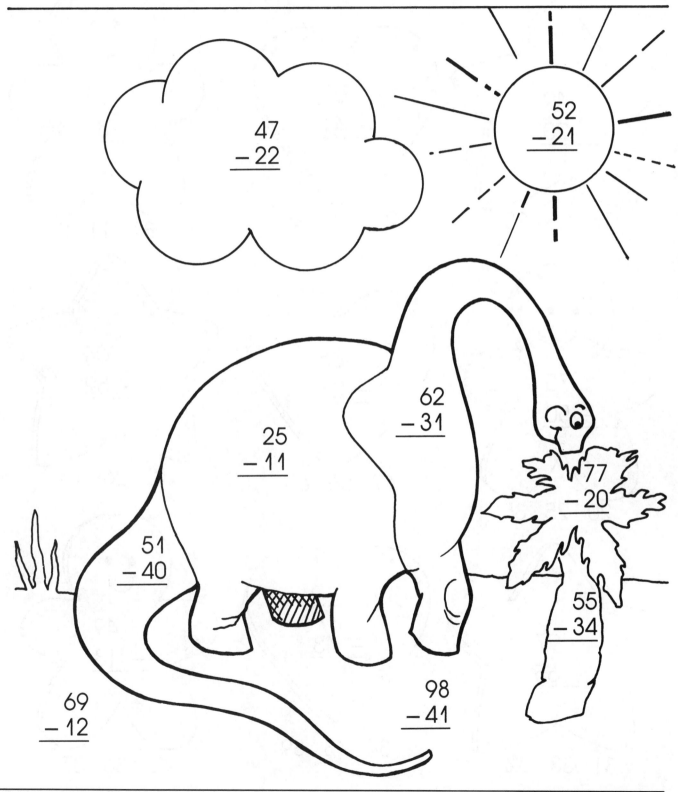

$$\begin{array}{r} 47 \\ -\ 22 \\ \hline \end{array}$$

$$\begin{array}{r} 52 \\ -\ 21 \\ \hline \end{array}$$

$$\begin{array}{r} 62 \\ -\ 31 \\ \hline \end{array}$$

$$\begin{array}{r} 25 \\ -\ 11 \\ \hline \end{array}$$

$$\begin{array}{r} 77 \\ -\ 20 \\ \hline \end{array}$$

$$\begin{array}{r} 51 \\ -\ 40 \\ \hline \end{array}$$

$$\begin{array}{r} 55 \\ -\ 34 \\ \hline \end{array}$$

$$\begin{array}{r} 69 \\ -\ 12 \\ \hline \end{array}$$

$$\begin{array}{r} 98 \\ -\ 41 \\ \hline \end{array}$$

MATH

Name _____

Cookie Craze!

Subtract. Circle the difference. Color the cookies with differences greater than 30.

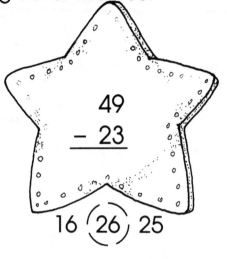

49
− 23

16   (26)   25

67
− 41

26   15   62

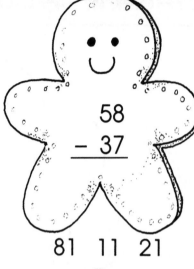

58
− 37

81   11   21

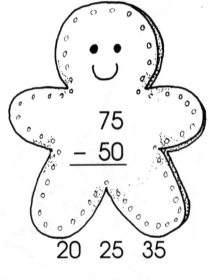

75
− 50

20   25   35

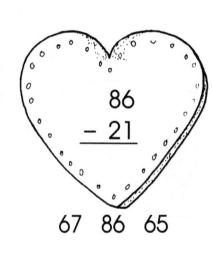

86
− 21

67   86   65

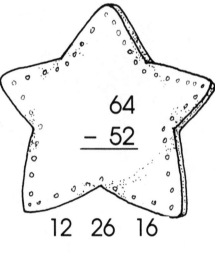

64
− 52

12   26   16

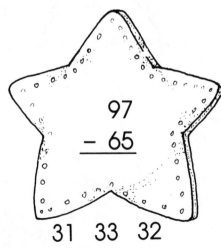

97
− 65

31   33   32

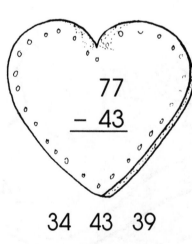

77
− 43

34   43   39

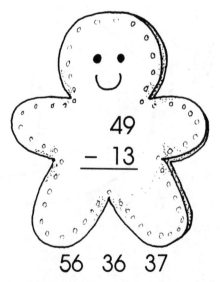

49
− 13

56   36   37

Name _____

Shell Subtraction

Ellen found 32 shells on the beach. She gave 15 shells to Cindy. How many shells does Ellen have now? To find out:

1. Put numbers on ten's and one's table.

tens	ones
3	2
− 1	5

2. Subtract ones. Ask: Do I need to regroup?

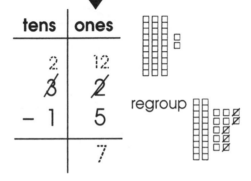

tens	ones
2	12
3	2
− 1	5
	7

regroup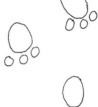

32 = 2 tens and 12 ones

3. Subtract tens.

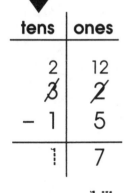

tens	ones
2	12
3	2
− 1	5
1	7

Ellen has __17__ shells now.

Try this. Subtract. Regroup as needed.

tens	ones
4	1
− 1	7

tens	ones
7	5
− 3	8

tens	ones
5	0
− 2	6

tens	ones
3	6
− 1	9

MATH

Name _____

Driving You Crazy
Match the drivers to their cars.

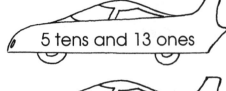
5 tens and 13 ones

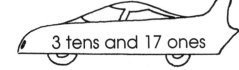
4 tens and 18 ones

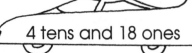
3 tens and 17 ones

0 tens and 16 ones

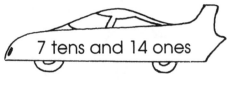
7 tens and 14 ones

1 ten and 10 ones

Regroup. Write how many tens and ones.

_____ tens and _____ ones

_____ tens and _____ ones

_____ tens and _____ ones

Name _____

Hatta Boy!

Subtract. Regroup as needed. Write your answers on the hats.

66 – 49

43 – 25

34 – 16

42 – 29

52 – 17

72 – 34

46 – 28

67 – 28

Name _____

Subtraction on the Beach

Subtract. Regroup as needed. Color the spaces with differences of:

10-19	red	30-39	green
50-59	brown	20-29	blue
40-49	yellow	60-69	orange

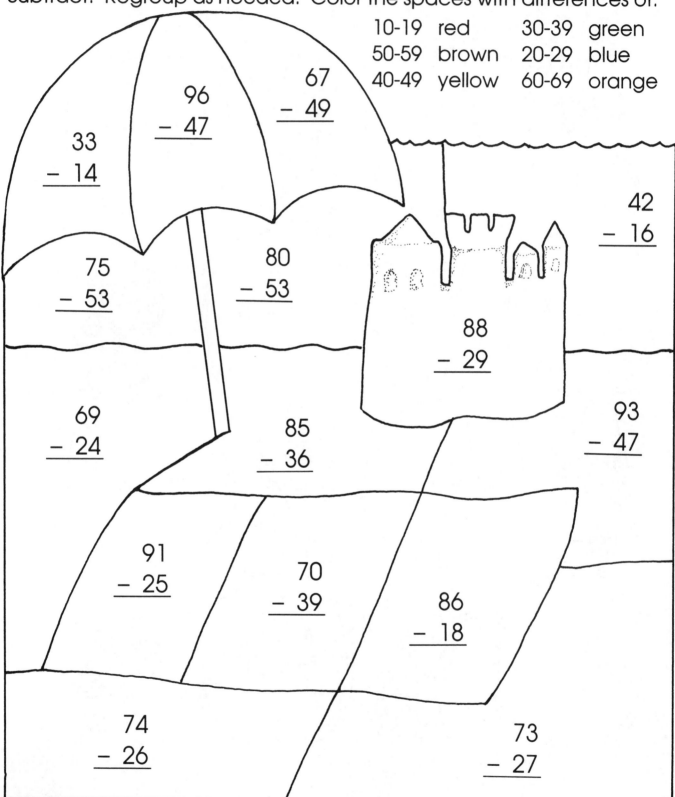

$$96 - 47$$

$$67 - 49$$

$$33 - 14$$

$$75 - 53$$

$$80 - 53$$

$$42 - 16$$

$$88 - 29$$

$$69 - 24$$

$$85 - 36$$

$$93 - 47$$

$$91 - 25$$

$$70 - 39$$

$$86 - 18$$

$$74 - 26$$

$$73 - 27$$

Name _____

How's Your Pitch?

Subtract. Write each answer.

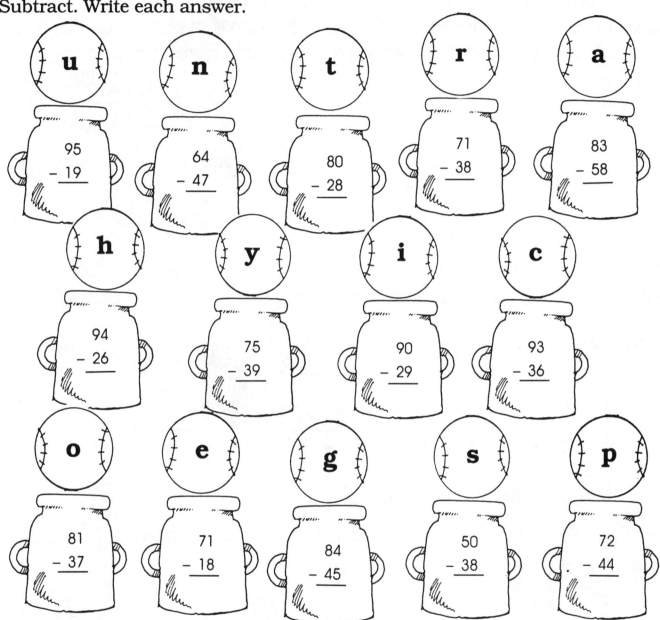

Use the answers and the letters on the baseballs to solve the code.

___ ___ ___ ___   ___ ___ ___ ___ ___   ___ ___
36 44 76 33   28 61 52 57 68   61 12

___ ___ ___ ___ ___   ___ ___   ___ ___ ___ ___ ___ ___!
33 61 39 68 52   44 17   52 25 33 39 53 52

Name _____

Airport Action

To find out if the answer to a subtraction problem is correct, add the answer to the number taken away. If the sum is the same as the first number in the subtraction problem, then the answer is correct.

Example 1

$$
\begin{array}{r}
{\scriptstyle 3\ 13} \\
4\cancel{3} \\
-\ 27 \\
\hline
16
\end{array}
\quad\longrightarrow\quad
\begin{array}{r}
{\scriptstyle 1} \\
16 \\
+\ 27 \\
\hline
43
\end{array}
$$

Since the sum is the same as the first number in the subtraction problem, the answer to the subtraction problem must be correct.

Example 2

$$
\begin{array}{r}
{\scriptstyle 6\ 11} \\
7\cancel{1} \\
-\ 28 \\
\hline
43
\end{array}
\quad\longrightarrow\quad
\begin{array}{r}
{\scriptstyle 1} \\
43 \\
+\ 28 \\
\hline
71
\end{array}
$$

Check the subtraction by adding.

$$
\begin{array}{r}
52 \\
-\ 37 \\
\hline
25
\end{array}
\quad\longrightarrow\quad +\ \rule{2cm}{0.4pt}
$$

Is the subtraction problem correct? _____
How do you know?

Subtract. Then add to check.

$$
\begin{array}{r}
52 \\
-\ 37 \\
\hline
\end{array}
\ \longrightarrow\ +\ \rule{1.5cm}{0.4pt}
\qquad
\begin{array}{r}
80 \\
-\ 26 \\
\hline
\end{array}
\ \longrightarrow\ +\ \rule{1.5cm}{0.4pt}
\qquad
\begin{array}{r}
64 \\
-\ 48 \\
\hline
\end{array}
\ \longrightarrow\ +\ \rule{1.5cm}{0.4pt}
$$

Name _____

Playing in the Park

Circle **Add** or **Subtract**. Then, write a number sentence to solve each problem. Think and check to see if your answer makes sense.

1. There are 6 swings. Four children are swinging. How many swings are empty?

   Add   Subtract

   ____ swings

2. The slide has 8 steps. Craig climbed 3 steps. How many more steps must he climb?

   Add   Subtract

   ____ steps

3. Ellen went across the monkey bars 5 times. So did Brooke. How many times did both girls go across?

   Add   Subtract

   ____ times

4. Three girls sat on one park bench. Three boys sat on another bench. How many children are sitting on both benches?

   Add   Subtract

   ____ children

Name _____

Superstar Students

Fill in the table using the information given. Then answer the questions.

Second Grade Students at Superstar School

Class	Boys	Girls	Total
A		17	28
B	12	15	
C	9		23
Total			

1. Which class has the most students? _____

2. Which class has the least students? _____

3. How many more girls than boys are in second grade? _____

4. Which class has the most boys? _____

5. Which class has the least girls? _____

6. If each boy in class A gave his teacher an apple, how many apples would she get? _____

7. How many students are in second grade at Superstar School? _____ Outline in red the box that tells this.

8. How many more students are in class A than class C? _____

9. If each boy in class B gave a girl in class A an apple, how many girls would not get an apple? _____

10. If 9 students move away, how many students would be in second grade then? _____

Name _____

Tree Troubles

Help the squirrels get to their trees. Add or subtract in your head.
Write the final answer on the tree.

$3 + 4 + 5 - 3 - 2 =$

$5 - 2 + 6 + 3 - 4 =$

$9 - 3 + 5 - 4 + 2 =$

$6 + 6 - 5 + 3 - 2 =$

$8 + 4 - 6 + 5 - 3 =$

Roll Call

Name _____

Look at the animals at the top of the page. Write the correct word to tell where each animal is standing in the line.

 1. _____

 2. _____

 3. _____

 4. _____

 5. _____

 6. _____

 7. _____

 8. _____

 9. _____

 10. _____

Word Bank

first
second
third
fourth
fifth
sixth
seventh
eighth
ninth
tenth

Name _____

My First Treat Will Be . . .

Circle the ordinal number word for each treat.

1.

2.

3.

4.

16.

 third, sixteenth, (fifth)

 fifteenth, fourth, first

5.

twelfth, second, seventh

15.

third, eleventh, fifteenth

6.

14.

 eighth, first, tenth

sixteenth, thirteenth, third

7.

ninth, second, thirteenth

13.

 sixth, seventh, ninth,

8.

12.

11.

10.

9.

Name _____

Two by Two

Finish counting.

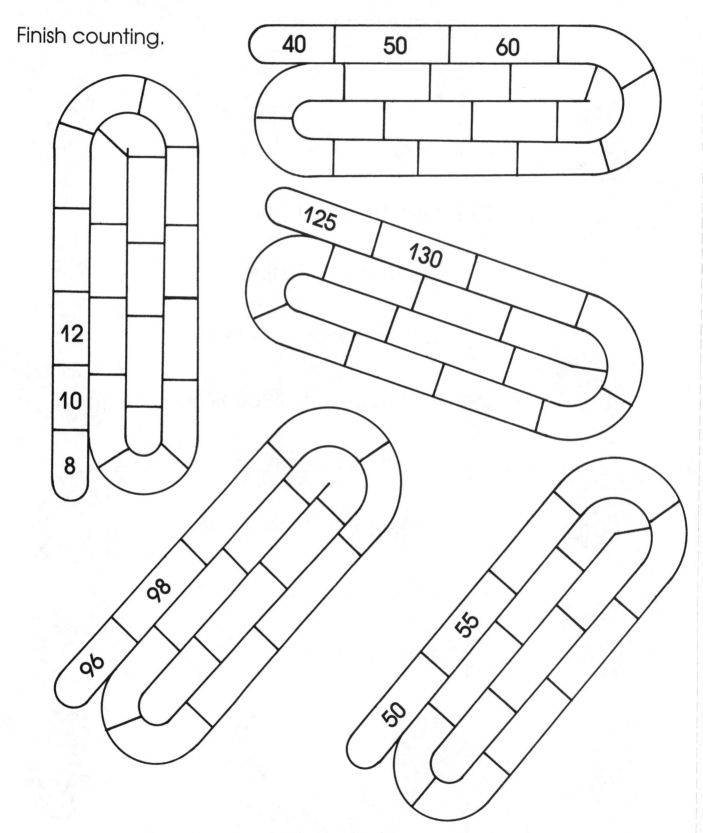

Name _____

Critter Count

Number of 's found.    = 5

    = 2 0

    = _____

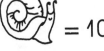   = _____

Number of 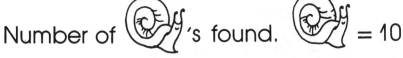's found.   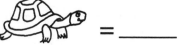 = 10

       = _____

   = _____

    = _____

Number of 's found.   = 2

   = _____

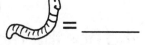 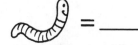   = _____

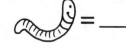      = _____

Name _____

Who Has the Most?
Circle the right answer.

1.

Jane has 3 🐷's.
Bob has 4 🐷's.
Bill has 5 🐷's.

Who has the most 🐷's?

Jane   Bob   Bill

2.

Pam has 7 🐶's.
Joe has 5 🐶's.
Jane has 6 🐶's.

Who has the most 🐶's?

Pam   Joe   Jane

3.

Amy has 23 🐰's.

Sandy has 19 🐰's.

Jack has 25 🐰's.

Who has the most 🐰's?

Amy   Sandy   Jack

4.

Ann has 19 🐔's.

Burt has 18 🐔's.

Brent has 17 🐔's.

Who has the most 🐔's?

Ann   Burt   Brent

5.

The boys have 14 🐱's.
The girls have 16 🐱's.
The teachers have 17 🐱's.

Who has the most 🐱's?

boys   girls   teachers

6.

Rose has 12 🐄's.

Betsy has 11 🐄's.

Ann has 13 🐄's.

Who has the most 🐄's?

Rose   Betsy   Ann

Name _____

Who Has the Least?
Circle the right answer.

1.
Pat had 4 🏈's.
Charles had 3 🏈's.
Jane had 5 🏈's.

Who had the least number of 🏈's?

Pat   Charles   Jane

2.
Jeff has 5 🏀's.
John has 4 🏀's.
Bill has 6 🏀's.

Who has the least number of 🏀's?

Jeff   John   Bill

3.
Jane has 7 ⚾'s.
Peg has 9 ⚾'s.
Fred has 8 ⚾'s.

Who has the least number of ⚾'s?

Jane   Peg   Fred

4.
Charles bought 12 ⛳'s.
Rose bought 6 ⛳'s.
Mother bought 24 ⛳'s.

Who bought the least number of ⛳'s?

Charles   Rose   Mother

5.
John had 9 ⚽'s.
Jack had 8 ⚽'s.
Jeff had 7 ⚽'s.

Who had the least number of ⚽'s?

John   Jack   Jeff

6.
Alma bought 12 🎾's.
Nina bought 16 🎾's.
Marty bought 13 🎾's.

Who bought the least number of 🎾's?

Alma   Nina   Marty

Name _____

Munch a Bunch

Gertrude Goat and her friends Ginger, George, and Gus are making special popcorn balls. Each piece of popcorn has a number on it.

Read the clues to find out which pieces of popcorn each goat will use for his/her popcorn ball. Write the numbers on the popcorn.

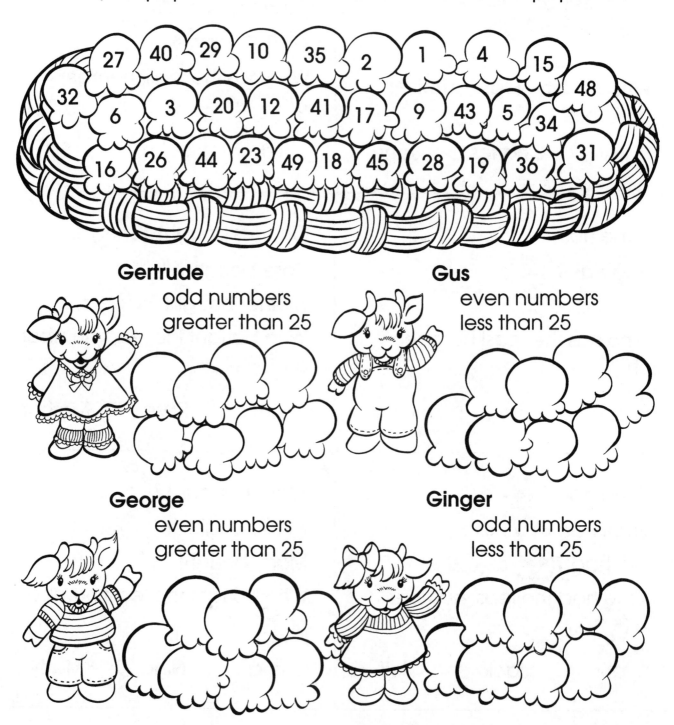

Gertrude
odd numbers
greater than 25

Gus
even numbers
less than 25

George
even numbers
greater than 25

Ginger
odd numbers
less than 25

Name _____

"Mouth" Math

Write < or > in each circle. Make sure the "mouth" is open toward the greater number!

36 ◯ 49   35 ◯ 53

20 ◯ 18   74 ◯ 21

53 ◯ 76   68 ◯ 80

29 ◯ 26   45 ◯ 19

90 ◯ 89   70 ◯ 67

Name _____

Right on Time

Cut out the time signs at the bottom of the page. Paste each sign on the engine next to the correct clock.

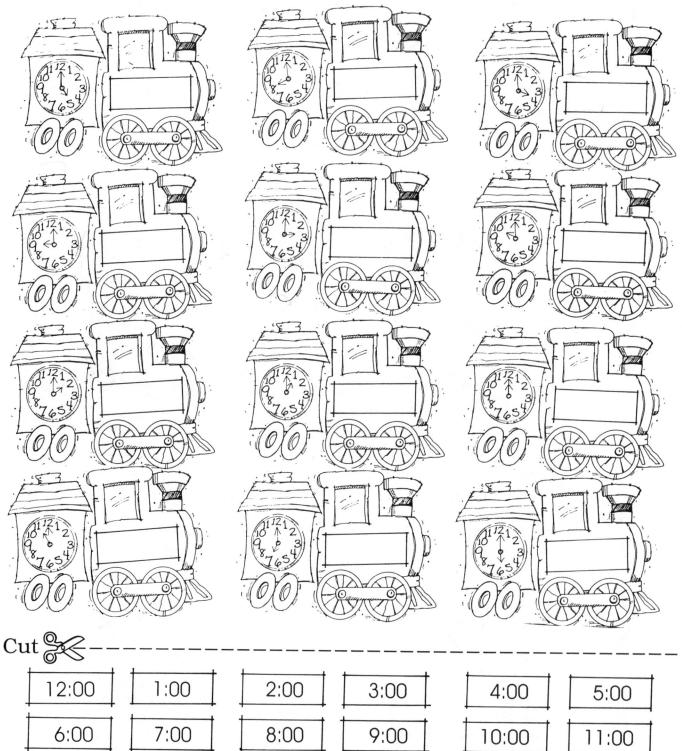

Cut ✂ -

12:00	1:00		2:00	3:00		4:00	5:00
6:00	7:00		8:00	9:00		10:00	11:00

Name _____

Space Time

What time is it?

3:00

_____

_____

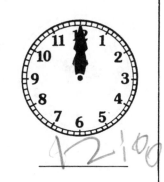

12:00

8:00

_____

2:00

_____

_____

_____

7:00

11:00

MATH

Name _____

Turtle Time
What time is it?

_____   _____

_____   _____   _____

_____   _____   _____

_____   _____   _____

Name _____

My Family Time Tree

Write the time.
Draw the hands on each clock.

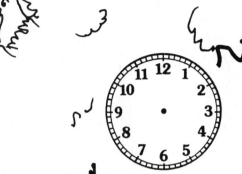

I get up at_____.

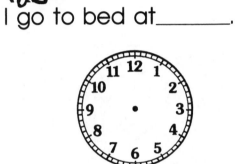

I go to bed at_____.

School starts at_____.

I watch TV at_____.

Lunch is at 12:00.

Dinner is at_____.

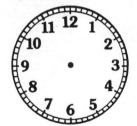

Recess is at_____.

School ends at_____.

I play at_____.

MATH

Name _____

Time to Clean Up

Match the digital time with each clock face by cutting and pasting each lid on the correct trash can.

Cut ✂

12:25	1:30	2:55	3:10
4:15	5:40	6:45	7:35
8:00	9:05	10:50	11:20

Name _____

It's About Time!

✏️ Trace each 🐭 with red if it has a time word.

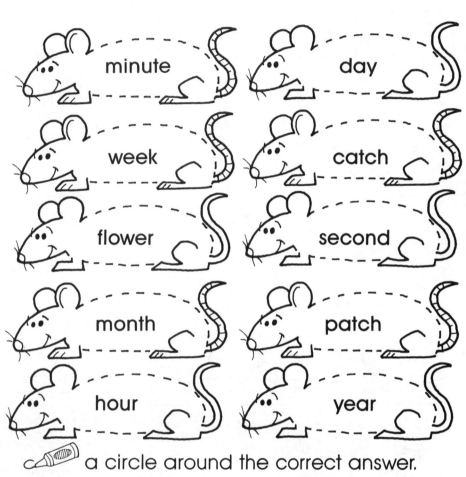

minute	day
week	catch
flower	second
month	patch
hour	year

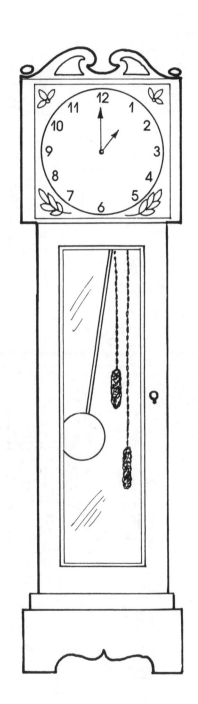

✏️ a circle around the correct answer.

1. There are sixty seconds in a   minute.
                              year.

2. There are sixty minutes in an   second.
                              hour.

3. There are 24 hours in a   minute.
                              day.

4. There are 365 days in a   year.
                              week.

5. There are seven days in a   week.
                              hour.

6. There are twelve months in a   year.
                              week.

MATH

Name _____

Postage Stamp, Please

Add up the coins on each envelope. Write the total on the stamp.

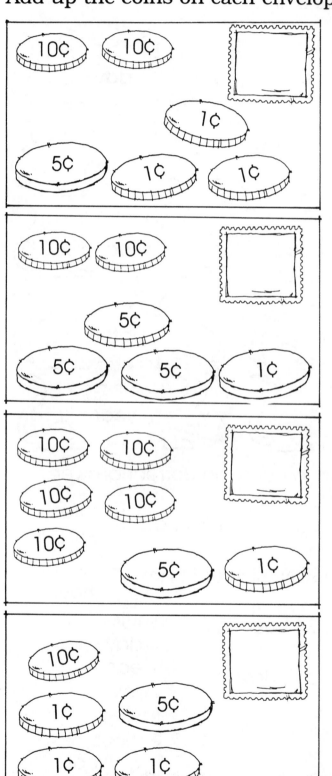

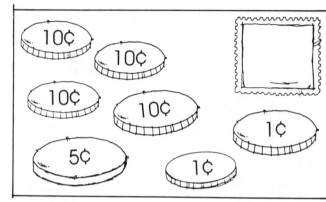

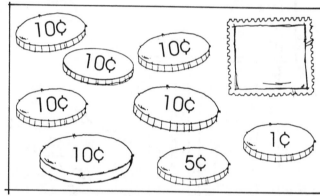

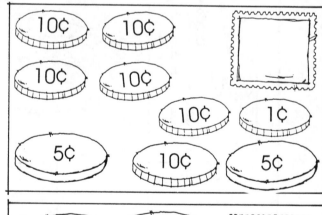

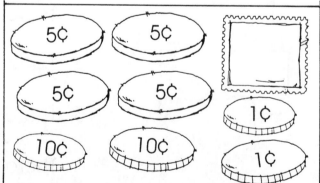

Name _____

Pencil Topper Purchases

Peggy wants to buy three different pencil toppers. Look at the cost of each topper.

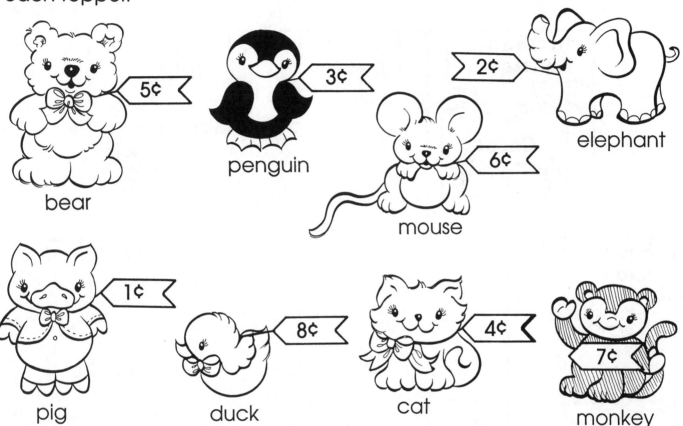

bear — 5¢

penguin — 3¢

mouse — 6¢

elephant — 2¢

pig — 1¢

duck — 8¢

cat — 4¢

monkey — 7¢

Peggy has 12¢ to spend. Write the names of the different pencil topper combinations she might pick.

1. _____   1. _____   1. _____

2. _____   2. _____   2. _____

3. _____   3. _____   3. _____

1. _____   1. _____   1. _____

2. _____   2. _____   2. _____

3. _____   3. _____   3. _____

Daily Learning Drills Grade 2

Name _____

Mall Mania

Count the coins in each purse. Then draw a line from each coin purse to the store where that amount is given.

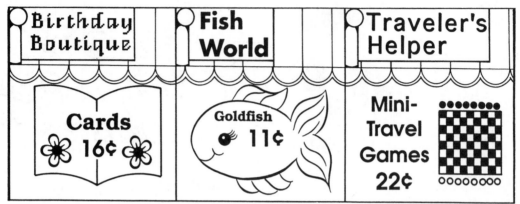

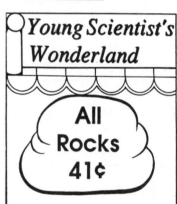

In which store did you not spend any money? _____

Name _____

So Many Choices!

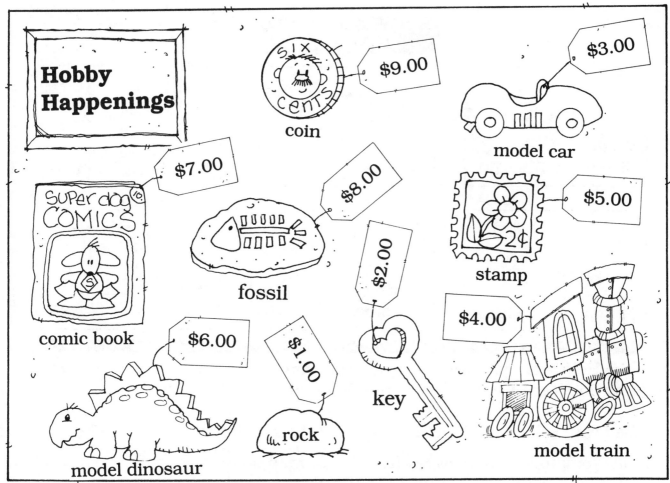

Hobby Happenings

$9.00 — coin

$3.00 — model car

$7.00

$8.00 — fossil

$5.00 — stamp

$2.00

comic book

$6.00

$1.00 — rock

key

$4.00

model dinosaur

model train

You want to buy 3 **different** items in the hobby store. You have $16.00. Write
all the different combinations of items you can buy using the entire $16.00.

1. _____   1. _____   1. _____   1. _____

2. _____   2. _____   2. _____   2. _____

3. _____   3. _____   3. _____   3. _____

1. _____   1. _____   1. _____   1. _____

2. _____   2. _____   2. _____   2. _____

3. _____   3. _____   3. _____   3. _____

Name _____

Earnings Add Up!

Help Wanted

Wash dishes $1.50

Feed cat $.95

Mow lawn $3.50

Mop floors $1.25

Pick tomatoes $2.75

Wash windows $2.85

Use the Help Wanted poster above to help you find out how much you can earn by doing each set of jobs. Write the total amount for each set.

1. feed cat	1. wash dishes	1. wash windows	1. feed cat
2. pick tomatoes	2. mow lawn	2. mop floors	2. wash windows
3. wash dishes	3. wash windows	3. mow lawn	3. mop floors

1. pick tomatoes	1. feed cat	1. pick tomatoes	1. mop floors
2. wash windows	2. wash dishes	2. wash windows	2. pick tomatoes
3. feed cat	3. mop floors	3. mow lawn	3. wash windows

Name _____

Here's Your Order

Count the money on each tray. Write the name of the food that costs that amount.

hamburger ..$2.45	milk ....$.64	cake $2.85
hot dog $1.77	soda pop $1.26	pie $2.25
sandwich $1.55	milkshake ...$1.89	sundae......$.95

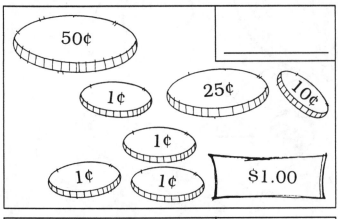

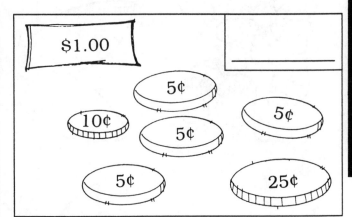

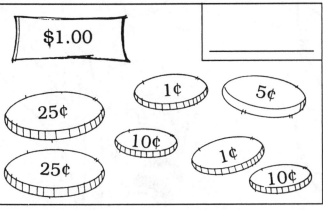

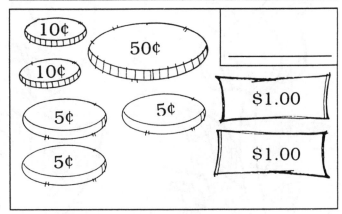

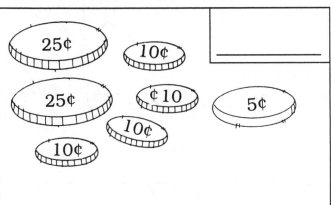

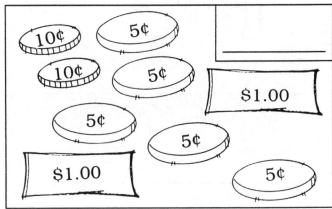

Daily Learning Drills Grade 2

Name _____

Flowers That "Measure" Up

Cut out the centimeter ruler at the bottom of the page. Use the ruler to measure how tall each flower is from the bottom of the stem to the top of the flower. Write the answer below the bee.

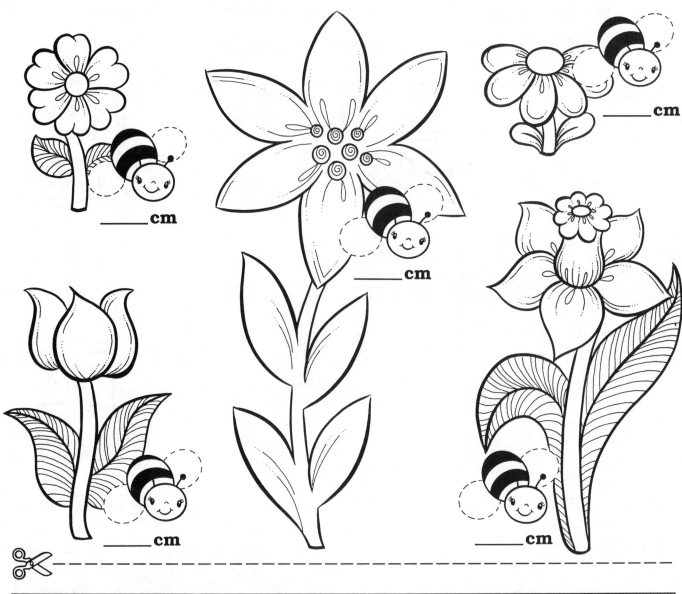

Name _____

Brush Up on Measuring!

Use your centimeter ruler to measure
these brushes to the nearest centimeter.

about _____ centimeters

about _____ centimeters

about _____ centimeters

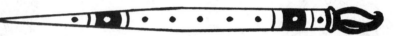

about _____ centimeters

about _____ centimeters

about _____ centimeters

about _____ centimeters

about _____ centimeters

about _____ centimeters

about _____ centimeters

Daily Learning Drills Grade 2

MATH

Name _____

Jungle Journey

Use a centimeter ruler to measure the line segments. Write the total length on each hut.

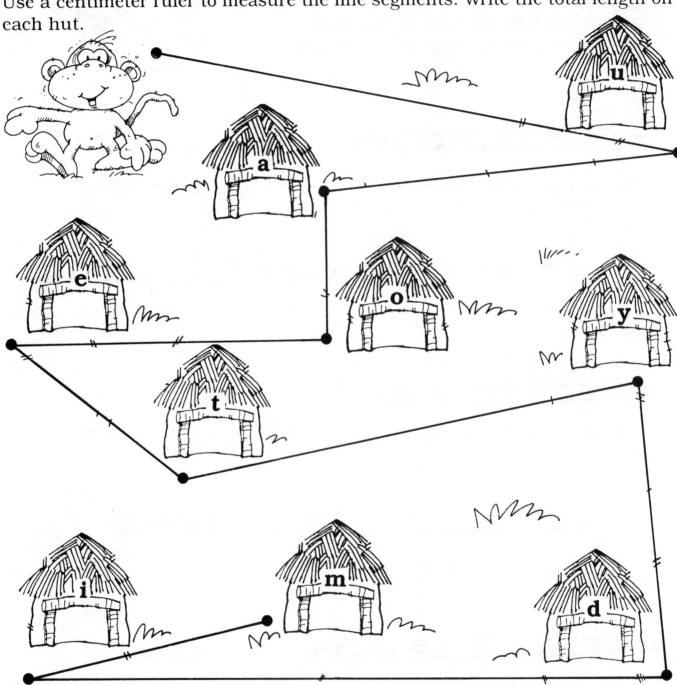

Use the numbers and the letters on the huts to solve the code.

___ ___ ___   ___ ___ ___ ___   ___ ___ !
13   4   15   7   10   8   9   18   6

Name _____

Jumping Jellybeans

Use an inch ruler to measure the line segments. Write the total length on each candy jar.

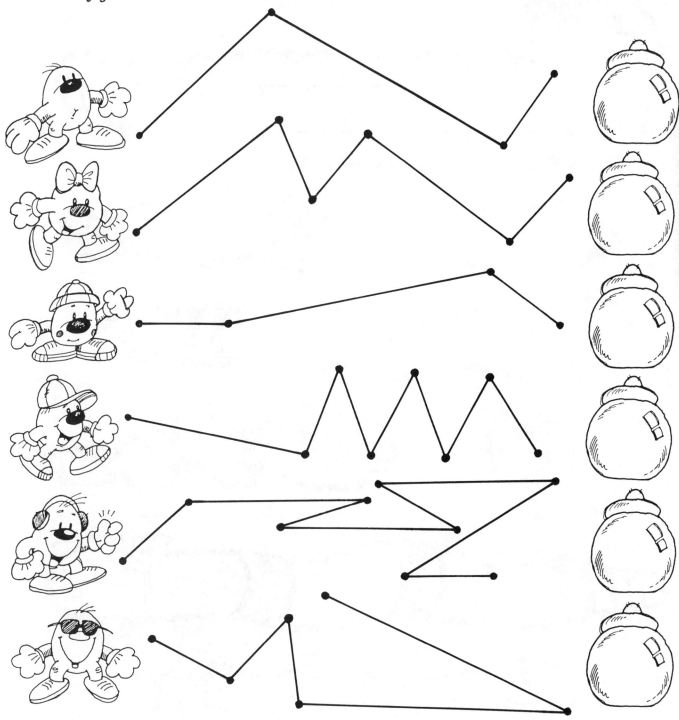

MATH

Name _____

The Inch Worm

Measure these worms to the nearest inch.

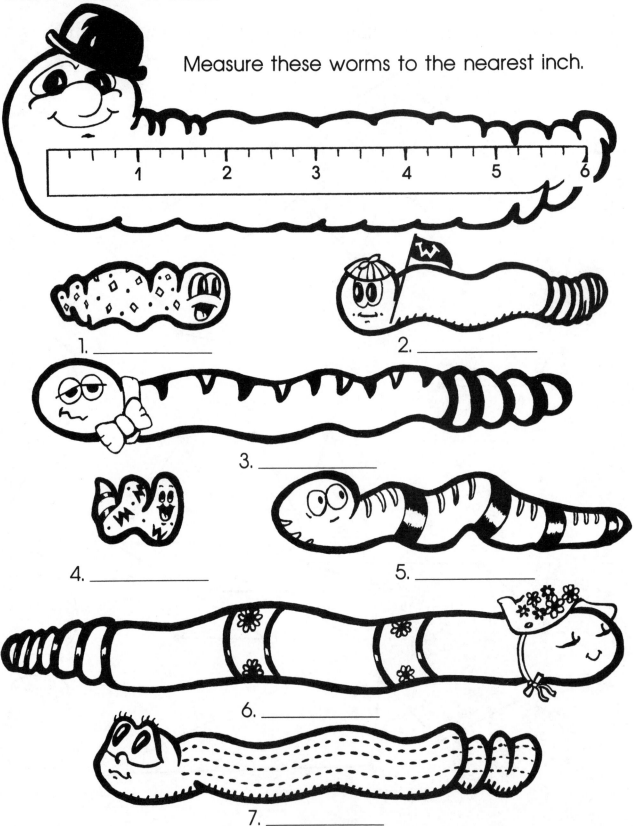

1. _____

2. _____

3. _____

4. _____

5. _____

6. _____

7. _____

Name _____

How Big Are You?

You are getting so big! Every day, you grow a little more. Estimate how long some of your body parts are. Then, using a ruler, work with a friend to find the actual measurements.

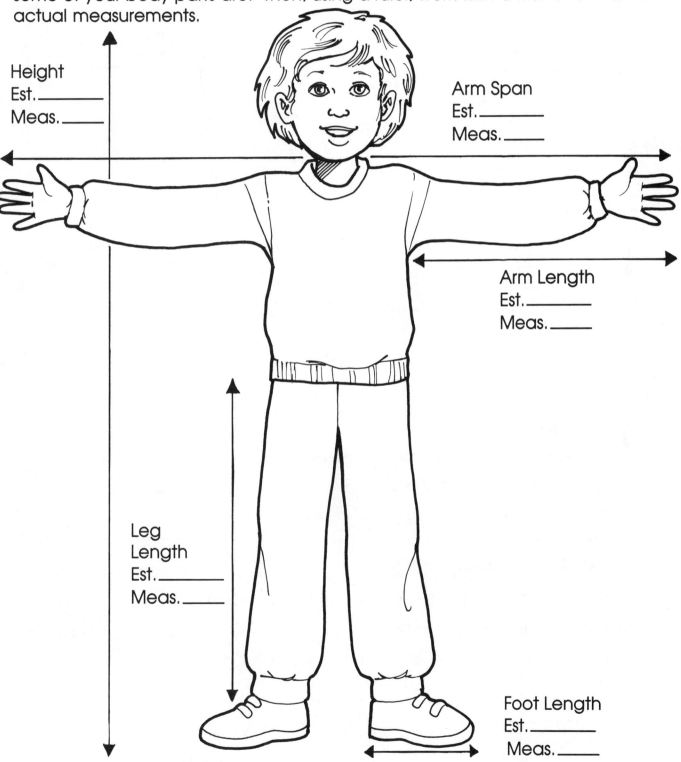

Height
Est. _____
Meas. _____

Arm Span
Est. _____
Meas. _____

Arm Length
Est. _____
Meas. _____

Leg
Length
Est. _____
Meas. _____

Foot Length
Est. _____
Meas. _____

MATH

Name _____

How Far Is It?

Use your ruler to measure each distance on the map. Then use the letters on the tires and your answers to solve the message at the bottom of the page.

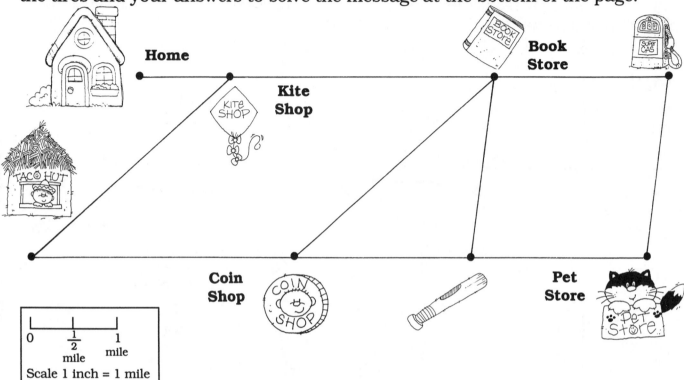

Home   **Kite Shop**   **Book Store**

Coin Shop   **Pet Store**

0    $\frac{1}{2}$ mile   1 mile

Scale 1 inch = 1 mile

How far is it from . . .

1. home to the Kite Shop? _____ **s**

2. home to the Book Store to the Gas Station? _____ **e**

3. home to the Kite Shop to the Taco Hut? _____ **p**

4. the Taco Hut to the Coin Shop to the Book Store to the Gas Station? _____ **a**

5. the Taco Hut to the Coin Shop? _____ **u**

6. the Baseball Field to the Book Store to the Kite Shop? _____ **d**

7. the Pet Store to the Gas Station? _____ **r**

8. the Gas Station to the Pet Store to the Baseball Field to the Coin Shop to the Taco Hut? _____ **m**

You __ __ __ __ __ __ __ __ __ __ !
     9 6 8 1 3 2 6 5   3 4

Name _____

Liquid Limits

Draw a line from the containers on the left to the containers on the right that will hold the same amount of liquid. **Hint:** 2 pints = 1 quart.

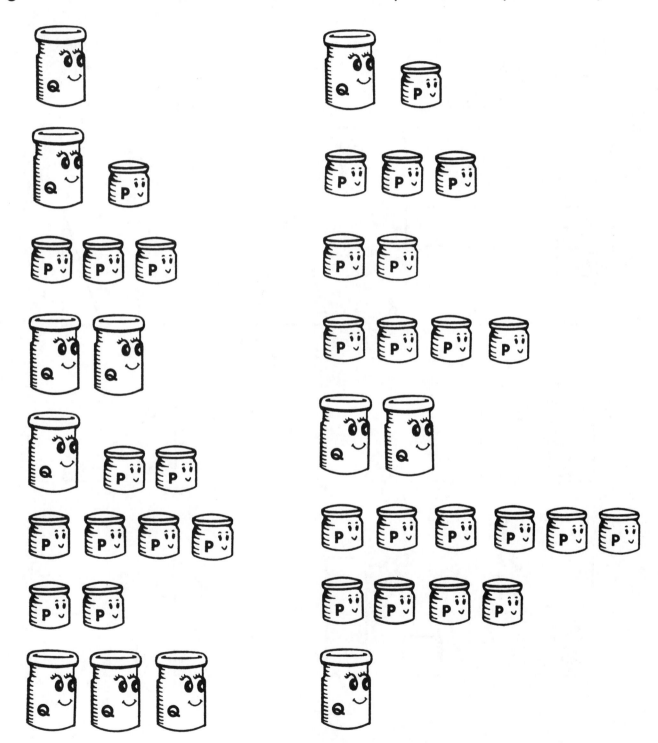

Name _____

Shape Sort

Color the ones in each row that are the same size and shape. Write **T** for triangle, **R** for rectangle and **S** for square.

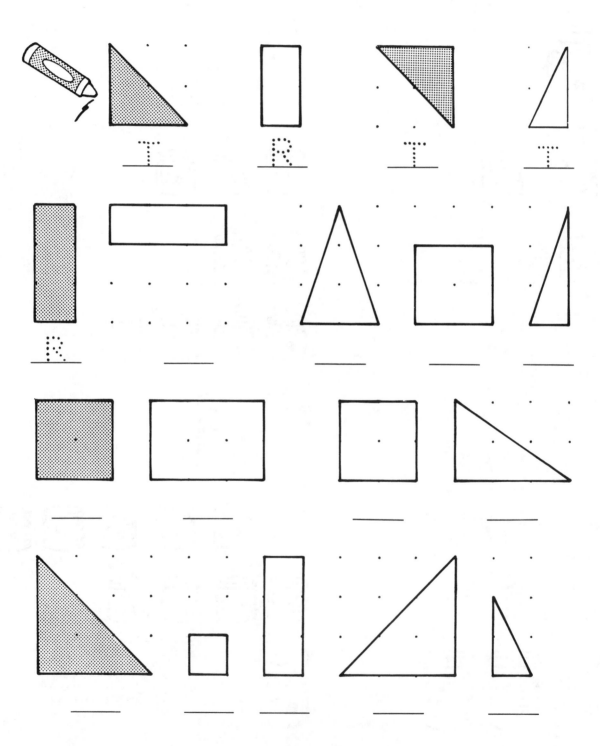

Name _____

Sea Shapes

Find the shapes and color them using the code.

 red   blue   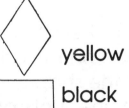 yellow

green   orange   black

Name _____

Equal and Unequal Parts

Cut out each shape below along the solid lines. Then fold the shape on the dotted lines. Do you get equal or unequal parts? Sort the shapes into two piles: those with equal parts and those with unequal parts.

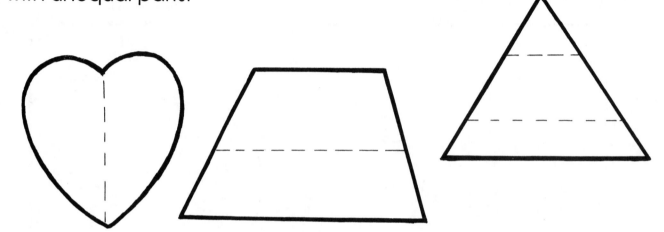

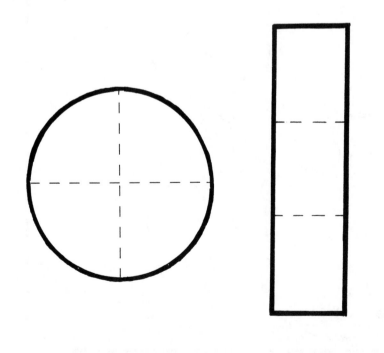

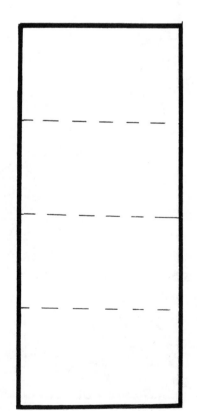

Name _____

Mean Monster's Diet

Mean Monster has to go on a diet. He is so fat he popped all the buttons off his shirt. Help him choose the right piece of food.

1. Mean Monster may have 1/4 of this chocolate pie. Color in 1/4 of the pie.

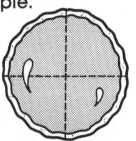

2. Mean Monster may eat 1/3 of this pizza. Color in 1/3 of the pizza.

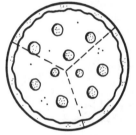

3. For a snack, he wants 1/3 of this chocolate cake. Color in 1/3 of the cake.

4. For lunch, Mean Monster gets 1/2 of the sandwich. Color in 1/2 of the sandwich.

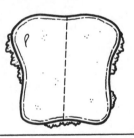

5. For an evening snack, he can have 1/4 of the candy bar. Color in 1/4 of the candy bar.

6. He ate 1/2 of the apple for lunch. Color in 1/2 of the apple.

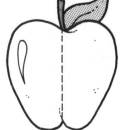

Daily Learning Drills Grade 2

MATH

Name _____

Shaded Shapes

Draw line from fraction to correct shape.

 shaded

 shaded

 shaded

 shaded

 shaded

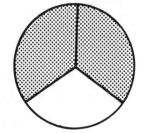 shaded

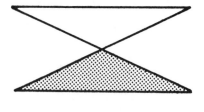

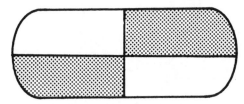

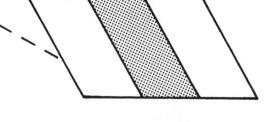

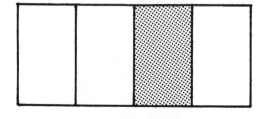

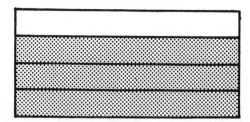

Name _____

Fraction Food

Count the equal parts. Circle the fraction that names one of the parts.

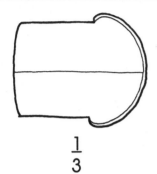

$\frac{1}{2}$ $\frac{1}{3}$ $\frac{1}{4}$

$\frac{1}{2}$ $\frac{1}{3}$ $\frac{1}{4}$

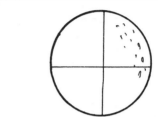

$\frac{1}{2}$ $\frac{1}{3}$ $\frac{1}{4}$

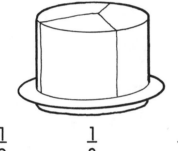

$\frac{1}{2}$ $\frac{1}{3}$ $\frac{1}{4}$

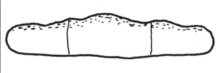

$\frac{1}{2}$ $\frac{1}{3}$ $\frac{1}{4}$

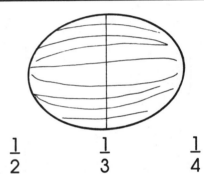

$\frac{1}{2}$ $\frac{1}{3}$ $\frac{1}{4}$

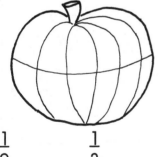

$\frac{1}{2}$ $\frac{1}{3}$ $\frac{1}{4}$

$\frac{1}{2}$ $\frac{1}{3}$ $\frac{1}{4}$

$\frac{1}{2}$ $\frac{1}{3}$ $\frac{1}{4}$

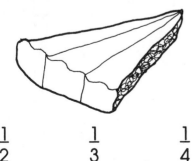

$\frac{1}{2}$ $\frac{1}{3}$ $\frac{1}{4}$

$\frac{1}{2}$ $\frac{1}{3}$ $\frac{1}{4}$

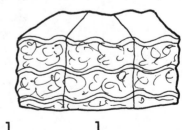

$\frac{1}{2}$ $\frac{1}{3}$ $\frac{1}{4}$

Daily Learning Drills Grade 2

MATH

Name _____

Fortunate Fractions

Read the fraction on each tray. Color the correct number of fortune cookies to show each fraction.

Name _____

Turtle Spots

Count the spots on the turtles.
Color the boxes to show how many spots.

MATH

Name _____

Wormy Apples

Color the boxes to show how many worms.
Answer the questions.

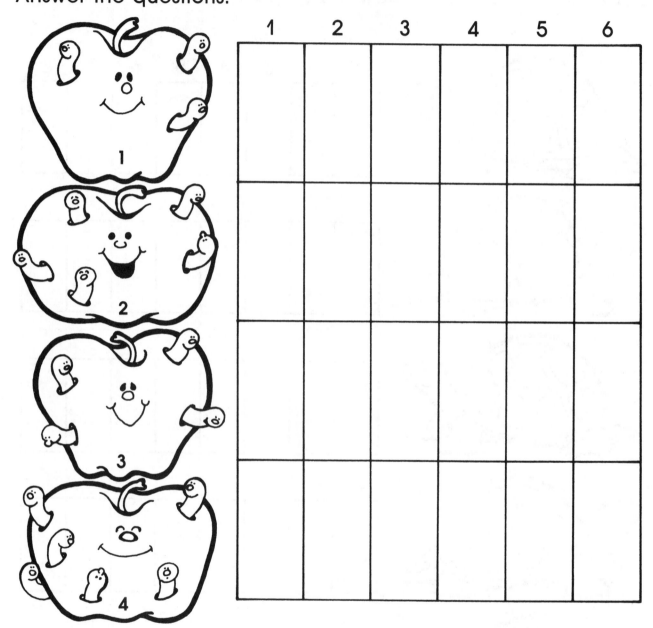

	1	2	3	4	5	6

How many worms in apple 1? ____ 2? ____ 3? ____ 4? ____

In apples 1 and 3? ____ In apples 2 and 4? ____

How many more worms in apple 4 than in apple 2? ____

How many more worms in apple 3 than in apple 1? ____

Name _____

Pat's Fish

This picture graph shows how many fish Pat caught.

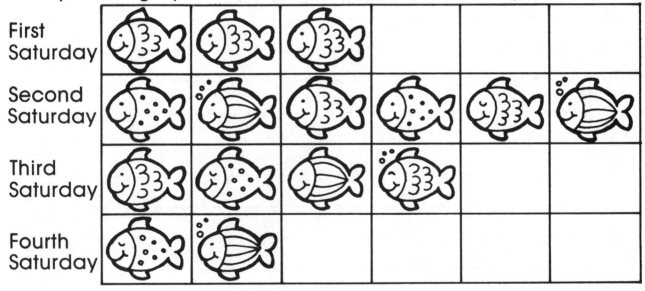

Color the fish Pat caught on the third Saturday red.
Color the fish he caught on the first Saturday blue,
the second Saturday yellow, and the fourth Saturday green.
How many fish did he catch on the first Saturday? ____
second Saturday? ____ third Saturday? ____ fourth Saturday? ____

Name _____

Honey Bear's Bakery

Look at the picture of the bakery. Fill in the graph to show how many of each treat are in the picture.

Number of Bakery Treats

12						
11						
10						
9						
8						
7						
6						
5						
4						
3						
2						
1						
0						

Name _____

Treasure Quest

Read the directions. Draw the pictures where they belong on the grid.

Start at 0 and go . . .

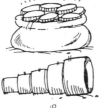

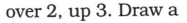

over 2, up 5. Draw a   over 7, up 1. Draw a

over 9, up 3. Draw a   over 6, up 4. Draw a

over 8, up 6. Draw a   over 2, up 3. Draw a

over 5, up 2. Draw a   over 3, up 1. Draw a

over 1, up 7. Draw a   over 4, up 6. Draw a

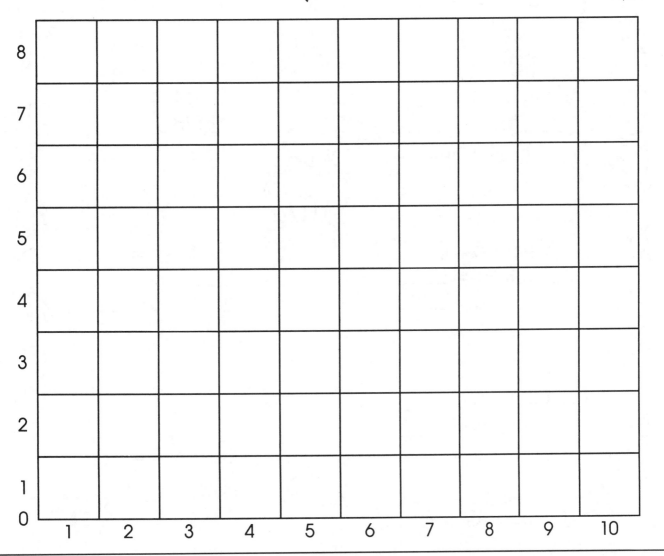

Daily Learning Drills Grade 2

Name _____

Multiplying Rabbits

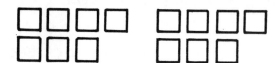

$$7 + 7 = \underline{14}$$
2 sevens = _____
$$2 \times 7 = \underline{}$$

$$\underline{8} + \underline{8} = \underline{16}$$
2 eights = _____
$$2 \times \underline{8} = \underline{}$$

$$2 + 2 + 2 + 2 = \underline{}$$
_____twos = _____
$$\underline{} \times 2 = \underline{}$$

$$3 + 3 + 3 + 3 + 3 = \underline{}$$
_____threes = _____
$$\underline{} \times 3 = \underline{}$$

$$4 + 4 + 4 = \underline{}$$
_____fours = _____
$$\underline{} \times 4 = \underline{}$$

$$9 + 9 = \underline{}$$
2 nines = _____
$$\underline{} \times 9 = \underline{}$$

$$5 + 5 + 5 = \underline{}$$
_____fives = _____
$$\underline{} \times 5 = \underline{}$$

$$6 + 6 = \underline{}$$
_____sixes = _____
$$\underline{} \times 6 = \underline{}$$

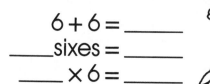
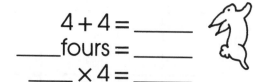

$$3 + 3 + 3 + 3 = \underline{}$$
_____threes = _____
$$\underline{} \times 3 = \underline{}$$

$$4 + 4 = \underline{}$$
_____fours = _____
$$\underline{} \times 4 = \underline{}$$

Name _____

Mr. X and His Cookies

Draw a line from each picture to its matching problem.

    $4 \times 3 = 12$

 $3 \times 3 = 9$

 $2 \times 9 = 18$

       $4 \times 4 = 16$

  $3 \times 6 = 18$

     $3 \times 5 = 15$

    $5 \times 2 = 10$

Daily Learning Drills Grade 2

Name _____

Move That Body

Read a task on the chart. Color the spaces on the chart which show the parts of the body that would be used for the task.

Tasks	head	arm	hand	leg	feet
wash dishes					
pull weeds					
play soccer					
play on a slide					
use a skateboard					
$1 + 1 = 2$ do homework					
play catch					

Name _____

Body Works

Read the clues. Write the words in the puzzle.

Across:

2. You use these to breathe.
4. You need to do this when you're tired.
5. This breaks down food.
7. This tells your body what to do.
9. A gas you breathe.
10. It pumps blood.

Down:

1. It carries oxygen to your body.
3. Microscopic living things that can make you sick.
6. This helps when you are sick.
8. These support and shape your body.

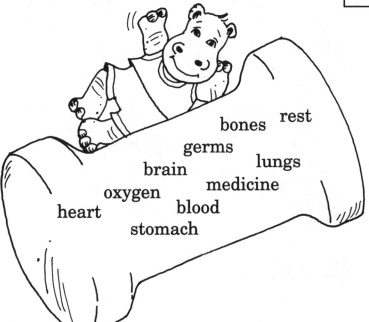

bones   rest
germs
brain   lungs
oxygen   medicine
heart   blood
stomach

SCIENCE

Name _____

My Bones

Bones give your body shape. They let you stand up tall. You cannot see your bones. But you can feel many of your bones under your skin.

Draw a line from each bone to the part of the body where it is found. Write the name of the bone(s).

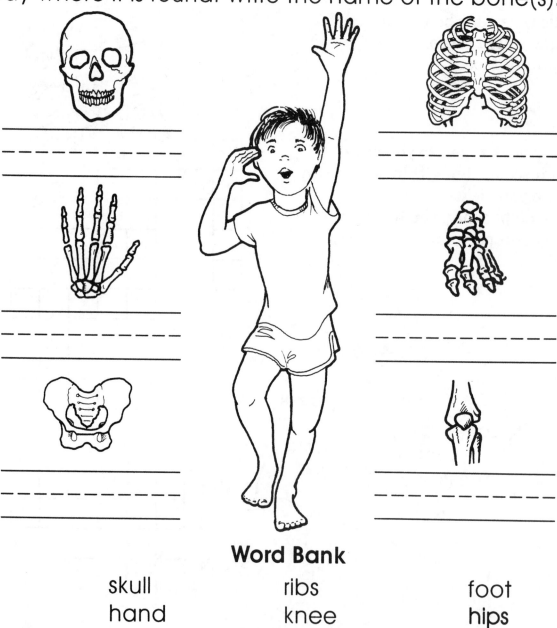

Word Bank

| skull | ribs | foot |
| hand | knee | hips |

Name _____

Name That Bone

Name these bones of your skeleton.

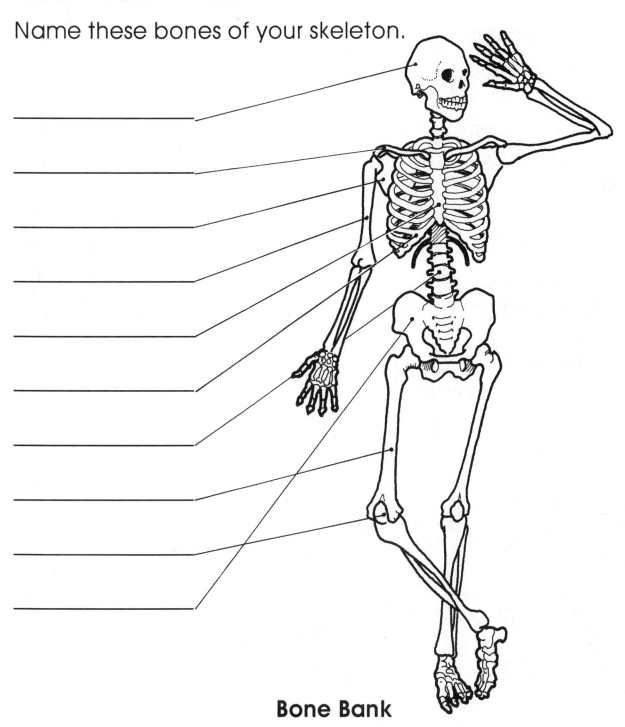

_____

_____

_____

_____

_____

_____

_____

_____

Bone Bank

hipbone	arm bone	backbone	rib
collarbone	breastbone	leg bone	skull
knee bone	shoulder blade		

SCIENCE

Crossbones

Name _____

Across

3. protects your heart and lungs
6. all of your bones
7. connects your leg and foot

Down

1. on the end of your hands
2. on the end of your feet
4. spine
5. makes your leg bend
6. protects your brain

Bone Chest

ribs toes fingers
knee skull backbone
ankle skeleton

Name _____

Outfitted for Health

Read the phrases in the Word Bank. Write only the **good** health habits on the lines.

Word Bank	Take a bath. Drink water. Sit all day. Exercise.	Eat a lot of sweets Get plenty of sleep. Never wash your hands. Eat healthy foods.	Stay up all night. Keep cuts clean. Brush your teeth.

1. _____
   - - - - - - - - - - - - - - - - - -
   _____

2. _____
   - - - - - - - - - - - - - - - - - -
   _____

3. _____
   - - - - - - - - - - - - - - - - - -
   _____

4. _____
   - - - - - - - - - - - - - - - - - -
   _____

5. _____
   - - - - - - - - - - - - - - - - - -
   _____

6. _____
   - - - - - - - - - - - - - - - - - -
   _____

7. _____
   - - - - - - - - - - - - - - - - - -
   _____

SCIENCE

Name _____

Solving the Pyramid's Mystery
Use with page 181.

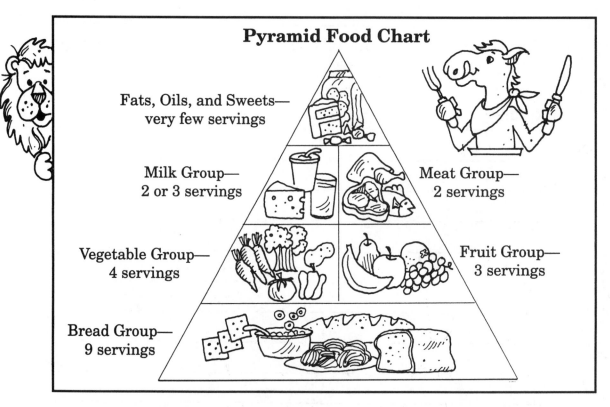

Pyramid Food Chart

Fats, Oils, and Sweets—
very few servings

Milk Group—
2 or 3 servings

Meat Group—
2 servings

Vegetable Group—
4 servings

Fruit Group—
3 servings

Bread Group—
9 servings

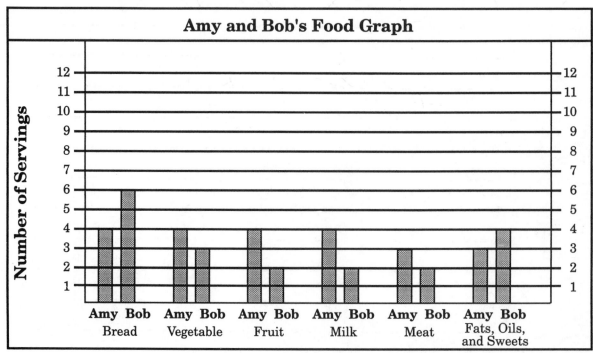

Amy and Bob's Food Graph

Number of Servings

Amy Bob — Bread
Amy Bob — Vegetable
Amy Bob — Fruit
Amy Bob — Milk
Amy Bob — Meat
Amy Bob — Fats, Oils, and Sweets

Name _____

Solving the Pyramid's Mystery (cont.)

Use the graph and Pyramid Food Chart on page 180 to help you answer the questions. Then use your answers and the circled letters to solve the code at the bottom of the page.

1. How many servings of bread did Amy eat? _____ Ⓞ

2. How many servings of bread did Bob eat? _____ Ⓘ

3. How many more servings of vegetables did Amy eat than Bob? _____ Ⓐ

4. Which person ate less servings of fruit? _____ Ⓕ

5. Did Bob drink more or less servings of milk than Amy? _____ Ⓖ

6. Which person ate the most servings of meat? _____ Ⓣ

7. Did Bob eat more or less servings of fats, oils, and sweets than Amy?
   _____ Ⓜ

8. How many less servings of fruit did Bob eat than Amy? _____ Ⓢ

9. Did Amy and Bob eat the needed number of servings of food in the bread
   group? _____ Ⓓ

10. Did they eat at least the needed number of servings of food in the meat
    group? _____ Ⓤ

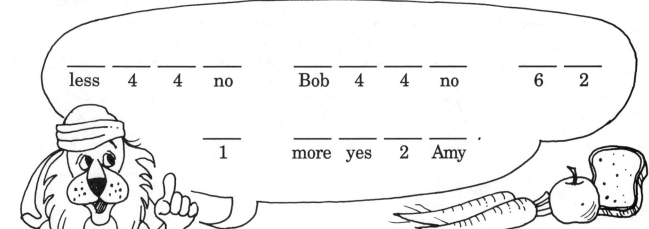

less   4   4   no   Bob   4   4   no   6   2

        1   more yes   2   Amy

Name _____

A "Sense"-ible Arrangement

Cut out the flowers at the bottom of the page. Pick one flower and look at the object and word on it. Paste the flower on the vase that tells which sense you would mainly use with the object on that flower.

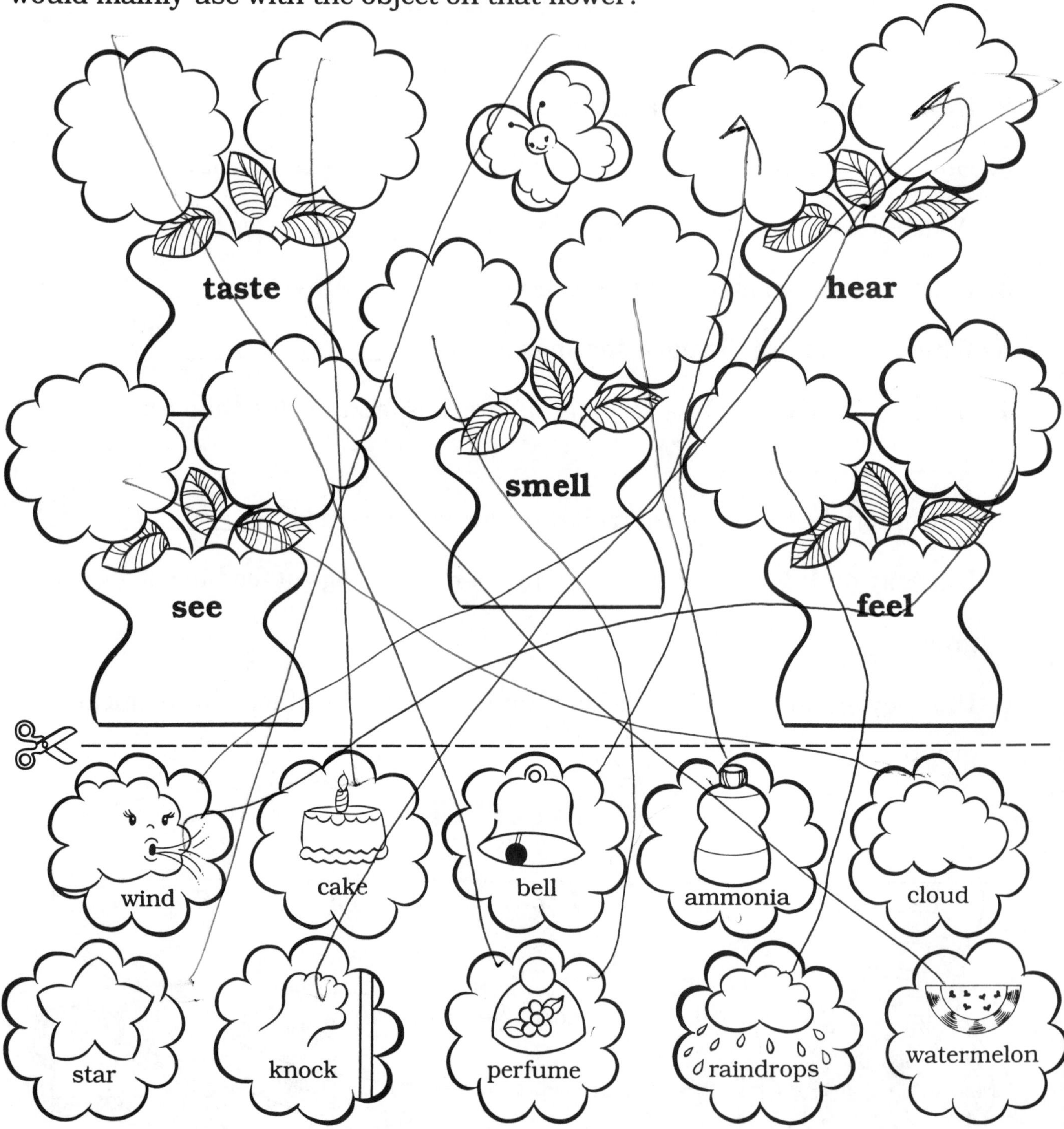

taste

hear

smell

see

feel

wind

cake

bell

ammonia

cloud

star

knock

perfume

raindrops

watermelon

Name _____

Identifying Prints

Cut out the fingerprints at the bottom of the page. Use a magnifying glass to match the cut-out fingerprints to those on the page. Paste each fingerprint next to the one it matches.

Exhibit A | Exhibit B | Exhibit C | Exhibit D | Exhibit E | Exhibit F

SCIENCE

Name _____

Interesting Invertebrates

Invertebrates are animals that have no backbone or inside skeleton. Some have soft bodies protected by shells. Others have soft bodies that are not protected. Some invertebrates are so small that they can only be seen with a microscope.

Below are some examples of invertebrates. Use the clues to name each one.

_____ I P E D E

S ___ ___ ___ F ___ ___ ___

J ___ ___ ___ ___ ___

E ___ ___ ___ ___ ___ W ___ ___ ___

F ___ ___ ___

S ___ ___ ___ ___

D ___ ___ ___ ___ ___ ___

S ___ ___ ___ ___ ___

S ___ ___ ___ C ___ ___ ___ ___ ___ ___ ___

A "Class"-y Group

Name _____

Read a word. If it names a mammal, write **M** above the word. If it names a reptile, write **R** above the word. If it names an amphibian, write **A** above the word. If it names an insect, write **I** above the word. If it names a bird, write **B** above the word. If it names a fish, write **F** above the word. Then draw a line to show where three of these letters are the same in a row.

eel	dragonfly	penguin
turtle	frog	snake
camel	moose	hippopotamus

moth	panda	goldfish
woodpecker	beetle	pig
seagull	ape	fly

Name _____

From the Inside Out

Animals whose skeletons have backbones are called **vertebrates**. The backbone, or spine, is made up of bones called **vertebrae**.

Look at the skeletons below. Use the riddle and the Word Bank to write the name of each vertebrate.

1.  I stand tall and proud. So please don't ask me to eat from the ground.

I am a _____.

5.  I am thankful to be alive at holidays. People might "gobble me up!"

I am a _____.

2.  I have wings, but I cannot fly. I love to strut around in my "tuxedo."

I am a _____.

6. 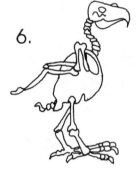 They say I have no hair, and they're right. I represent a great country.

I am a _____.

3.  I am not a bird, but I can fly. Bruce Wayne used me as a model for his costume.

I am a _____.

4. 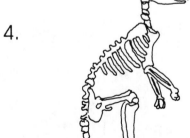 My legs and tail are very strong. I even come with a pocket.

I am a _____.

Word Bank
bald eagle
kangaroo
turkey
penguin
giraffe
bat

Name _____

Fine, Feathered Friends

Do the puzzle about birds.
Color only the birds.

Down

1. _____ keep a bird's body warm and dry.
4. A bird uses its _____ to pick up food.

Across

2. A bird is a _WarM_ -blooded animal.
3. Baby birds are hatched from _eggs_.
5. Birds breathe with their _lungs_.

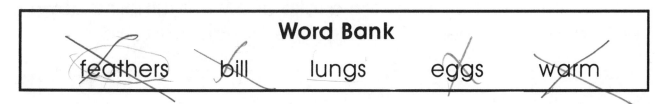

Word Bank				
feathers	bill	lungs	eggs	warm

Daily Learning Drills Grade 2

Name _____

Birds of a Feather

Birds are the only animals that have feathers. All birds have wings, but not all can fly. They all hatch from eggs, have backbones, and are warm-blooded.

The eggs in the nest contain names of different birds. When filling in the puzzle, the last letter of one name becomes the first letter of the next name. Write the names of the birds in the puzzle in the correct order. Start at the outside edge and spiral in toward the center. The first three names are written for you.

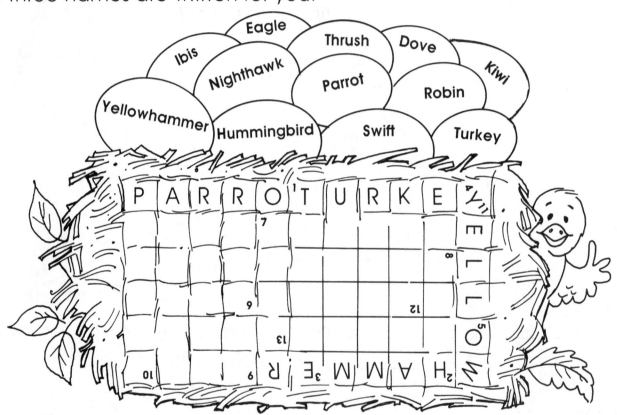

Complete this story. Write the letters from the sections with numbers in the blanks.

A sly and hungry fox quietly crept into the hen house one night. Carefully, he took a basket and began filling it with eggs. As he turned to leave, he tripped on a rake and went tumbling down, eggs and all. The hens awoke, laughed loudly, and said,

" ___ ___ ___   ___ ___ ___ ___ ___ '   ___ ___   ___ ___ ___ !"
  1 2 3   4 5 6 7 8   9 10   11 12 13

A Fish Story

Name _____

Fish live almost anywhere there is water. Although fish come in many different shapes, colors, and sizes, they are alike in many ways.

- All fish have backbones.
- Fish breathe with gills.
- Most fish are cold-blooded.

- Most fish have fins.
- Many fish have scales and fairly tough skin.

Professor Fish teaches a *school* of fish in the ocean. He decided that he would make name tags for everyone. But, he decided to have some fun, and he jumbled the fish' names on their name tags.

Use the clues to unscramble the fish names. Write each name correctly at the top of the name tag. Then use your imagination to draw each fish.

_____ rparto fish (a talking bird)	_____ oinlfish (king of the beasts)	_____ gknifish (opposite of queen)
_____ tbturelfy fish (an insect with colorful wings)	_____ ogatfish (a nanny – or a billy –)	_____ opprucneifish (animal with quills)

SCIENCE

Name _____

A Mixture of Mammals

Mammals live in many different places. They are a special group because they . . .

- can give milk to their babies.
- protect and guide their young.
- are warm-blooded.

- have hair at some time during their lives.
- have a large, well-developed brain.

Below are some silly pictures made from two mammals put together. Write the names of the two real mammals on the lines. The last letter(s) in the name of the first animal is the first letter(s) in the name of the second animal. The first one is done for you.

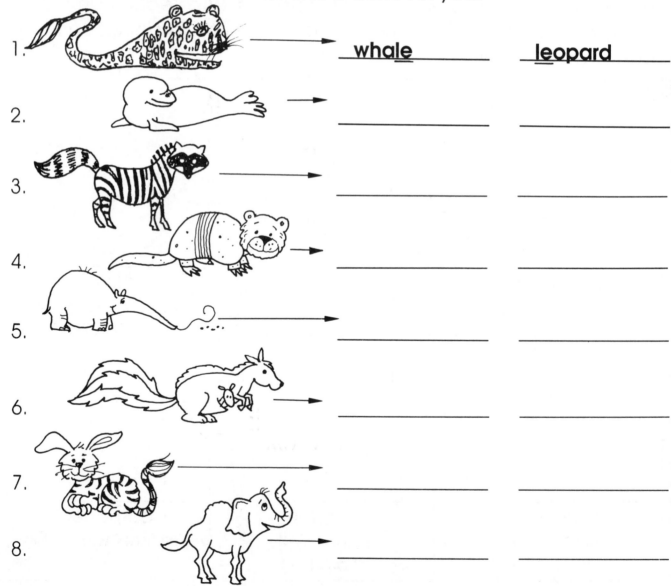

1.   __whale__   __leopard__

2.   _____   _____

3.   _____   _____

4.   _____   _____

5.   _____   _____

6.   _____   _____

7.   _____   _____

8.   _____   _____

Name _____

The Reptile House

There are about 6,000 different kinds of reptiles. They come in all sorts of shapes and colors. Their sizes in length range from 2 inches to almost 30 feet. Reptiles can be found on every continent except Antarctica. Even though reptiles can seem quite different, they all . . .

- breathe with lungs.
- are cold-blooded.
- have dry, scaly skin.
- have a backbone.

In the Reptile House at the zoo, each animal needs to be placed in the correct area. Read the information about each reptile. Then use the clues and the pictures to write the name of each reptile in its area.

Giant Tortoise can live over 100 years. It can hide under its shell for protection.

Reticulated Python is the longest snake. One was almost 33 feet long.

Saltwater Crocodile is one of the largest reptiles. It can weigh 1,000 lbs.

Komodo Dragon is a dragon-like reptile. It is the largest living lizard.

Tuatara is closely related to the extinct dinosaur.

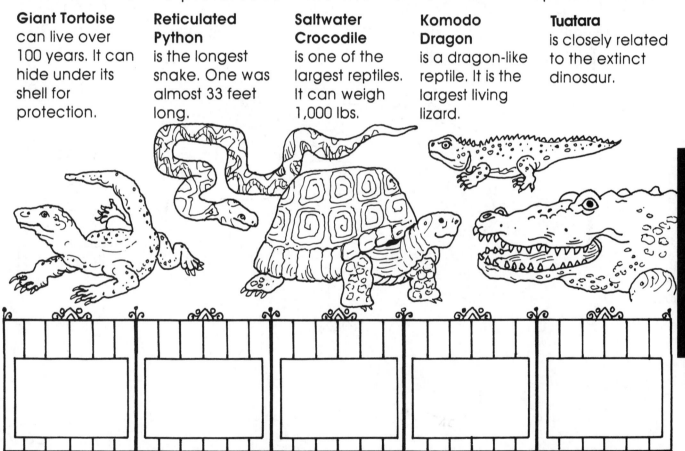

SCIENCE

Clues:
- The snake is between the largest lizard and the largest member of the turtle family.

- A relative of the alligator is on the far right side.

- The reptile who carries its "house" is in the middle.

Name _____

Amazing Amphibians

Amphibians are cold-blooded vertebrates (animals with backbones). They have no scales on their skin. Most amphibians hatch from eggs laid in water or on damp ground. Many amphibians grow legs as they develop into adults. Some live on land and have both lungs and gills for breathing. Frogs and toads are examples of amphibians.

Santjie, a South African sharp-nosed frog, holds the record for the longest triple jump. He jumped a total of more than 33 feet!

The frogs below won 1st, 2nd, and 3rd place in a recent triple-jump contest. Each jump after each frog's first jump was two feet shorter than the jump before. How many total feet did each frog jump? Fill in the answers on the trophies.

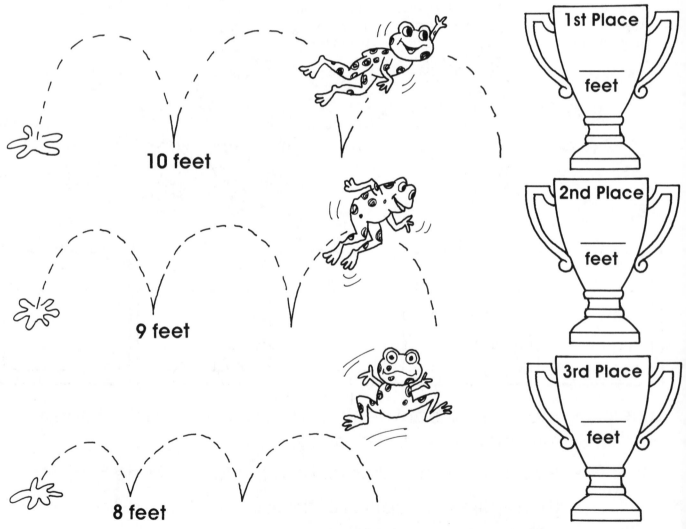

10 feet

9 feet

8 feet

1st Place
_____ feet

2nd Place
_____ feet

3rd Place
_____ feet

Name _____

Plotting Plants

Follow Rupert Rabbit as he learns about plants. Use the words in the Word Bank to help you.

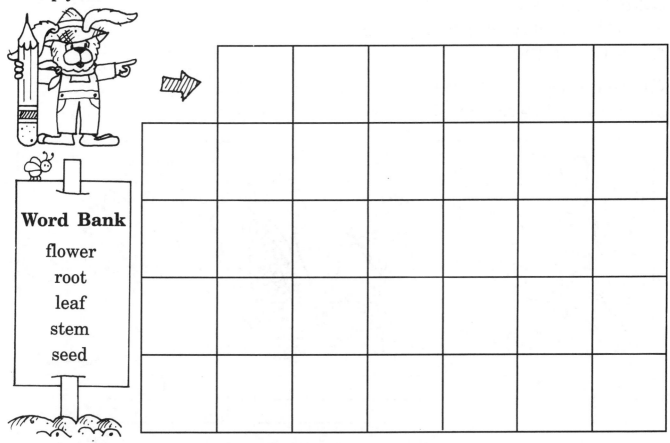

Word Bank

flower
root
leaf
stem
seed

Read and follow the directions. Start at Rupert Rabbit.

1. Go right 5 spaces. Then go down 3 spaces and left 5 spaces. Write the word that names what grows into a new plant here.

2. Now go up 2 spaces. Then go right 6 spaces and down 3 spaces. Write the word that names the part of the plant that is underground here.

3. Now go up 3 spaces. Then go left 3 spaces and down 1 space. Write the word that names the part of the plant that makes the food here.

4. Now go right 2 spaces. Then go up 1 space and left 4 spaces. Write the word that names the part of the plant that carries food and water to the rest of the plant here.

5. Now go down 2 spaces. Then go right 5 spaces and up 3 spaces. Write the word that names the part of the plant that makes the seeds here.

     Daily Learning Drills Grade 2

SCIENCE

Name _____

Those Nutty Seeds

Seeds are found in different
parts of the plant. Some seeds are
found in the flower. Some seeds
are found in the fruit or the nut.

Circle the part of the plant that has the
seed. Write the name of the seed.

Name _____

Traveling Seeds

Seeds travel from one place to another. Sometimes people move the seeds. Sometimes they are moved in other ways.

Finish the sentences to tell how seeds travel.

Word Bank
people
animals
animals
wind
water

Seeds travel with _____ .

Seeds travel in _____ .

Seeds travel on _____ .

Seeds travel in _____ .

Seeds travel in the _____ .

SCIENCE

Daily Learning Drills Grade 2

Name _____

Eyes in the Dark

What has eyes, but cannot see? A potato! The little white bumps that grow on a potato's skin are called "eyes." An eye can grow into a new potato plant.

You will need:
potato
potting soil
flowerpot or plastic glass

1. Put the potato in a dark cupboard or closet. Check it daily for small bumps called "eyes."

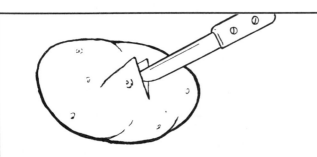

2. When the eyes appear ask an adult to cut them off the potato.

3. Fill a flowerpot half full of potting soil and lay the piece of potato on it with the "eyes" facing up.

Record what happened after . . .

1 week

2 weeks

4. Cover the "eyes" with 1 inch of soil. Water. Keep moist—but not wet. Watch closely for about two weeks.

What happened?

A potato is a tuber. A tuber is a fat underground stem with little buds that can grow into new plants. The "eye" that you planted was really a potato bud that grew into a new plant.

Name _____

Dynamic Dinosaurs

Dinosaurs were reptiles that lived millions of years ago. Some of them were the biggest animals to ever live on land. Some were as small as chickens. Some dinosaurs ate plants, while others were meat-eaters.

Scientists have given names to the dinosaurs that often describe their special bodies, sizes, and habits.

Look at the object(s) placed in the picture with each dinosaur. Use the objects as clues to fill in the blanks and finish each dinosaur's name.

T R I C E R A ___ ___ ___ ___ ___

___ ___ ___ T R O D O N

___ ___ ___ ___ ___ A S A U R U S

___ ___ ___ E O S A U R U S

___ ___ ___ ___ ___ O S A U R U S

SCIENCE

Name _____

Dial a Dinosaur

Danny loves dinosaurs. In fact, he loves them so much that everyone calls him Dinosaur Danny! Find out what Dinosaur Danny's favorite dinosaur is by decoding the message below. To do this, use the numbers on the telephone and the directional markers.

For example: `3` points to the letter D.

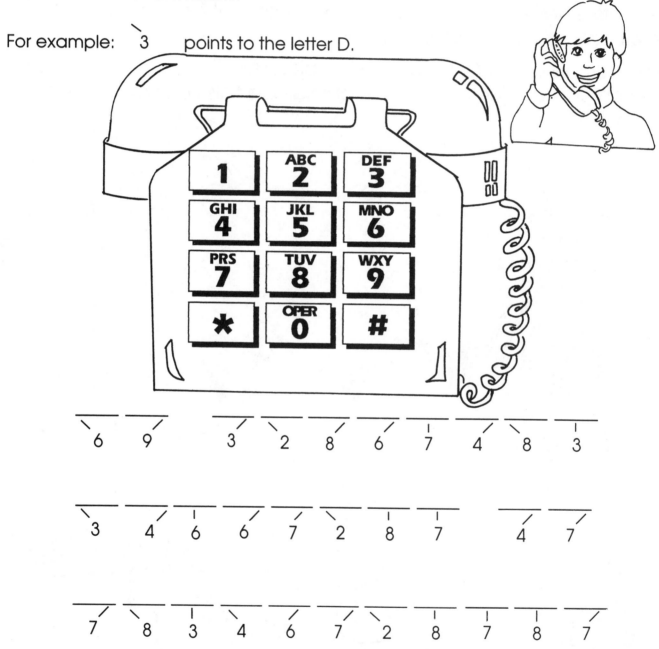

Write your own message and share it with a classmate.

Name _____

Magic Square Mania

Did you know that the word dinosaur comes from two Greek words meaning terrible lizard? Dinosaurs were not lizards at all! To further improve your dinosaur vocabulary, read Column A. Choose an answer from Column B. Write the number of the answer in the Magic Square. The first one has been done for you.

Column A

A.   Person who studies fossils
B.   Petrified remains of animals and plants
C.   Meat-eating dinosaurs
D.   Plant-eating dinosaurs
E.   Movement of animals over long distances
F.   Large bony plates on dinosaur's neck
G.   Bones on the top of a dinosaur's head
H.   The Age of Dinosaurs
I.   Large groups of animals that live together

Column B

1. skeleton
2. Mesozoic Age
3. carnivores
4. herbivores
5. paleontologist
6. migration
7. herds
8. frills
9. crest
10. fossils

A 5	B ___	C ___
D ___	E ___	F ___
G ___	H ___	I ___

Add the numbers across, down and diagonally. What answer do you get? _____

Why do you think this is called a magic square? _____

Name _____

Weather Watch

Weather is the condition of the air around the earth for a period of time. The weatherman's job is to predict the weather.

There were some very unusual weather patterns recorded for a recent month. Use the key to draw the correct weather symbols for each day.

- Every Monday and Tuesday it rained. Then it was sunny for the following three days.
- On the first and third weekends, the first day was cloudy, and the second day was snowy.
- On the second and fourth weekends, it was just the opposite.

Key

sunny

cloudy

rainy

snowy

Sun.	Mon.	Tues.	Wed.	Thurs.	Fri.	Sat.
		1	2	3	4	5
6	7	8	9	10	11	12
13	14	15	16	17	18	19
20	21	22	23	24	25	26
27	28	29	30	31		

Write the word that tells about the weather on these dates:

- 6th day of the month _____
- 13th day of the month _____
- last day of the month _____

Name _____

Gauging the Weather

Cut out the centimeter ruler at the bottom of the page. Use the ruler to measure the amount of rainfall from the bottom of the gauge to the top of the water. Write the measurement on the raindrop.

SCIENCE

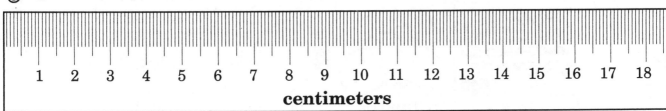

centimeters

Daily Learning Drills Grade 2

Name _____

A Cloudy Day

Clouds bring us many kinds of weather. Some clouds give us fair weather. Other clouds bring rain.

Paste the picture of the cloud next to its description.

	How the Clouds Look	Weather
	Big, puffy clouds	Nice day, but there might be a small shower.
	Tall, dark, piles of clouds.	Thunderstorm
	Whispy clouds that look like feathers.	Fair
	Layers of gray clouds that cover the whole sky.	Steady drizzle.

Stratus   Cumulus   Cumulo-nimbus   Cirrus

Name _____

Lacy Patterns

Kim likes to look at the lacy patterns of snowflakes with her magnifying glass. Most of them have six sides or six points. But she has never seen two snowflakes that are alike. Kim catches them on small pieces of dark paper so that she can see them better. Some of the snowflakes are broken because they bump into each other as they fall from the clouds.

Color.

What does Kim use to make the snowflakes look bigger?

Check.

Most snowflakes have ☐ seven ☐ six ☐ five   sides or points.

Kim looks at them on dark pieces of paper so that she can...

☐ take them to school. ☐ make a picture. ☐ see them better.

Write.

Why are some of the snowflakes broken?

_____

- -

_____

• Finish the snowflake.

SCIENCE

Name _____

Sink or Float?

Why do some objects float? Why do other objects sink? Is it because of their shape? Is it because of their color? Let's find out!

You will need:
   large bowl of water
   test objects such as –
      apple, nail, orange,
      eraser, wood, stone, egg,
      penny, crayon

Sinker or Floater?

1. List your objects.
2. Make guesses. Will they sink or float?
3. Test your objects to find the actual results.

Object	Guess	Actual Results

What happened?

If an object is heavy for its size, it will sink. If it is light for its size, it will float. A brick is heavy for its size so it will sink. A piece of wood the same size will float.

Names _____

Salty Water Evaporation

1. With a partner, decide which of you will be responsible for each job below.

    Experimenter—responsible for following the given directions, gathering materials, and cleaning up.

    Recorder—responsible for reading the directions and questions out loud and for recording the answers.

2. Gather the following materials:
    - spoon
    - salt
    - paper cup
    - 1/4 cup water

3. Stir the salt into the water.

4. Put the cup in a warm place.

5. Use what you already know about science to predict:

    What do you think will happen to the water? _____

    _____

    What do you think will happen to the salt? _____

    _____

6. Check the cup in a few days and record:

    What has happened to the water? _____

    _____

    What has happened to the salt? _____

    _____

    What do you think happens to ocean water when it is exposed to the sun?

    _____

    _____

    What do you think happens to the ocean salt when the water evaporates?

    _____

    _____

Name _____

Anti-Freeze

Water turns into a solid at a temperature of 32°F. This is called the freezing point. Does all water freeze at 32°F? Let's find out!

You will need:
- 2 small paper cups
- 4 teaspoons of salt
- water
- marking pen
- freezer

1. Fill both cups with water.

2. Mix 4 teaspoons of salt in one of the cups. Write "salt" on that cup.

3. Put both cups in the freezer. Check on them every hour for four hours.

I found out . . .

the cup of plain water _____

_____

the cup of salt water _____

_____

What happened?

When the temperature of water gets very cold, the particles of water hook together to make ice crystals. Salt gets in the way of this process, and an even lower temperature is needed before ice crystals will form.

Names _____

Layers of the Ocean Floor

Have you ever wondered what is under the sand on a beach? Some beaches are really layers of rock, pebbles, shells, and sand. Work in a group of four students and choose one of these materials to bring to school for your group. Write your name next to the material that you will bring:

sand _____   shells _____

rock _____   pebbles _____

Your teacher will provide a glass jar and water.

1. Gather the materials and take turns adding them to the jar. Add the same amount of each material.

2 Fill the jar to the top with water.

3. Close the lid tightly!

4. Take turns shaking the jar 10 times each.

5. Set the jar aside for one day.

6. Each student should draw and label one layer of the jar on the worksheet. Then put your names on the paper.

7. For follow-up, draw a picture of the layers of the ocean floor. Think about the layers you saw in your jar.

SCIENCE

Name _____

Ocean Temperatures

Where do you think the ocean temperatures are the warmest? Do you think the salt makes the ocean warmer or cooler? Do you think the sun makes the ocean warmer or cooler? Try this experiment to find out!

1. Get 4 clear glasses of water.
2. Add salt to 2 of the glasses and stir well.
3. Set one freshwater glass and one saltwater glass in the shade outside.
4. Set the other 2 glasses in the sun outside.
5. Set thermometers in each of the 4 glasses.
6. Divide into 4 equal groups and start at a different glass.
7. Wait 15 minutes, then read the thermometer and record below.
8. On signal, rotate to the next glass.

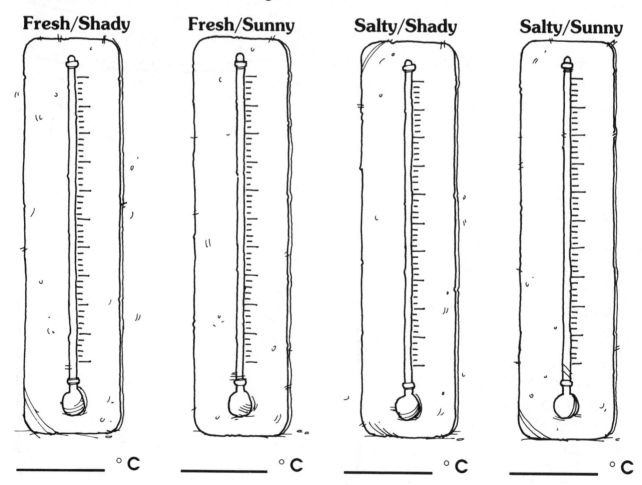

Fresh/Shady **Fresh/Sunny** **Salty/Shady** **Salty/Sunny**

_____ °C   _____ °C   _____ °C   _____ °C

Name _____

The Dancing Coin

You can make a coin dance on the top of a bottle as if a ghost were pushing on it. Let's try!

You will need:
glass soft-drink bottle
coin

1. Wet the rim of an empty bottle and one side of the coin.

2. Place the wet side of the coin on rim of the bottle.

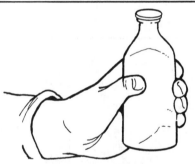

3. Hold the bottle with your warm hands. Watch closely!

What happened to the coin? _____

_____

What happened to the temperature of the air in the bottle when you put your hands around the bottle? _____

_____

What happened?

Your warm hands heated the cool air in the bottle. The air expanded and tried to escape. It pushed on the coin and made it dance.

Name _____

The Crusher

I'll bet you can crush a plastic soft-drink bottle without even touching it. Of course there is a little trick. Let's try it!

You will need:
plastic soft-drink bottle
hot water
cold water

1. Fill the bottle with hot water from the faucet. Be careful. Let the bottle stand for a minute.

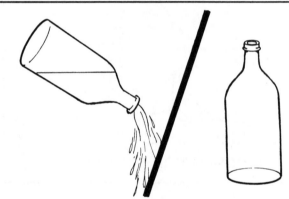

2. Pour out the hot water. Quickly screw on the cap. Make sure the cap is on tight.

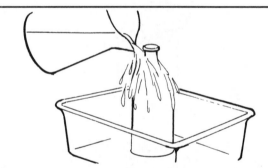

3. Pour a pitcher of very cold water over the bottle or hold the bottle under the cold water faucet. Watch what happens!

What happened?

The hot water made the air in the bottle very warm. The bottle cap captured the warm air in the bottle. The cold water made the warm air become cold. Cold air takes less space and the air pressure outside the bottle pushed in the sides of the bottle.

Name _____

Powerful Push-Up

Can air hold up water? It can with a little help from you.
Let's find out how!

You will need:
drinking glass
card the size of a postcard
water

1. Fill the glass to overflowing.

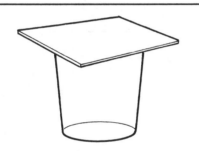

2. Lay the card on top of the glass.

3. Hold the card down with one hand. Turn the glass over. Remove your hand. Wow!

What happened to the water in the glass? _____

_____

What happens if you tilt the glass? _____

_____

What happened?

Air pushes in all directions. The air pressure pushing up under the card is greater than the pressure of the water pushing down. The card stays in place.

SCIENCE

Name _____

High and Dry

Can you put a piece of paper under water without getting it wet?
You can do it with a little help from air pressure. Let's try!

You will need:
drinking glass
sheet of paper
sink full of water

1. Crumple a sheet of paper. Push it into the bottom of a glass so that it stays in place.

2. Hold the glass upside down.

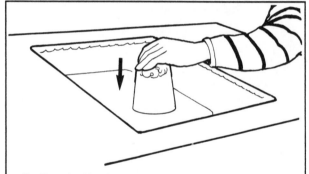

3. Push it straight down into the water.

What happens to the paper if you pull the glass straight up? _____

_____

What happens if you tilt the glass when putting it in the water? _____

_____

What happened?

The glass is full of air. The air cannot come out because it is lighter than the water. If you tilt the glass, the air escapes and water enters.

Name _____

The Last Straw

Sodas, milkshakes and root beer are all fun to sip through a straw. It would be fun to sip them through two straws. Could you sip liquid through three straws? four straws? What is the most you could use? Let's find out!

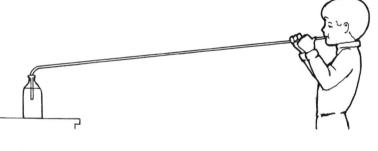

You will need:
plastic straws
clear tape
plastic pop bottle
water

1. Fill the bottle with water.

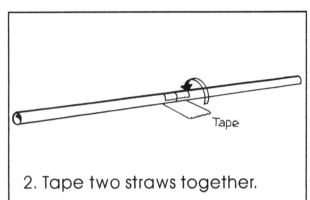

Tape

2. Tape two straws together.

3. Now try to drink through the two straws. Was it hard?

4. Add one more straw. Suck hard! Did it work? Try adding more!

SCIENCE

How many straws can you tape together and still drink through? _____

What happened?

Air pressure pushes down on the water in the bottle and also down on the water in the straw. When you suck the air out of the straw there will be no air pressure pushing down on the water in the straw, only air pressure pushing on the rest of the water in the bottle. The air pressure in the bottle pushes the water up the straw.

Name _____

What's the Matter?

All things are made of **matter**. Matter takes up space. It can take three forms – solid, liquid or gas.

Solids have shape and volume. They do not change shape easily.

Liquids have volume, but they have no shape of their own. They take the shape of the container they are in.

Gases have no shape or volume. Most gases are invisible.

Find and circle the words in each wordsearch that are examples of each kind of matter. Then write the words on the lines.

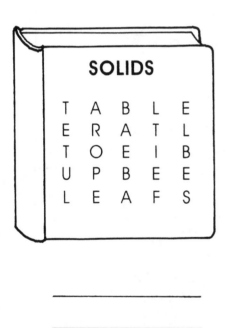

SOLIDS

```
T  A  B  L  E
E  R  A  T  L
T  O  E  I  B
U  P  B  E  E
L  E  A  F  S
```

LIQUIDS

```
A  P  O  P  K
B  C  O  L  A
J  U  I  C  E
A  M  L  I  T
W  A  T  E  R
```

GASES

```
A  B  T  O  E  P
C  I  G  L  T  O
E  B  R  A  H  D
O  X  Y  G  E  N
W  O  T  E  R  T
H  E  L  I  U  M
```

_____   _____   _____

_____   _____   _____

_____   _____   _____

_____   _____   _____

_____   _____   _____

_____   _____

_____

Name _____

"Shadowing" Shadows

Cut out the pictures at the bottom of the page. Read the directions and paste the objects where they belong.

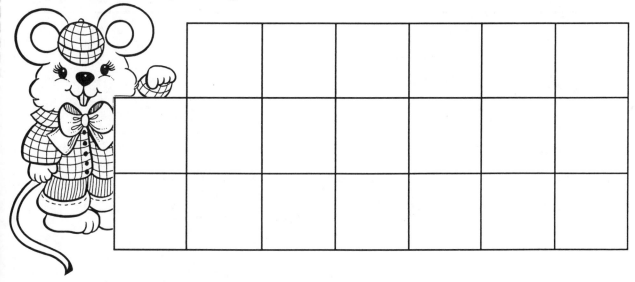

Start at Detective Mouse.

1. Go down 1 space and right 4 spaces. Paste the picture here of what would make this shadow.

2. Now go left 3 spaces and down 1 space. Paste the picture here of what would make this shadow.

3. Then go right 5 spaces and up 1 space. Paste the picture here of what would make this shadow.

4. Go up 1 space and left 4 spaces. Paste the picture here of what would make this shadow.

5. Go down 1 space and left 2 spaces. Paste the picture here of what would make this shadow.

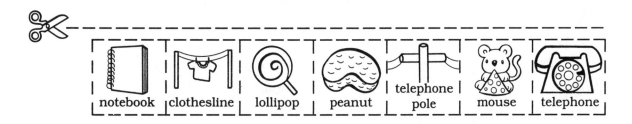

notebook | clothesline | lollipop | peanut | telephone pole | mouse | telephone

SCIENCE

Name _____

Volume Control

If the words name something that makes a loud sound, color the space **gray**.
If the words name something that makes a soft sound, color the space **red**.

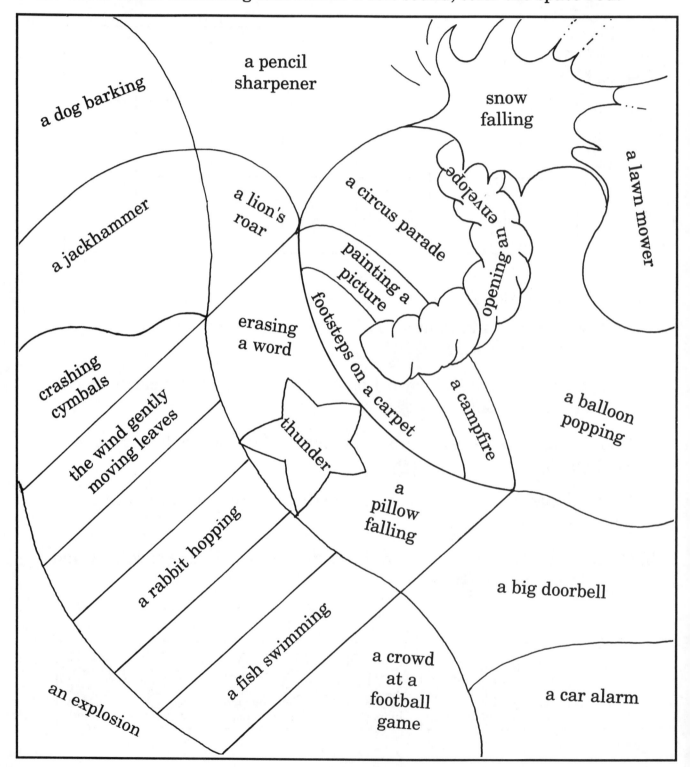

a pencil sharpener

a dog barking

snow falling

a lawn mower

a jackhammer

a lion's roar

a circus parade

painting a picture

opening an envelope

erasing a word

footsteps on a carpet

crashing cymbals

the wind gently moving leaves

thunder

a campfire

a balloon popping

a rabbit hopping

a pillow falling

a big doorbell

a fish swimming

an explosion

a crowd at a football game

a car alarm

Name _____

Energetic "Source"-ry

Write the sources of energy from the Word Bank above the correct cauldron.

SCIENCE

Name _____

Keep It Clean!

Have you ever cleaned a penny? Let's try it!

Materials:

4 dirty pennies	soap	window cleaner
salt	water	steel wool pad
vinegar	taco sauce	paper towels

Directions:

1. In the "I predict . . . " section on the chart, explain what you think each penny will look like after you clean it with one of the materials.

2. Your teacher will place a small amount of each material in the center of each table.

3. Try cleaning one penny using window cleaner. Explain what it looks like in the "I observed . . . " section.

4. Now try cleaning another penny using soap, water, and the steel wool pad. Explain what it looks like.

5. Clean a different penny in salt and vinegar. Explain what it looks like.

6. Now clean the last penny in taco sauce. Explain what it looks like.

Materials	I predict . . .	I observed . . .
window cleaner		
soap, water, and steel wool pad		
salt and vinegar		
taco sauce		

Name _____

Magnetic Attraction

The word **magnet** begins with the same three letters as the word magic, and sometimes magnets do seem a little magical.

Every magnet has two poles — north and south. The north pole of one magnet attracts and pulls toward the south pole of another magnet. Two poles that are the same (two north poles or two south poles) do **not** attract each other. Instead, they push away from each other.

Using the information above, continue labeling the horseshoe and bar magnets below with **N** (for north) and **S** (for south).

SCIENCE

Name _____

"Attractive" Magnets

Cut out each object and paste it on the chart where it belongs. Use a crayon to graph the results.

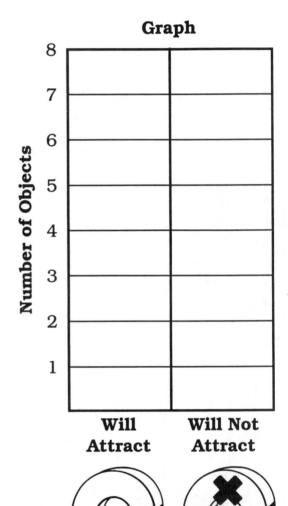

Will Attract	Will Not Attract

Graph

Number of Objects: 8, 7, 6, 5, 4, 3, 2, 1

Will Attract · Will Not Attract

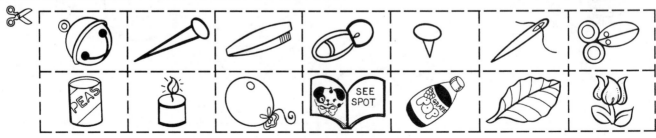

Name _____

Lifting with Levers

A lever is a simple machine used to lift or move things. It has two parts. The **arm** is the part that moves. The **fulcrum** supports the arm and does not move.

Name the parts of this lever.

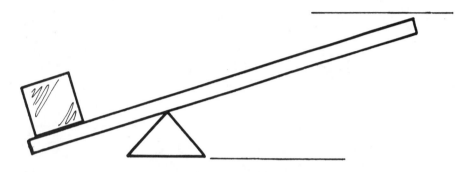

Unscramble the names of these levers.

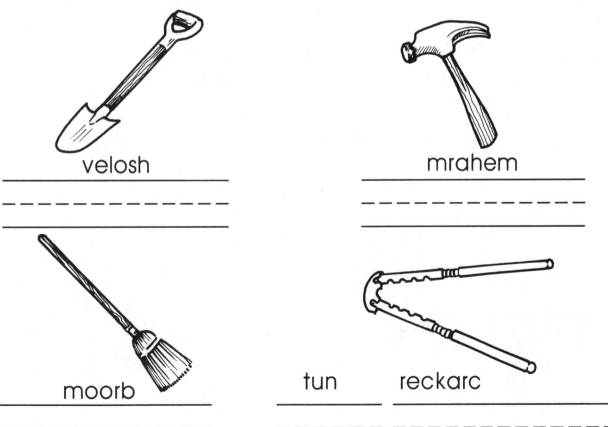

velosh

_____

- - - - - - - - - - -

mrahem

_____

- - - - - - - - - - -

moorb

_____

- - - - - - - - - - -

tun   reckarc

____ _____

- - - - - - - - - - - -

SCIENCE

Name _____

Levers at Work

Levers help make our work easier. Circle all the levers. Then find their names in the wordsearch.

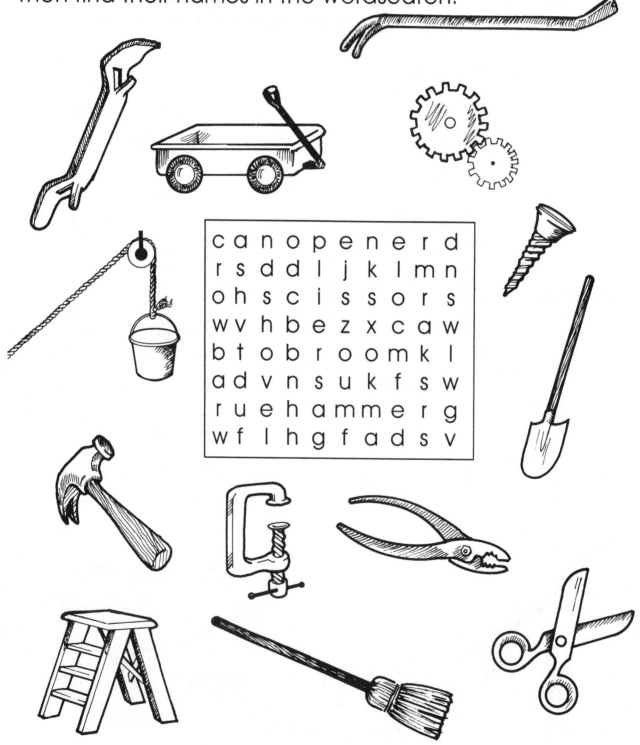

```
c a n o p e n e r d
r s d d l j k l m n
o h s c i s s o r s
w v h b e z x c a w
b t o b r o o m k l
a d v n s u k f s w
r u e h a m m e r g
w f l h g f a d s v
```

Name _____

The Right Tool for the Job

Mother gave Tyrone and Kim a list of jobs. Help them pick the right tool for each job. Draw a line from the job to the tool.

What will help Kim raise the flag up the flagpole?

What will Tyrone use to help him get the cat out of the tree?

inclined plane

What will Kim use to carry sand to her new sandbox?

pulley

What will Tyrone use to get the nail out of the board?

lever

What will Kim use to hang the mirror on her bedroom door?

screw

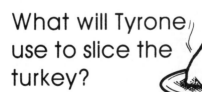

What will Tyrone use to slice the turkey?

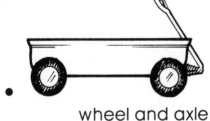

wheel and axle

wedge

SCIENCE

Name _____

Slanted Machines

An inclined plane has a slanted surface. It is used to move things from a low place to a high place. Some inclined planes are smooth. Others have steps.

Color the inclined planes in the picture.

Name _____

The Wedge

A wedge is a type of inclined plane. It is made up of two inclined planes joined together to make a sharp edge. A wedge can be used to cut things. Some wedges are pointed.

Color only the pictures of wedges.

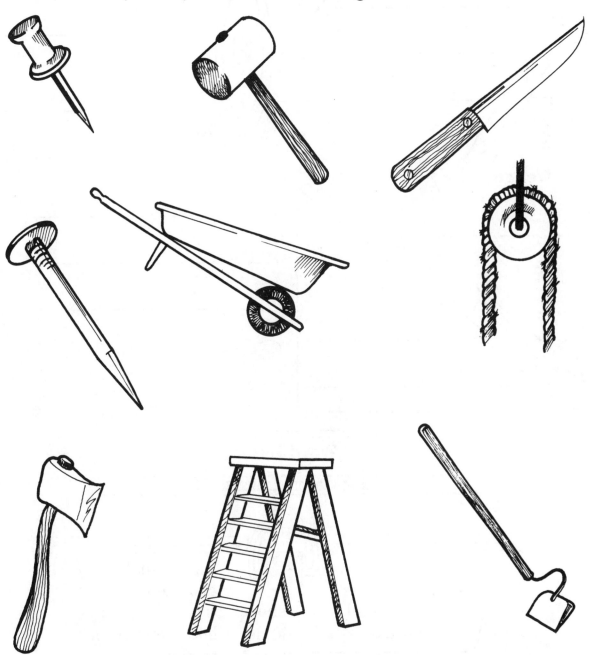

SCIENCE

Name _____

Ready for Work!

Read the names of the objects in the Word Bank. Write the objects under the correct kind of simple machine.

Inclined Plane

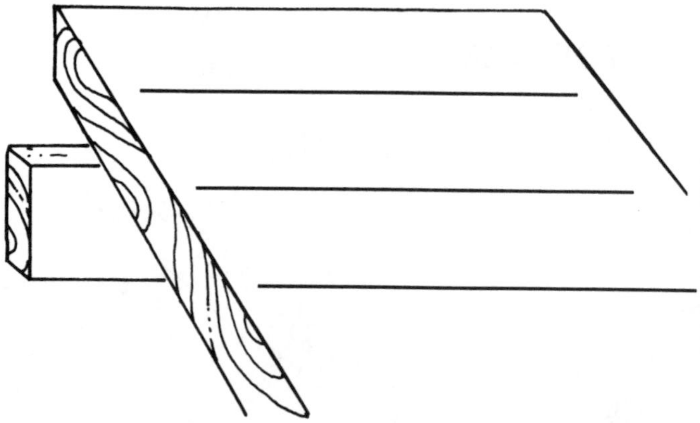

Wheel and Axle

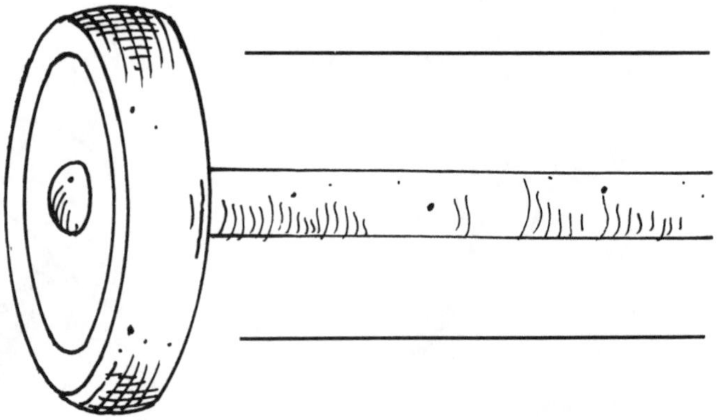

Wedge

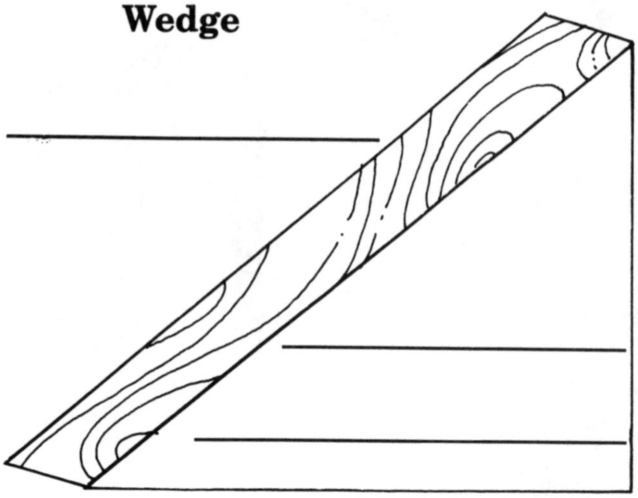

Lever

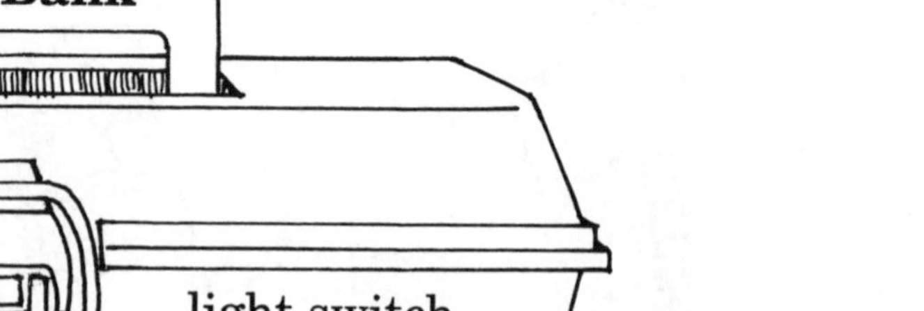

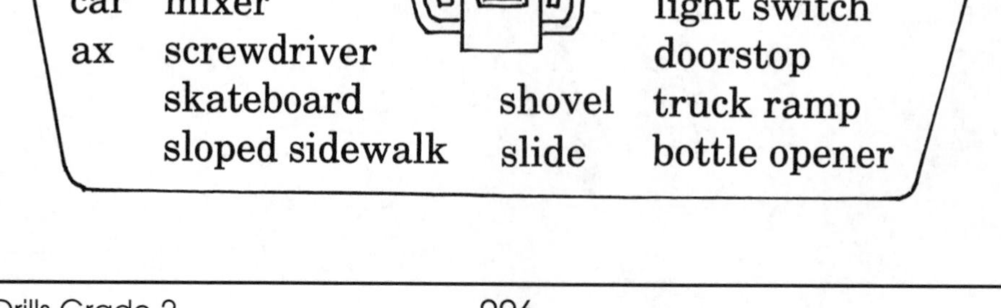

Word Bank

car	mixer		light switch
ax	screwdriver		doorstop
	skateboard	shovel	truck ramp
	sloped sidewalk	slide	bottle opener

226

Name _____

Faraway and Close Up

Kim's favorite subject is science. She has a telescope and a microscope in her bedroom. At night, she looks through her telescope. Things that are far away, like the moon, stars and planets, look bigger. When she looks through her microscope, she can see tiny things close up, like a drop of water or a bit of salt.

Unscramble and write.

_____

Kim's favorite subject is _. _ _ _ _ _ _ _ .

niecsec

Circle.

She has a   bicycle   and a   microscope   in her bedroom.
             telescope   planet

Color.

What faraway things look bigger with a telescope?

Check.

When Kim looks through her microscope, she can see ...

☐ tiny things close up.   ☐ big things far away.

• **SOMETHING EXTRA** •

What is your favorite subject? Why?

SCIENCE

Name _____

Planets

There are nine planets that move around the sun. Our planet is Earth. Earth is closest to Mars and Venus. Jupiter is the largest planet. It is many times larger than Earth. Saturn is the planet with seven rings around it. The smallest planet is called Mercury!

Circle.

How many planets are there?   three   nine   seven

| Mercury | Earth | Jupiter | Mars | Venus | Saturn |

Write.

_____ I am your planet.

_____
_____ } We are closest to Earth.

_____ I am the largest planet.

_____ I am the planet with seven rings.

_____ I am the smallest planet.

Color.

Draw three red rings around Saturn.

• Draw what you think you would find on the planet Mercury.

Position the Planets

Write the names of the planets on the lines according to their distance from the sun. Use the Word Bank to help you spell the words correctly.

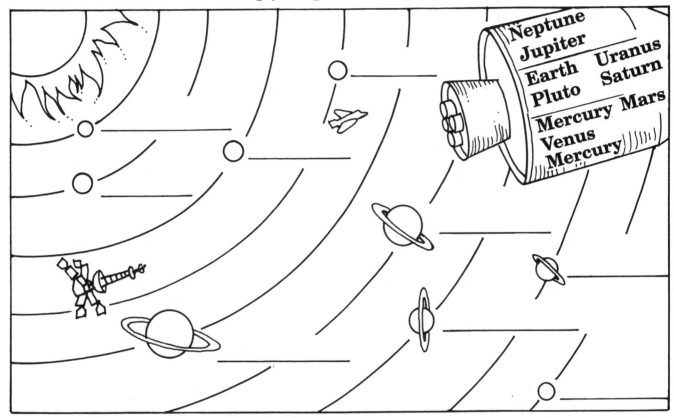

Read the sentences. Record the information on the chart.

1. *Viking 2* took close-up pictures of Mars on September 3, 1976, but scientists still are not sure if there is life on the planet.

2. Two of Saturn's outer rings were very clear in pictures taken by *Pioneer-Saturn* on September 1, 1979.

3. In March of 1979, the probe *Voyager 1* discovered that Jupiter has a thin ring around it.

Name of Probe	Planet Destination	Date	Results or Discoveries

Daily Learning Drills Grade 2

SCIENCE

Name _____

Spacing Out

Read a clue. Find the matching word in the puzzle and write it on the line.
Then connect the puzzle dots in the same order as your answers.

Clues

1. The planet we live on _____

2. The closest star _____

3. They shine in the sky at night

   _____

4. Earth is a _____ .

5. Planets, stars, and moons are

   in _____ .

6. Time when the sun shines

   _____

7. A group of stars

   _____

8. A person who travels in space

   _____

9. The path a planet follows to travel
   around the sun

   _____

10. It gives us light at night

    _____

11. People who study the stars

    _____

12. You use this to see the stars

    close up _____

13. Time when the sun does not

    shine _____

14. We feel this from the sun

    _____

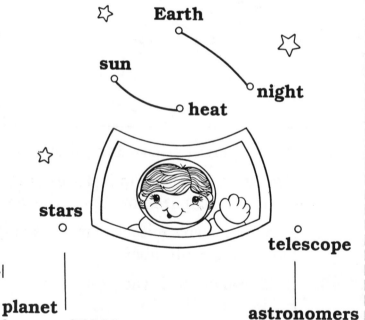

Name _____

Birthday Surprise!

1. Complete sentences 1 and 2.

2. Connect the numbers in the dot-to-dot.

3. Color 2 presents red and 3 presents blue.

4. Draw candles on the dot-to-dot picture to show how old you are.

5. Color the dot-to-dot.

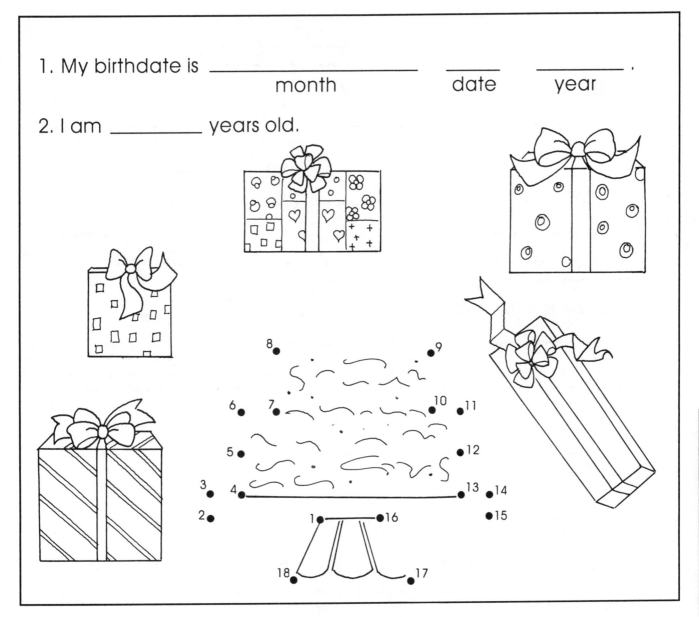

1. My birthdate is _____ ____ _____ .
   month   date   year

2. I am _____ years old.

SOCIAL STUDIES

Name _____

I Like Me!

Complete the sentences below to tell about you.

Most people like the way I _____

_____

_____ .

I feel happy when _____

_____

_____ .

The thing I like best about me is

_____

_____ .

I feel sad when _____

_____

_____ .

I feel special when _____

_____

_____ .

At home I _____

_____

_____ .

At school I _____

_____

_____ .

Name _____

Featuring the One and Only Me

In each box write about a different event in your life. Draw a picture to go with each event.

____I was born.____ _____	_____ _____	_____ _____
_____ _____	_____ _____	_____ _____
_____ _____	_____ _____	_____ _____

SOCIAL STUDIES

Name _____

My Body Homework

You know how special your body is! To keep your body working and looking its best, you should start developing good habits now and keep them as you grow older. Use this check list to keep yourself on track for the next week. Keep it on your bathroom mirror or next to your bed where it will remind you to do your "homework!"

	Sun.	Mon.	Tues.	Wed.	Thurs.	Fri.	Sat.
I slept at least 8 hours.							
I ate a healthy breakfast.							
I brushed my teeth this morning.							
I ate a healthy lunch.							
I washed my hands after using the bathroom.							
I exercised at least 30 minutes today.							
I drank at least 6 glasses of water.							
I stood and sat up straight.							
I ate a healthy dinner.							
I bathed.							
I brushed my teeth this evening.							

Name _____

People Scavenger Hunt

Get to know the kids in your class. Find someone to fit each description. Try not to use the same name twice!

How We Look

1. _____ has freckles on his/her arms.

2. _____ is wearing a watch, ring or necklace.

3. _____ has red on his/her socks.

4. _____ has 3 buttons on his/her shirt.

5. _____ is missing 3 baby teeth.

How We Feel

1. _____ likes green beans.

2. _____ wants a baby brother or sister.

3. _____ is scared during thunderstorms.

4. _____ would like a snake as a pet.

5. _____ would like his/her room painted blue.

What We Do

1. _____ ate cereal for breakfast.

2. _____ played a sport last weekend.

3. _____ can dive into a swimming pool.

4. _____ made his/her bed today.

5. _____ is taking lessons to learn how to do something.

SOCIAL STUDIES

Name _____

Shooting for My Goals

What is something new you want to do? Maybe you want to improve at something you already do. Fill in the sentences below.

There are two goals I have for the rest of the school year.

One is _____

_____

_____

Two is _____

_____

_____

I will do this by

day _____

month _____

year _____

_____
signed

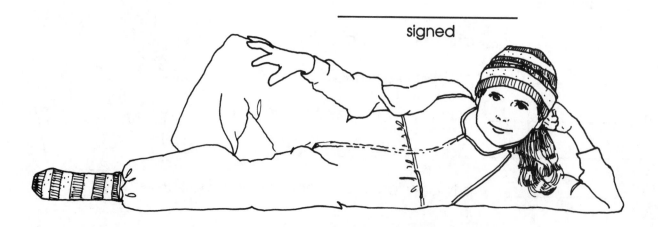

Name _____

My Personal Shield

Let your friends learn more about how special you are. Complete each sentence and draw a picture to go with it.

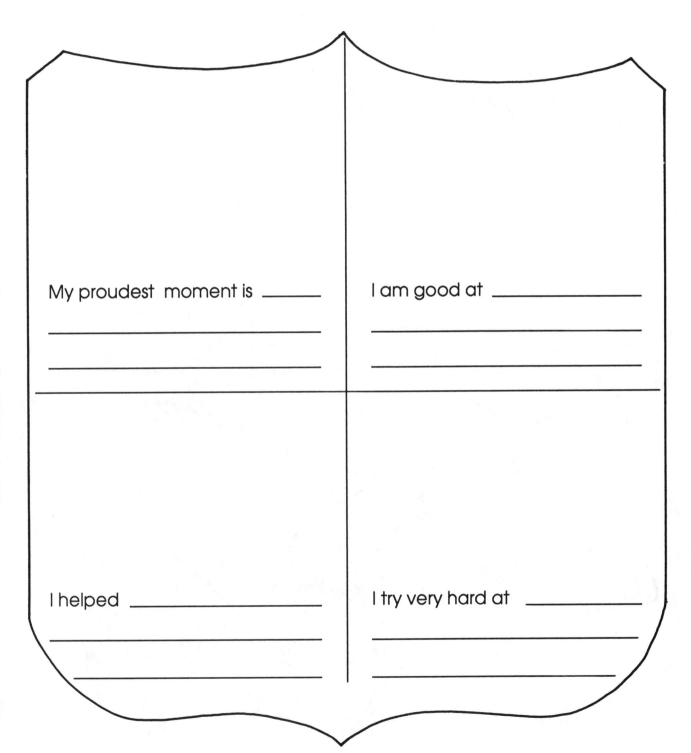

My proudest moment is _____
_____
_____

I am good at _____
_____
_____

I helped _____
_____
_____

I try very hard at _____
_____
_____

SOCIAL STUDIES

Name _____

Interview a Friend

Interview your friend and then fill out the information below.

My friend is _____ .

Favorite Colors

Favorite Book

Favorite Activities

Favorite Foods

Name _____

Create a Comrade!

Imagine that you could create a perfect friend. Describe your "creation" on the lines below.

Name _____
Age _____

Favorite Pastime _____
_____

Personal Qualities

_____
_____
_____
_____

Special Interests/Hobbies

_____
_____
_____
_____

Talents

_____
_____
_____
_____

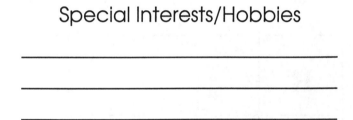

What we could do together

_____
_____
_____
_____

SOCIAL STUDIES

Name _____

Friendly Favorites

Think of the names of favorite animals, food and places that begin with the letters in the word FRIENDS. Write the names in the correct boxes below. One word in each column has already been done for you. For extra fun, play with a friend. The one who can think of the most names is the winner.

	Animal	**Food**	**Place**
F			
R			
I		ice cream	
E			
N			New York
D	dog		
S			

Name _____

Buddy's Lists

Buddy likes to make lists. Yesterday, he wrote a list of his favorite things to do with friends. Today, he wants to divide this list into three more lists. Help Buddy by filling in these three lists with one-syllable, two-syllable and three-syllable words from his word list. The first word has been done for you.

One-syllable words

1. golf _____
2. _____
3. _____
4. _____
5. _____

Buddy's Word List
Things to Do with Friends

golf	basketball
Ping-Pong™	camp
swim	snorkeling
backpacking	biking
volleyball	skate
baseball	canoeing
fishing	soccer
swing	

Two-syllable words

1. _____
2. _____
3. _____
4. _____
5. _____

Three-syllable words

1. _____
2. _____
3. _____
4. _____
5. _____

SOCIAL STUDIES

Name _____

Cars and Colors

What is the color of your family car? _____

If you have more than one car, what are the other colors? _____

_____

Record the colors of all the cars in your class on the bar graph below. If a color is not shown, include it in "Other."

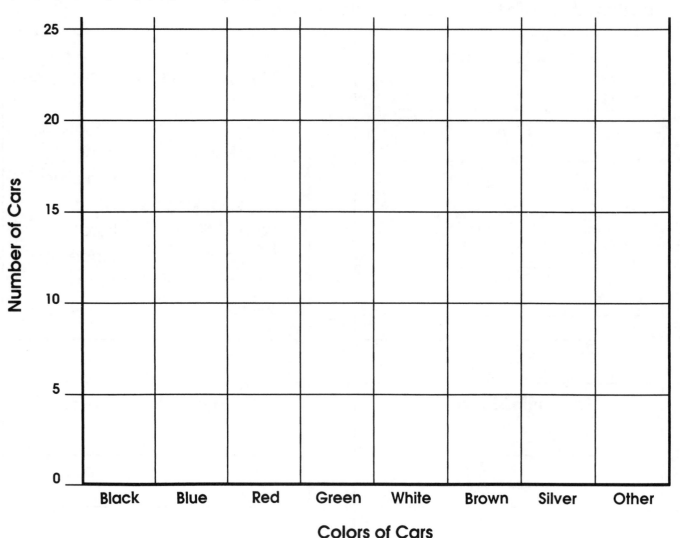

1. What is the most popular color of car? _____

2. What is the least popular color of car? _____

3. What is the total number of cars that were counted? _____

4. Were there any colors that were equally popular? _____

Name _____

Comparing a Car and a Truck

In some ways, cars and trucks are alike. In other ways, they are different. On the car, write words and phrases that are true about it but are not true about the truck. Do the same with the truck. Where the car and the truck overlap, write words and phrases that are common to both of them.

SOCIAL STUDIES

Name _____

Sightseeing by Train

Follow the train as it travels through the countryside.
Identify by number the places where the train:

goes through a forest _____   goes through a covered bridge _____
comes to a stop _____   passes through a plowed field _____
crosses a high bridge _____   comes down the mountain _____
passes a water tower _____   passes a volcano _____
exits a tunnel _____   goes through rocks _____
crosses a low bridge _____   crosses a lake _____
passes a school _____   goes by a small town _____
enters a tunnel _____   passes cows _____

Name _____

Sights and Sounds of Travel

Look at the numbered pictures below. Write the numbers
of the pictures by each question.

What can carry more than one person? _____

What moves on wheels? _____

What moves on just two wheels? _____

What makes a very loud noise? _____

What moves through water? _____

What has a motor to make it run? _____

What can hold large, heavy objects? _____

What can travel very fast? _____

What has to be pushed or pulled? _____

1	2	3
4	5	6
7	8	9
10	11	12

SOCIAL STUDIES

Daily Learning Drills Grade 2

Name _____

Transportation Sort

Study the examples of transportation below. Sort the objects into three groups. Think how each type travels.

Draw a ◯ around objects in group one.

Draw a △ around objects in group two.

Draw a ▢ around objects in group three.

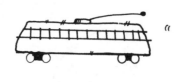

Name _____

How Many Wheels?

Cut out the pictures of the vehicles at the bottom of the page.

Paste the vehicles with no wheels in section 1.
Paste the vehicles with two wheels in section 2.
Paste the vehicles with three wheels in section 3.
Paste the vehicles with four wheels in section 4.
Paste the vehicles with more than four wheels in section 5.

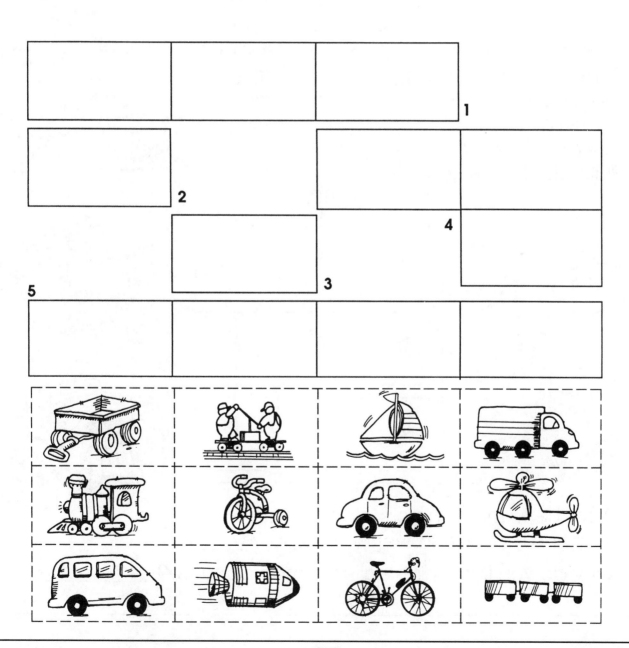

Daily Learning Drills Grade 2

SOCIAL STUDIES

Name _____

Transportation Magic Square

1. Read Column A. Choose an answer
   from Column B. Write the number of
   the answer in the correct square.
   The first one has been done for you.

Column A

A. Filled with helium
B. Runs on gasoline
C. Powered by wind
D. Burns coal or wood
E. Runs on nuclear energy
F. Moves on snow or ice
G. Moves by pedals
H. Powered by oars
I. Pulled by horses or oxen

Column B

1. jet plane
2. rowboat
3. sailboat
4. steam locomotive
5. blimp
6. submarine
7. wagon
8. sled
9. bicycle
10. car

A 5	B ___	C ___
D ___	E ___	F ___
G ___	H ___	I ___

2. Add the numbers across, down, and
   diagonally. What answer do you get? _____

   Why do you think this is called a magic square? _____

   _____

Name _____

Traveling to a Large City

1. Circle the correct answer. Then follow the directions.
   A large truck used for moving furniture is called a:
   a.   dump truck - Mark out all letter M's below.
   b.   van - Mark out all letter C's below.
   c.   pickup truck - Mark out all letter I's below.

   A large vehicle for transporting children to school is called a:
   a.   bus - Mark out all letter B's below.
   b.   yacht - Mark out all letter A's below.
   c.   jet - Mark out all letter F's below.

   A vehicle pulled by horses or oxen is called a:
   a.   hot air balloon - Mark out all letter D's below.
   b.   tricycle - Mark out all letter O's below.
   c.   wagon - Mark out all letter P's below.

   A long line of boxcars that runs on a track is called a:
   a.   submarine - Mark out all letter L's below.
   b.   train - Mark out all letter N's below.
   c.   bicycle - Mark out all letter R's below.

   A vehicle that sails through water is called a:
   a.   ship - Mark out all letter E's below.
   b.   tank - Mark out all letter M's below.
   c.   sled - Mark out all letter A's below.

C	M	B	N	I	P	E	C
A	P	C	M	B	N	E	I
B	F	N	C	P	E	B	N
P	C	L	B	N	P	E	C
B	E	C	P	B	O	E	N
R	B	N	C	I	P	B	E
C	D	B	P	N	B	A	C

2. Start at the top. Write the name of the remaining letters in the spaces below.

   I will travel to what city? __ __ __ __ __ , __ __ __ __ __ __ __

Daily Learning Drills Grade 2

Name _____

By Land, by Sea, and by Air

Write the first letter of the names of the objects below.
The letters form words.
Underline the word in red if it travels "By Land."
Underline the word in green if it travels "By Sea."
Underline the word in orange if it travels "By Air."

_____ _____ _____

_____ _____ _____

_____ _____ _____

_____ _____ _____

Name _____

Follow That Sign!

Look at the road sign symbols below. Each sign is matched to a letter. Use the road sign code to find the names of four vehicles that travel on roads.

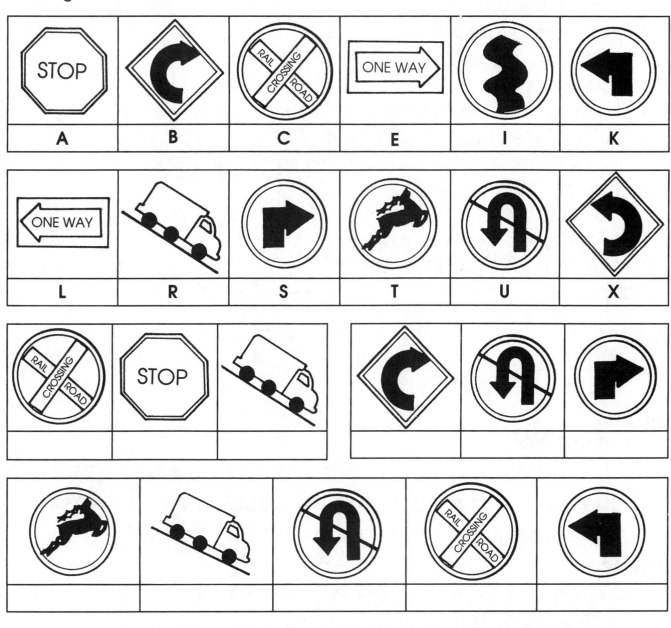

SOCIAL STUDIES

Name _____

The Subway

Some big cities have a subway. A subway is a railroad that is under the ground. The trains carry people from one part of the city to another. The trains stop often to let people off and on. Many people ride to work on a subway. Others ride to school or to go shopping. Subways are nice because they do not take up space in a city.

Write.

A _____ is a railroad that is under the ground.

shop   subway

Circle.

Yes or No

The subway takes people to parts of the city.	Yes	No
The subway stops only one time each day.	Yes	No
The subway stops to let people off and on.	Yes	No

Circle.

Where are some people on the subway going?

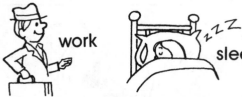

Color the subway train red.

• Draw where **you** would go on the subway.

Name _____

A Helicopter

Would you like to ride in a helicopter? A helicopter flies in the air. It can fly **up** and **down**. It can fly **forward** and **backward**. It can fly **sideways**. A helicopter can even stay in one spot in the air! Helicopters can be many sizes. Some helicopters carry just one person. Some carry 30 people. Helicopters can be used for many jobs.

Write.

A _____ flies in the air.

     trailer   helicopter

Write.

Which way can a helicopter fly? (Look at story.)

4→u __   3→d __ __ __   5→f __ __ __ __ __ __

2→b __ __ __ __ __ __ __   1→s __ __ __ __ __ __ __ __

Write the answers in the puzzle above.

Circle.

Yes or No

A helicopter can stay in one spot in the air.   Yes   No

Helicopters come in many sizes.   Yes   No

All helicopters can carry 10 people.   Yes   No

• Draw a big green helicopter.

SOCIAL STUDIES

Name _____

Hot Air Balloons

Would you like to fly in a hot air balloon? A hot air balloon can fly when it is filled with hot air or a gas, called helium. Most hot air balloons use helium to fly. People can ride in a basket that is tied to the balloon. The wind moves the balloon in the sky. To come down, the people must let some of the air or gas out of the balloon.

Circle.

What does a hot air balloon need to fly?

hot air   music   gas

Write.

Most hot air balloons use _____ to fly.

helmets   helium

Circle.

What do people ride in?

cart   basket

Circle.

The   moon
          wind   moves the balloon in the sky.

Color.

1 - red   **2** - purple   **3** - green

• Draw a hot air balloon with two people in the basket.

Name _____

What's New?

Inventions help to make life easier. Various inventors from all around the world try to come up with ways to improve upon things presently used.

Below are pictures of inventions that have changed as inventors improved them. Number them in the correct order each version appeared by writing 1, 2, and 3 in the boxes.

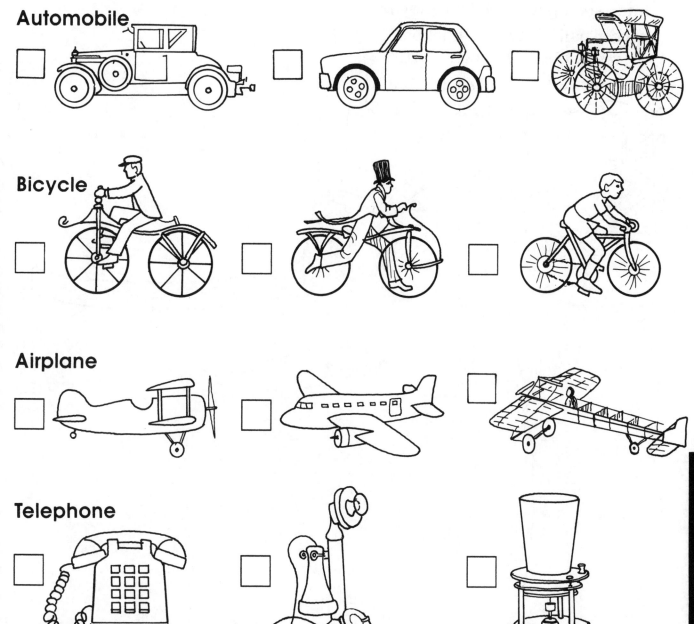

Automobile

Bicycle

Airplane

Telephone

SOCIAL STUDIES

Name _____

Selecting Supplies

Read each word in the Word Bank. If a word names a **need**, write it on the sack of flour. If a word names a **want**, write it on the pickle barrel.

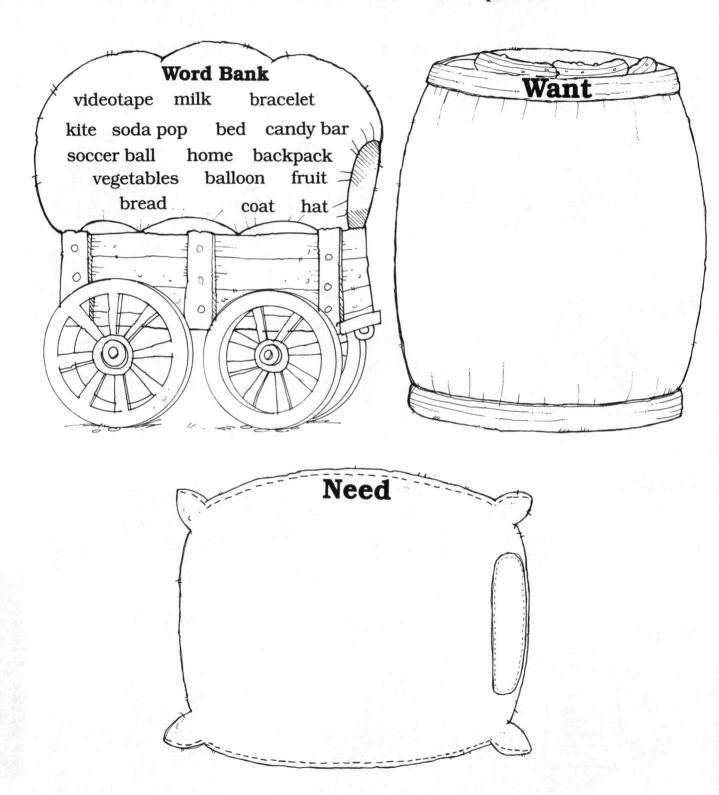

Word Bank

videotape   milk   bracelet

kite soda pop   bed   candy bar

soccer ball   home   backpack

vegetables   balloon   fruit

bread   coat   hat

Want

Need

Name _____

"Good Service" Delivery

Read each word. If it names an occupation that provides goods, mark **G** on the word. If it names an occupation that provides a service, mark **S** on the word. Then draw a line to show where three answers are the same in a row.

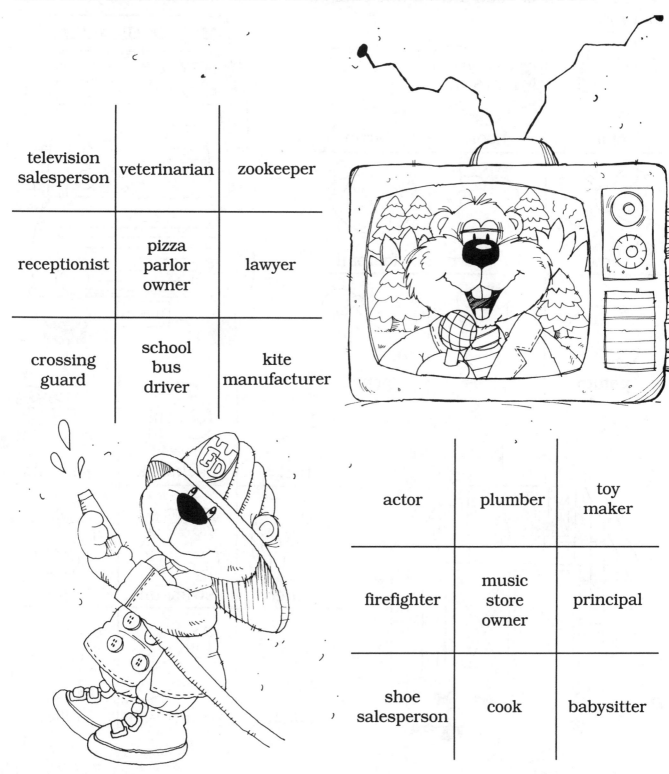

television salesperson	veterinarian	zookeeper
receptionist	pizza parlor owner	lawyer
crossing guard	school bus driver	kite manufacturer

actor	plumber	toy maker
firefighter	music store owner	principal
shoe salesperson	cook	babysitter

SOCIAL STUDIES

Daily Learning Drills Grade 2

Name _____

Brought to You from . . .

Look at each picture. If the picture shows something that comes from a farm, mark **X** on the picture. If it shows something that comes from a factory, mark **O** on the picture. Then draw a line to show where three answers are the same in a row.

chair	book	carrot
bow	strawberry	football
potato	glass	pencil

Made in the U.S.A.

U.S.A.

nail	backpack	peanuts
lettuce	swimsuit	apple
radish	paintbrush	pillow

Name _____

"Time"-ly Toy Gifts

Use the time line to answer the questions.

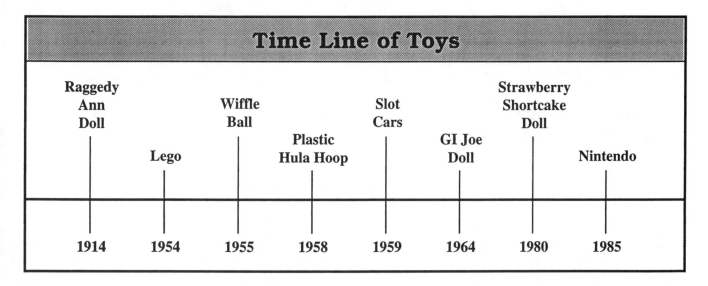

1. When was Nintendo first sold? _____

2. Could you play a game with a Wiffle Ball in 1940? _____

3. What new toy was sold in 1964? _____

4. In what year were plastic Hula Hoops first sold? _____

5. How many years passed between the first Raggedy Ann Doll
   and the first GI Joe Doll? _____

6. What toys were invented during the 1950s? _____

   _____

7. How many toys on the time line were invented in the 1970s? ____

8. Could you have played with a plastic Hula Hoop in 1960? _____

9. In what year was the Strawberry Shortcake Doll first sold? _____

10. What new toy was first sold in 1954? _____

SOCIAL STUDIES

Name _____

It's Time to Eat

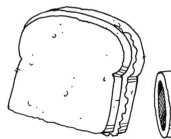  

Cut out the pictures at the bottom of this page. Follow the clues to paste them where they belong on the time line.

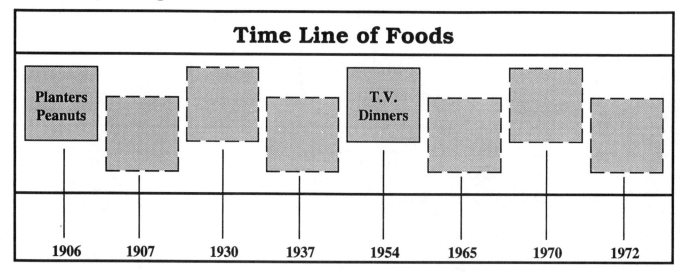

Time Line of Foods

Planters Peanuts				T.V. Dinners			
1906	1907	1930	1937	1954	1965	1970	1972

1. You could begin to eat Corn Flakes for breakfast 1 year after you could munch on Planters Peanuts.

2. Twinkies were first sold 23 years after Corn Flakes and 7 years before Spam.

3. You could top your favorite piece of pie with Cool Whip 35 years after you first tasted Twinkies.

4. A quick dinner could be made with Hamburger Helper two years before one could be made with Tuna Helper.

Cut ✂ –

Name _____

Build a Community

Cut out the pictures at the bottom of this page. Read the directions. Paste the pictures where they belong.

1. Place the school **west** of the house and **east** of the row of trees.

2. Place the train at the **southwest** edge of the railroad tracks.

3. Place the Police Station **west** of the Train Station and **east** of the train.

4. Place the Grocery Store **east** of the house and **south** of the rising sun.

5. Place the Bank **north** of the train.

6. Place the Firehouse **south** of the Grocery Store and **east** of the Train Station.

Cut ✂ -

SOCIAL STUDIES

Daily Learning Drills Grade 2

Name _____

Just Being Neighborly

Go along with Percival Porcupine as he delivers the Welcome basket.

Follow the directions. Trace a path from one place to the next.

1. Start at Percival and go east 3 spaces. Write **library.**
2. Then go south 4 spaces. Write **market**.
3. Next go west 2 spaces. Write **gas station**.
4. Now go north 3 spaces. Write **school**.
5. Go west 2 spaces. Write **fire station**.
6. Go south 2 spaces. Write **park**.
7. Go east 6 spaces. Write **welcome**.

Name _____

Find the Ring

Look at the map. Read each clue and write the correct word on the line. Then draw a line from one place to the next to show where each clue takes you.

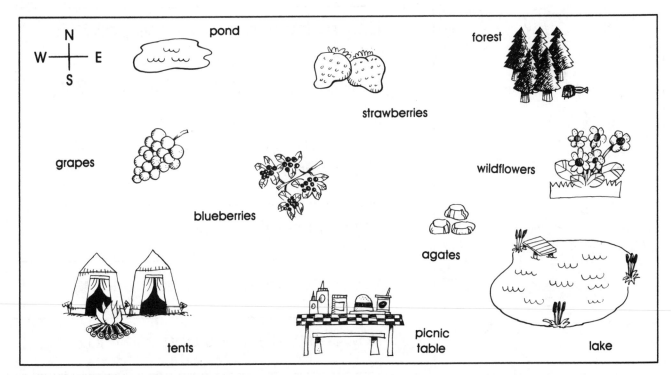

1. Begin where campers sleep. _____
2. Go north to a fruit that makes a purple-colored juice. _____
3. Go southeast to a place where you can sit and eat. _____
4. Then go east where you can row a boat. _____
5. Turn north to the small plants with colored petals. _____
6. Go southwest to find some special rocks. _____
7. Now go northwest to pick some sweet, red berries. _____
8. Go west to a place where you can swim. _____
9. Then go southeast and pick some round, blue-colored fruit. _____
10. At last, go northeast to a place where there are many trees. _____
11. Look closely to find the missing ring. Draw a circle around it.

SOCIAL STUDIES

Name _____

Follow the Map

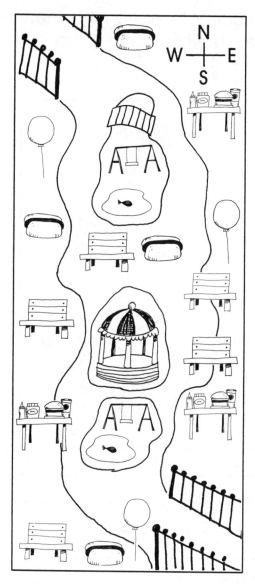

Use the map to answer the questions.

1. How many entrances do you see?

   _____

2. How many ponds are in the park?

   _____

3. How many picnic areas are there?

   _____

4. How many picnic areas are near a playground?

   _____

5. How many bridges do you see?

   _____

6. How many balloon sellers are there?

   _____

7. How many benches can you find?

   _____

8. How many places are there to buy food?

   _____

9. How many carousels are there?

   _____

Map Key

path _____	bridge	bench
pond	entrance	picnic area
carousel	balloon seller	food
playground		

Name _____

The Adventure Begins

One rainy Saturday morning, Patrick, Brenda, and Jamie decided they needed something new and exciting to do that morning. They took out the telephone book and turned to the yellow pages. In it they found these advertisements for special places to visit.

Aquarium

Open weekdays from
10:00 a.m. to 6:00 p.m.
Closed weekends

Call 123 - Fish

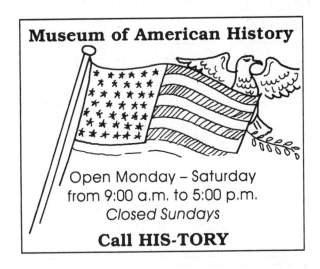

Museum of American History

Open Monday – Saturday
from 9:00 a.m. to 5:00 p.m.
Closed Sundays

Call HIS-TORY

Planetarium

Open Mon. – Friday
12:00 noon to 6:00 p.m.
Saturday 3:00 p.m. to 9:00 p.m.

Call 83S - TARS

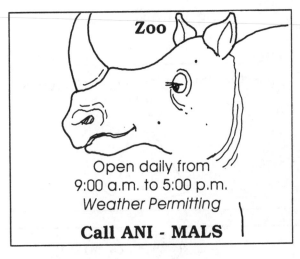

Zoo

Open daily from
9:00 a.m. to 5:00 p.m.
Weather Permitting

Call ANI - MALS

The children looked carefully at the ads. Which place did they choose to visit and why?

They chose to go to the _____

because _____

Name _____

Home Sweet Home

At the Museum of American History, Patrick, Brenda, and Jamie saw large exhibits of Native Americans and their homes.

Use the rebuses below to discover the different types of houses various nations of Native Americans lived in. Your answers will sound right, but the spellings won't be right. Get the the correct spellings from the Word Box.

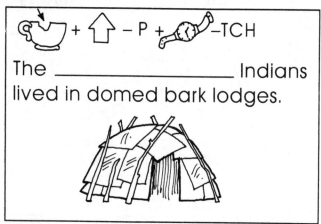

The _____ Indians lived in domed bark lodges.

The _____ Indians lived in long houses.

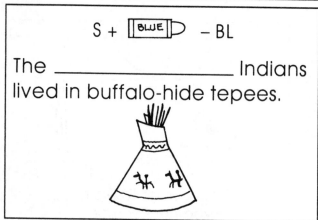

The _____ Indians lived in buffalo-hide tepees.

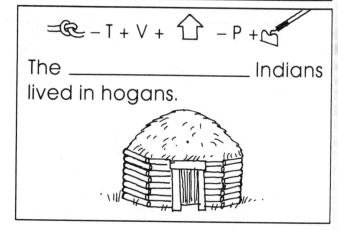

The _____ Indians lived in hogans.

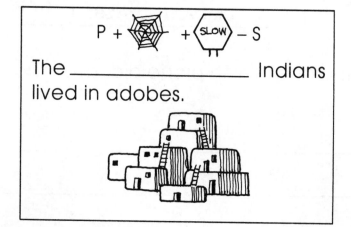

The _____ Indians lived in adobes.

Word Box		
Pueblo	Iroquois	Sioux
Navajo	Chippewa	

Name _____

Dinner Time

In the museum, the children saw a display on Eskimos. Eskimos get their name from a Native American word that means *eaters of raw meat*. Eskimos often ate their meat raw because they didn't have much wood or fuel for fires.

Each of the Eskimos below caught some fish for dinner. Read the clues. Then decide how many fish each person caught and write the number on the line under each one.

Circle the fisherman who caught the most fish.

Draw boxes around the two whose fish added together equals 14.

Daily Learning Drills Grade 2

SOCIAL STUDIES

Name _____

A Family of Friends

There was a great exhibit at the Museum of American History of figures of Native Americans and Pilgrims sharing the first Thanksgiving feast. When the Pilgrims came to Plymouth, Massachusetts, in 1620, they had a very difficult year. Native Americans helped the Pilgrims hunt and harvest food.

Read each riddle. Use the Word Box to write each food that the Native Americans helped the Pilgrims find or grow.

1. Water doesn't stick –
   It rolls off my back;
   And when it does,
   I loudly say, "Quack, quack!"

   I am _____ .

2. I'm not inside a whale,
   But I'm found in a "wheel."
   You'll also find me
   In a piece of "steel."

   I am _____ .

3. When your roof "leaks,"
   You may want to cry.
   You'll do the same thing
   When I'm near your eye.

   I am _____ .

4. Boil me or pop me
   When I am ripe.
   Cook me in bread
   Or use my cob as a pipe.

   I am _____ .

5. I like to "honk,"
   And I can fly.
   Ask the lady who rode me,
   Reciting rhymes in the sky.

   I am _____ .

Word Box		
a goose	a leek	a duck
corn	an eel	

Then and Now

Name _____

The museum had great examples of things the colonists used. Although their lives were different than ours today, many of their needs were the same.

Unscramble the names of objects we use today. (The first letter is underlined.) Then write the correct letter to match similar objects of the past and present.

Present

Past

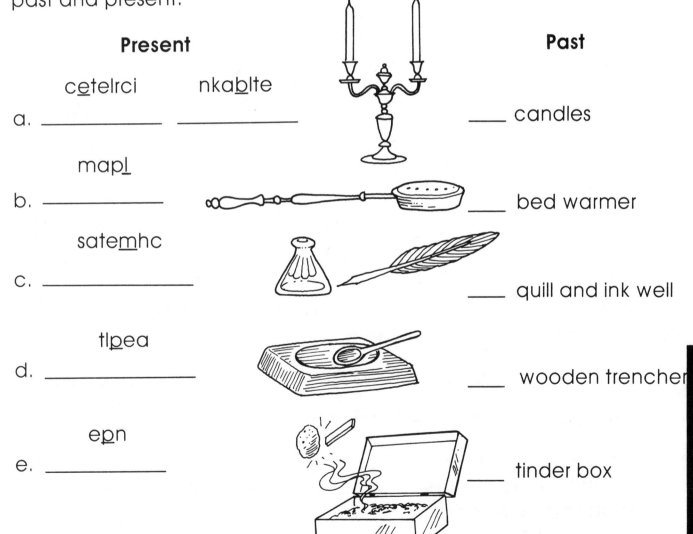

cetelrci   nkablte

a. _____   _____   ___ candles

mapl

b. _____   ___ bed warmer

satemhc

c. _____   ___ quill and ink well

tlpea

d. _____   ___ wooden trencher

epn

e. _____   ___ tinder box

SOCIAL STUDIES

Name _____

Down on the Farm

At the museum the children learned that though the colonists worked very hard, they also took time for some fun. One favorite form of fun was corn-husking competitions.

In the cornfield below, Thomas picked and husked corn from the cornstalks that have circles around the numbers.

Jonathon picked and husked corn from the cornstalks that have squares around the numbers.

James did the same with the cornstalks that have triangles around the numbers.

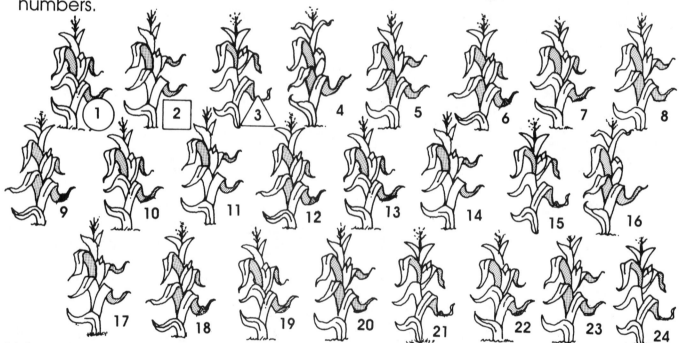

Using the pattern started above, finish drawing the circles, squares, and triangles. Then answer these questions.

1. Who picked and husked corn from cornstalk #20? _____

2. Who picked and husked corn from cornstalk #22? _____

3. If all of the even-numbered cornstalks had two ears of corn, and all of the odd-numbered cornstalks had one ear of corn, how many ears of corn did each boy husk?

   Thomas _____   Jonathon _____   James _____

Name _____

Sew What?

A favorite activity of colonial women and girls was getting together for a quilting bee. The quilts, made from scraps of linen, wool, and cotton, were frequently sewn together in a pattern.

Look carefully at the pattern in the unfinished quilt below. Then continue the pattern by drawing pictures in the blank sections to complete the quilt.

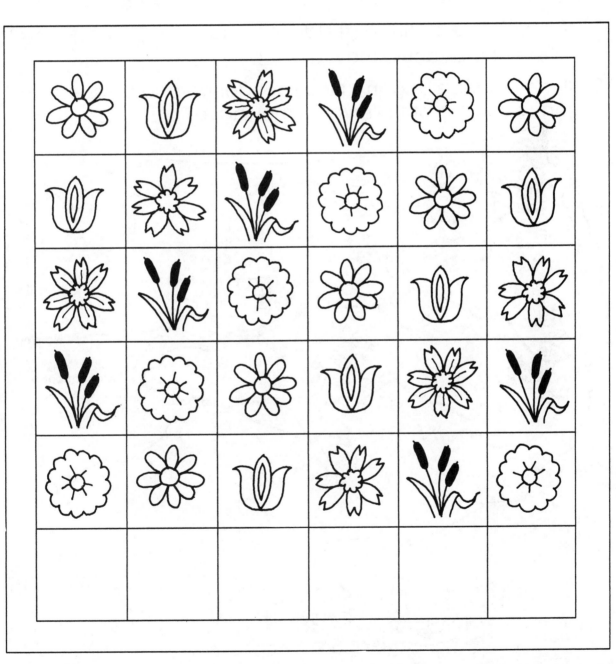

Daily Learning Drills Grade 2

SOCIAL STUDIES

Name _____

Go West, Young Man!

From about 1760 to 1850, pioneers moved westward across the United States. They traveled in big covered wagons called **Conestoga** wagons.

Some of the trails that the pioneers took in their Conestoga wagons are marked on the map below.

Look closely at the trails. Then answer the questions.

1. If the pioneers started at Nauvoo and traveled **west**, how many different trails could they take? _____

2. If the pioneers began at Independence and traveled **west**, how many choices of trails would they have? _____

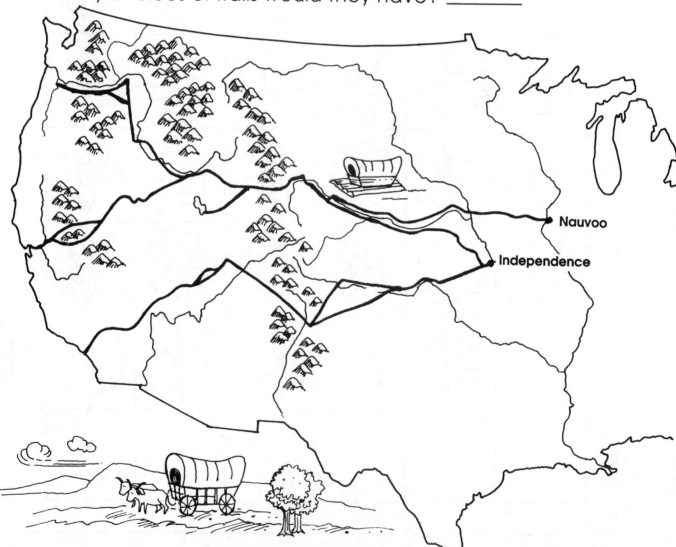

Name _____

A Man of Peace

A large picture of the Lincoln Memorial was on display at the museum. Abraham Lincoln was our 16th president. Shortly after he became President in 1861, America's Civil War began between the people living in the South and the people living in the North.

Abraham Lincoln made a famous speech in which he said that all people are created equal. He wanted all people in our country to live together in peace.

Look carefully at the tall columns around the outside of the building. If you walked around the whole building, how many columns would you pass? _____

SOCIAL STUDIES

Name _____

What's Your Brand?

The Museum of American History had a great display on cowboys who lived from the 1860's to the 1880's. These cowboys went on cattle drives for two to three months at a time and sometimes traveled 1,000 miles! They were often in danger from rattlesnakes, quicksand, cattle stampedes, and wild horses.

During cattle roundups in the spring and fall, cowboys branded the newborn calves to show what ranch they belonged to.

Look at the brands below. Use the Word Box to write what each brand meant.

A A   EZ   DL

_____   _____   _____

                 BQ

_____   _____   _____

   Z

_____   _____   _____

 WE   B

_____   _____   _____

Word Box

Twin Snakes	Double Z	Pair of Aces	Sunrise	Too Easy
Rocking Chair	Extra X	Big Deal	Sunset	Barbecue
Broken Wheel	Lazy S	Starlight	Tall Hat	Two Bees

Name _____

News Flash!

One large room in the museum had pages from calendars on its walls, listing events from America's past. Pretend that you were a newspaper reporter in the year 1888. You wrote a story about each event on the day it happened, as shown on the calendar below.

October – 1888

Sunday	Monday	Tuesday	Wednesday	Thursday	Friday	Saturday
	1	2	3	4	5	6
7	8	9 National Monument to George Washington opened	10	11	12	13
14	15	16	17	18 First school for agriculture set up in Minnesota	19	20 American baseball teams go on world tour
21	22	23	24	25 Double-decker ferry-boat launched in New York	26	27
28	29	30 J.J. Loud develops ball-point pen in Plymouth, Mass.	31			

Here are headlines for your newspaper stories. Write the date each story was written.

"Piggyback Ride Across River" _____

"A Hit 'Round The World" _____

"First President Honored" _____

"New Invention Makes Mark" _____

"Learning to Farm Is Fun" _____

SOCIAL STUDIES

Name _____

Help Wanted

America has often been called a "Land of Opportunity." Its people may choose from many types of careers.

Use the Word Box to write two different careers that have the following characteristics in common.

1. Place importance on books _____ _____

2. Consider water an important tool _____ _____

3. Work with needle and thread _____ _____

4. Work with food _____ _____

5. Make sure people follow rules _____ _____

6. Deliver mail and packages _____ _____

7. Takes care of medical needs _____ _____

8. Work with animals _____ _____

9. Use numbers quite often _____ _____

10. Provide entertainment _____ _____

Word Box

mathematician	veterinarian	teacher	chef
actor	police officer	nurse	doctor
accountant	mail carrier	seamstress	gardener
musician	fireman	librarian	tailor
delivery person	farmer	umpire	zookeeper

Name _____

Geography Magic Square

Read column A and choose an answer from column B. Write the number of the answer in the correct magic square. The first one has been done for you.

Column A

A. Large areas of water

B. A flat area of land that is higher than the land around it

C. One of the seven areas of land on Earth

D. A hot, wetland area of thick trees, plants and animals

E. A sun-dried clay brick used for building

F. A piece of land with water on three sides

G. A cone-shaped mountain made of ash and melted rock

H. A hot, dry area of land covered with sand

I. A group of mountains

Column B

1. peninsula
2. volcano
3. plateau
4. desert
5. continent
6. rain forest
7. ocean
8. adobe
9. range

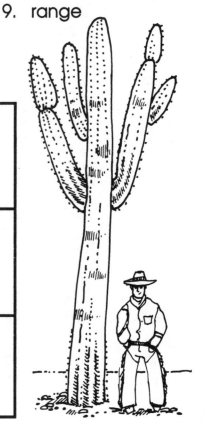

A 7	B	C
D	E	F
G	H	I

Add the numbers across and down. What answer do you get? _____

SOCIAL STUDIES

Name _____

Landform Riddles

Use the Word Bank to solve the riddles. Then color the pictures.

Word Bank					
lake	island	plain	river	mountain	peninsula

I have water on three sides. I am a

_ _ _ _ _ _ _ _ _

I have water all around me. I am an

_ _ _ _ _ _

I am wet and have land all around me. I am a

_ _ _ _

I am long and narrow and flow through the land. I am a

_ _ _ _ _

I am raised land, larger than a hill. I am a

_ _ _ _ _ _ _ _

I am low and flat. I am a

_ _ _ _ _

Name _____

Seeking the Sights

Read each clue. Use the map to locate the matching state. Write the abbreviation on the line.

1. The Space and Rocket Center is in the state south of Tennessee, **east** of Mississippi and **west** of Georgia. _____

2. Buffalo Bill's home is in the state **west** of Iowa and **south** of South Dakota.
_____

3. Elephant Rock is in the state **southeast** of Oregon and **west** of Utah.

_____

4. Casey Jones Railroad Museum is in the state **north** of Alabama and **south** of Kentucky. _____

5. Fossil National Monument is in the state **east** of Idaho and **south** of Montana. _____

6. The Corn Palace is in the state **southeast** of Montana and **northwest** of Iowa. _____

7. A life-size model of one of Columbus' ships, the *Santa Maria*, is in the state **west** of Pennsylvania and **east** of Indiana. _____

8. Gillette Castle is in the state **east** of New York and **south** of Massachusetts. _____

SOCIAL STUDIES

Name _____

The Seven Continents

Pretend you are a pilot. Your job is to land on each continent for a top-secret mission. You must learn what each continent looks like.

Write the name of each continent below its picture. Use the word bank below.

1. _____   2. _____   3. _____

4. _____   5. _____   6. _____

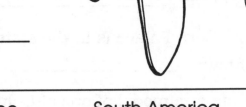

7. _____

Africa	Asia	Europe	South America
Antarctica	Australia	North America	

Name _____

Animals Around the World

Color the animals and the continents.

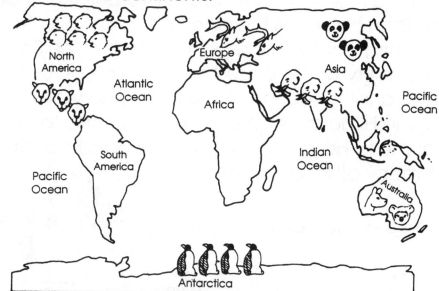

Color one square for each animal on the map.
Use a different color for each animal.

kangaroo						
elephant						
panda						
koala						
polar bear						
reindeer						
penguin						
jaguar						
	1	**2**	**3**	**4**	**5**	

SOCIAL STUDIES

Name _____

The Largest Continent

Asia is the world's largest continent. It stretches for thousands of miles. More than half of all the people in the world live in Asia. Asia contains the large area that was once called the Soviet Union. China, the country with the most people living in it, is also located in Asia. India, another country in Asia, has the world's highest mountains, the Himalayas. These mountains are so high that the snow never melts. Have you ever seen a panda or an elephant? These and many other animals live in Asia.

Follow the directions below.

1. Use a map of Asia to label:
   A. China
   B. India
   C. Saudi Arabia
   D. Soviet Union

2. Label the three oceans that surround Asia.

List two things you learned about Asia.

1. _____

_____

2. _____

_____

Name _____

Geography Crossword

Read each clue. Find an answer in the Word Bank. Write the words in the puzzle. Be sure to cross out the words you use in the Word Bank.

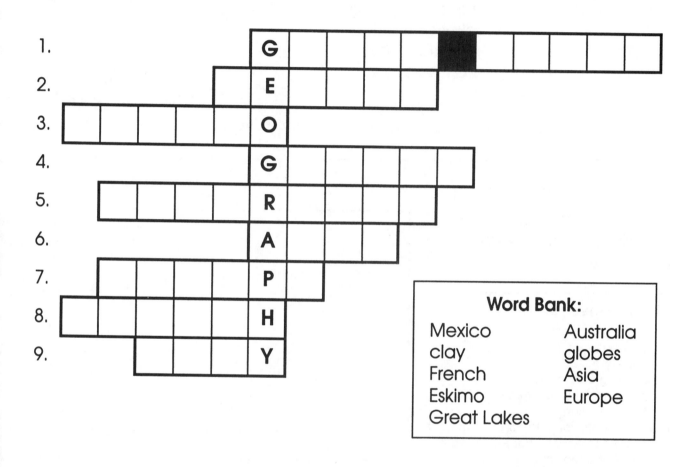

1.
2.
3.
4.
5.
6.
7.
8.
9.

G
E
O
G
R
A
P
H
Y

Word Bank:

Mexico	Australia
clay	globes
French	Asia
Eskimo	Europe
Great Lakes	

1. Bodies of fresh water that border Canada and the U.S.
2. A country that is south of the United States
3. A group of people sometimes called the Inuits
4. Models of Earth
5. Kangaroos and koalas live on this continent
6. The largest continent
7. A small continent that has many countries
8. A group of people who sailed across the Atlantic to Canada
9. Some Hispanics once used this to build their houses

Daily Learning Drills Grade 2

SOCIAL STUDIES

Name _____

Speaking Strine

Australians, like Americans, have their own "language" called Strine. An Aussie might say something like this, "I'm going to take my swag and tucker down to the billabong while my jumbucks are resting." That sounds like a foreign language!

In the box to the left below is a Strine dictionary so you can translate what the "bloke" said. _____

_____

Using the dictionary, write and illustrate two sentences of your own.

How to Speak Strine

billabong - water hole
billy - container for boiling tea
bloke - man
bonzer - great, terrific
bush - country away from the city
chook - chicken
dingo - Australian wild dog
dinkum, fair dinkum - honest, genuine
dinki-di - the real thing
fossick - to prospect for gold or gems
grazier - ranch
jumbuck - sheep
make a good fist - do a good job
ocker - basic down-to-earth Aussie
outback - remote bush
pom - English person
roo - a kangaroo
shout - buy a round of drinks
station - sheep or cattle ranch
Strine - what Aussies speak
swag - bedroll and belongings
tucker - food
ute - utility or pickup truck
waltz matilda - carry a swag

Name _____

Happy New Year!

In China, the most celebrated holiday is the New Year. The Lantern Festival is part of the celebration. That is when Chinese people welcome the first full moon of the year. The Chinese New Year is fixed according to the lunar calendar. It occurs somewhere between January 30 and February 20. Each Chinese year is represented by one of 12 animals.

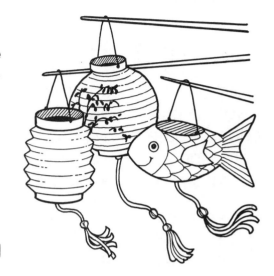

Look at the chart below to see what animal represents the year you were born.

RAT	OX	TIGER	HARE (RABBIT)	DRAGON	SNAKE	HORSE	RAM	MONKEY	ROOSTER	DOG	PIG
1900	1901	1902	1903	1904	1905	1906	1907	1908	1909	1910	1911
1912	1913	1914	1915	1916	1917	1918	1919	1920	1921	1922	1923
1924	1925	1926	1927	1928	1929	1930	1931	1932	1933	1934	1935
1936	1937	1938	1939	1940	1941	1942	1943	1944	1945	1946	1947
1948	1949	1950	1951	1952	1953	1954	1955	1956	1957	1958	1959
1960	1961	1962	1963	1964	1965	1966	1967	1968	1969	1970	1971
1972	1973	1974	1975	1976	1977	1978	1979	1980	1981	1982	1983
1984	1985	1986	1987	1988	1989	1990	1991	1992	1993	1994	1995
1996	1997	1998	1999	2000	2001	2002	2003	2004	2005	2006	2007
2008	2009	2010	2011	2012	2013	2014	2015	2016	2017	2018	2019

The Festival of the Lanterns is celebrated on the third day of the New Year. Make a colorful lantern to hang in your classroom.

1. Fold a bright-colored piece of construction paper vertically.

2. Cut strips from the folded side stopping 2" from the open edge.

3. Open, bend in circle, and staple.

4. Cut out a long paper strip and staple to make a handle.

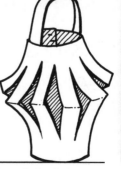

SOCIAL STUDIES

Name _____

The "Boot"

From America, Italy is across the Atlantic Ocean. It is part of a continent called Europe. Most of Italy is shaped like a boot. It also has two islands named Sicily and Sardinia. Its "boot," or mainland, extends into the Mediterranean Sea. The shape of the mainland is called a peninsula because it has water around three of its sides. Rome is Italy's capital and largest city. It has been an important city for more than 2,500 years. Italy got its name from the Romans who called its southern part Italia, meaning "land of oxen" or "grazing land."

Color Italy green.
Color the Mediterranean Sea blue.
Use the map to unscramble the names of some Italian cities below it.

ALSNEP _____   ENCLEOFR _____   MERO _____

LMNIA _____   AENOG _____   NCVEIE _____

OGBNLOA _____

Name _____

The American Alphabet

The United States attracts people from all over the world. We are sometimes called a nation of immigrants.

Write the alphabet in order in the boxes. Then use the Word Box and the letter in each box to write the name of each country where it belongs.

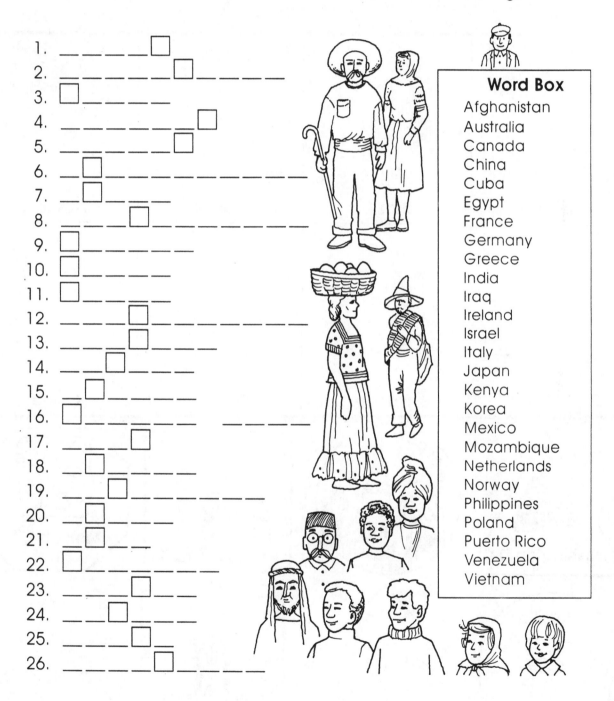

1. _ _ _ _ ☐
2. _ _ _ _ ☐ _ _
3. ☐ _ _ _
4. _ _ _ _ ☐ _
5. _ _ _ _ ☐ _
6. _ ☐ _ _ _
7. _ ☐ _ _
8. _ _ ☐ _ _ _ _ _
9. ☐ _ _
10. ☐ _ _
11. ☐ _ _ _
12. _ _ ☐ _ _ _ _ _ _
13. _ _ ☐ _ _
14. _ ☐ _ _ _
15. _ ☐ _ _ _
16. ☐ _ _ _ _ _ _ _ _ _ _
17. _ _ ☐ _ _ _
18. _ ☐ _ _ _ _
19. _ _ ☐ _ _ _ _ _ _
20. _ ☐ _ _
21. _ ☐ _ _ _
22. ☐ _ _ _ _
23. _ _ ☐ _ _
24. _ ☐ _ _ _ _ _
25. _ _ ☐ _ _
26. _ _ _ ☐ _ _ _

Word Box
Afghanistan
Australia
Canada
China
Cuba
Egypt
France
Germany
Greece
India
Iraq
Ireland
Israel
Italy
Japan
Kenya
Korea
Mexico
Mozambique
Netherlands
Norway
Philippines
Poland
Puerto Rico
Venezuela
Vietnam

SOCIAL STUDIES

Name _____

A Capital Idea

This is what Tommy's suitcase might have looked like after visiting the eight countries on his adventure. Color and cut out the travel stickers below. Paste them on the suitcase so each capital matches its country.

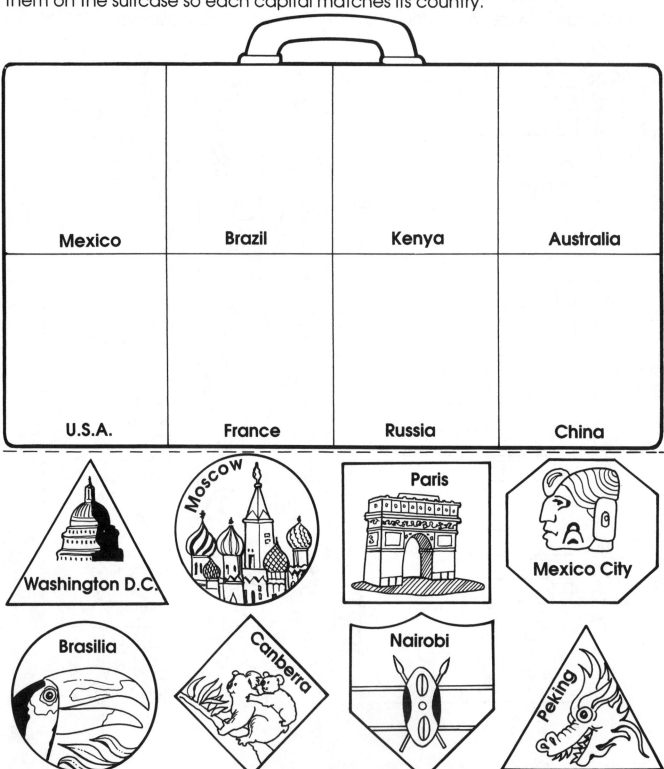

| Mexico | Brazil | Kenya | Australia |
| U.S.A. | France | Russia | China |

Washington D.C.

Moscow

Paris

Mexico City

Brasilia

Canberra

Nairobi

Peking

Answer Key

Food for Gregory

Print Gregory's food in ABC order. Then draw each meal on the plate

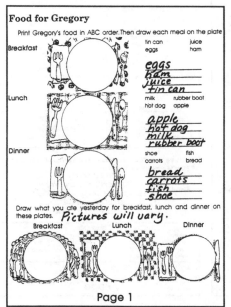

Breakfast
tin can | juice
eggs | ham

eggs
ham
juice
tin can

Lunch
milk | rubber boot
hot dog | apple

apple
hot dog
milk
rubber boot

Dinner
shoe | fish
carrots | bread

bread
carrots
fish
shoe

Draw what you ate yesterday for breakfast, lunch and dinner on these plates. Pictures will vary.

Breakfast | Lunch | Dinner

Page 1

Which Part Shall I Play?

Grace loves to act out stories. Read the list of characters. Then write them in alphabetical order.

Joan of Arc
Anansi
Peter Pan
Juliet
Captain Hook
Hiawatha
Wendy
Romeo
Mowgli
Aladdin

1. Aladdin
2. Anansi
3. Captain Hook
4. Hiawatha
5. Joan of Arc
6. Juliet
7. Mowgli
8. Peter Pan
9. Romeo
10. Wendy

Page 2

Which Way?

Read the words in the Word Bank. Write them in alphabetical order on the lines.

Word Bank
juggling
fiddled
whole
cookie
tight
pieces
easy
button
laces
somersaults

1. button
2. cookie
3. easy
4. fiddled
5. juggling
6. laces
7. pieces
8. somersaults
9. tight
10. whole

Write the missing lowercase letters in alphabetical order.

a b c d e f g h i j k l m
n o p q r s t u v w x y z

Page 3

ABC Potion

Write the words in alphabetical order.

1. always
2. baron
3. control
4. drink
5. flashed
6. hard
7. ketchup
8. lightning
9. monster
10. overhead
11. point
12. rumbled
13. scientist
14. thunder
15. world

point
scientist
world
lightning
hard
baron
flashed
monster
rumbled
control
ketchup
overhead
drink
thunder
always

Page 4

Crazy Creatures

Draw a line to each letter in ABC order to finish this dot-to-dot picture.

Now color and add details to the picture. Then write all the consonants in order on these lines.

1. b 5. g 9. l 13. q 17. v 21. z
2. c 6. h 10. m 14. r 18. w
3. d 7. j 11. n 15. s 19. x
4. f 8. k 12. p 16. t 20. y

Page 5

Alphabet Soup

Nan Cook has a special way of making alphabet soup. She mixes two boxes of soup together. Then she adds two secret ingredients — mystery and fun. After the soup is cooked, a strange thing happens. All the vowels rise to the top of the pot.

Write the consonant that can be used in both the front and back of each vowel or pair of vowels to make a word. One is done for you.

Answers may vary.

peep dad
pop gag mom deed
noon bib pup tot
wow mum did dud
bob nun kook pep
gig sees tat
sis

Page 6

Stretch and Grow

Goofy Gladys got new glasses. The glasses had springs on them which stretched words out and then added another vowel to each one.

Add a vowel to each word below to see what words Gladys saw through her glasses.

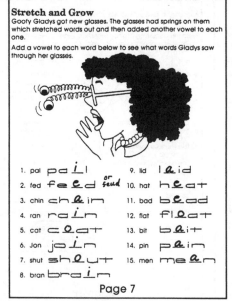

1. pal pail
2. fed feed or feud
3. chin chain
4. ran rain
5. cat coat
6. Jon join
7. shut shout
8. bran brain

9. lid laid
10. hat heat
11. bad bead
12. flat float
13. bit bait
14. pin pain
15. men mean

Page 7

Motorcycle Maze

Help Ralph move through the maze to the Mountain View Inn by tracing over the path in which all of the words have two syllables.

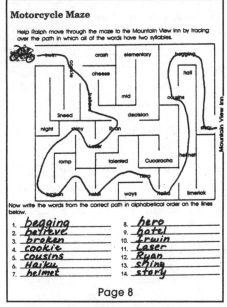

Mountain View Inn

Now write the words from the correct path in alphabetical order on the lines below.

1. begging
2. believe
3. broken
4. cookie
5. cousins
6. Haiku
7. helmet

8. hero
9. hotel
10. Irwin
11. Laser
12. Ryan
13. shiny
14. story

Page 8

Trick or Treat Syllables

Think about how many syllables are in each word in the Word Bank. Then write each word on the correct jack-o'-lantern.

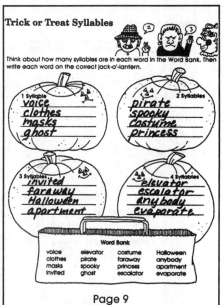

1 Syllable
voice
clothes
masks
ghost

2 Syllables
pirate
spooky
costume
princess

3 Syllables
invited
faraway
Halloween
apartment

4 Syllables
elevator
escalator
anybody
evaporate

Word Bank

voice	elevator	costume	Halloween
clothes	pirate	faraway	anybody
masks	spooky	princess	apartment
invited	ghost	escalator	evaporate

Page 9

Daily Learning Drills Grade 2

All Together Now
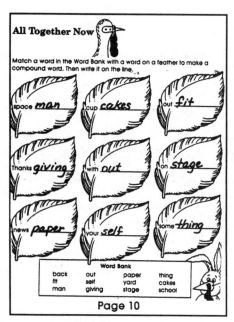

Match a word in the Word Bank with a word on a feather to make a compound word. Then write it on the line.

space *man*   cup *cakes*   out *fit*

Thanks *giving*   with *out*   on *stage*

news *paper*   your *self*   some *thing*

Word Bank

back	out	paper	thing
fit	self	yard	cakes
man	giving	stage	school

Page 10

Word Magic
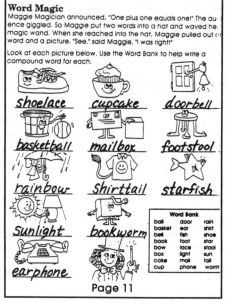

Maggie Magician announced, "One plus one equals one!" The audience giggled. So Maggie put two words into a hat and waved her magic wand. When she reached into the hat, Maggie pulled out one word and a picture. "See," said Maggie, "I was right!"

Look at each picture below. Use the Word Bank to help write a compound word for each.

shoelace   *cupcake*   *doorbell*

basketball   *mailbox*   *footstool*

rainbow   *shirttail*   *starfish*

sunlight   *bookworm*

earphone

Word Bank

ball	door	rain
basket	ear	shirt
bell	fish	shoe
book	foot	star
bow	lace	stool
box	light	sun
cake	mail	tail
cup	phone	worm

Page 11

Compound Your Effort
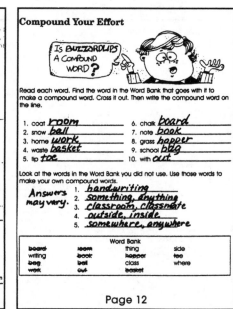

IS BUZZARDLIPS A COMPOUND WORD?

Read each word. Find the word in the Word Bank that goes with it to make a compound word. Cross it out. Then write the compound word on the line.

1. coat *room*
2. snow *ball*
3. home *work*
4. waste *basket*
5. tip *toe*
6. chalk *board*
7. note *book*
8. grass *hopper*
9. school *bag*
10. with *out*

Look at the words in the Word Bank you did not use. Use those words to make your own compound words.

Answers may vary.
1. *handwriting*
2. *something, anything*
3. *classroom, classmate*
4. *outside, inside*
5. *somewhere, anywhere*

Word Bank

~~board~~	~~room~~	thing	side
writing	~~book~~	~~hopper~~	toe
~~bag~~	~~ball~~	class	where
~~work~~	~~out~~	~~basket~~	

Page 12

Mystery Word Mix-Up

Put on your detective hat! How many words can you make using only the letters in the words:

N a t e   t h e   G r e a t

1. *neat*
2. *net*
3. *eat*
4. *ate*
5. *gate*
6. *get*
7. *treat*
8. *teeth*
9. *tea*
10. *green*
11. *ten*
12. *tan*
13. *teen*
14. *hear*
15. *heart*
16. *ear*
17. *gear*
18. *near*
19. *tear*
20. *greet*
21. *nag*
22. *tag*

Others possible.

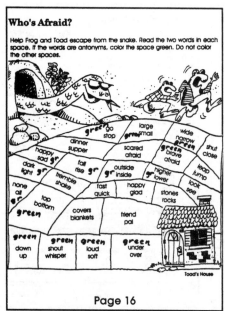

Page 13

Flower Fun
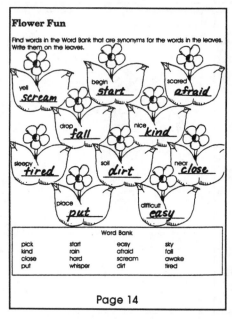

Find words in the Word Bank that are synonyms for the words in the leaves. Write them on the leaves.

yell *scream*   begin *start*   scared *afraid*

drop *fall*   nice *kind*

sleepy *tired*   soil *dirt*   near *close*

place *put*   difficult *easy*

Word Bank

pick	start	easy	sky
kind	rain	afraid	fall
close	hard	scream	awake
put	whisper	dirt	tired

Page 14

Where?
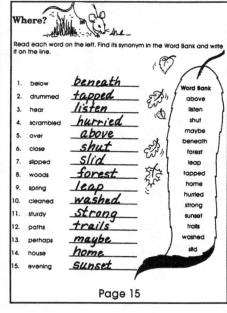

Read each word on the left. Find its synonym in the Word Bank and write it on the line.

1. below *beneath*
2. drummed *tapped*
3. hear *listen*
4. scrambled *hurried*
5. over *above*
6. close *shut*
7. slipped *slid*
8. woods *forest*
9. spring *leap*
10. cleaned *washed*
11. sturdy *strong*
12. paths *trails*
13. perhaps *maybe*
14. house *home*
15. evening *sunset*

Word Bank

above
listen
shut
maybe
beneath
forest
leap
tapped
home
hurried
strong
sunset
trails
washed
slid

Page 15

Who's Afraid?

Help Frog and Toad escape from the snake. Read the two words in each space. If the words are antonyms, color the space green. Do not color the other spaces.

Toad's House

Page 16

Should We Wake Them?

Read the words on each of the pillows. Find a word in the Word Bank that means the opposite and write it on the line.

sold *bought*   off *on*   first *last*

hated *loved*   warm *cool*   front *back*

remembered *forgotten*   small *big*   to *from*

yours *mine*   everybody *nobody*   early *late*

Word Bank

bought	on	all	tiny
nobody	big	last	late
ahead	mine	from	cool
forgotten	loved		back

Page 17

Flying Free Like an Eagle
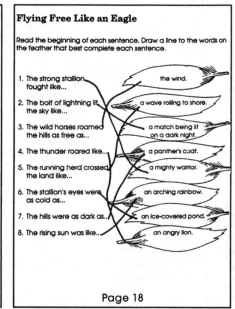

Read the beginning of each sentence. Draw a line to the words on the feather that best complete each sentence.

1. The strong stallion fought like...
2. The bolt of lightning lit the sky like...
3. The wild horses roamed the hills as free as...
4. The thunder roared like...
5. The running herd crossed the land like...
6. The stallion's eyes were as cold as...
7. The hills were as dark as...
8. The rising sun was like...

the wind.
a wave rolling to shore.
a match being lit on a dark night.
a panther's coat.
a mighty warrior.
an arching rainbow.
an ice-covered pond.
an angry lion.

Page 18

Rain, Rain Go Away!

Read the naming parts in the tent.
✏ one of the naming parts to begin each sentence.

Rain
Black clouds
A big wind
The campfire
Todd and Clint
The old green tent

1. **Todd and Clint** went camping.
2. **The old green tent** was hard to set up.
3. **A big wind** blew the trees.
4. **Black clouds** filled the sky.
5. **Rain** ran off the tent.
6. **The campfire** went out.

Page 19

It Takes Many Colors

Read the words in the Word Bank. If the word means one, write it on the paint jar. If the word means more than one, write it on the paintbrushes.

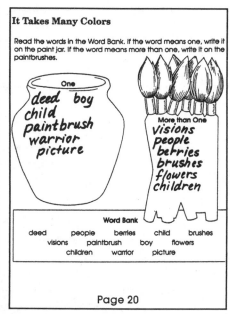

One
deed   boy
child
paintbrush
warrior
picture

More than One
visions
people
berries
brushes
flowers
children

Word Bank
deed   people   berries   child   brushes
visions   paintbrush   boy   flowers
children   warrior   picture

Page 20

Fun Around the Campfire

Word Bank
beat   sang   told
danced   sat   wore

✏ a verb in each sentence below. Use the word bank to help you.

1. The boys and girls **danced** around the campfire.
2. They **sang** songs.
3. Brian **beat** a drum.
4. Jerry and Helen **wore** Indian costumes.
5. They **sat** around the campfire.
6. The teacher **told** stories.

Page 21

It's Time

✏ these verbs in the correct Time Machine.

play   pull   barked   jumped   danced
looked   laugh   walk   listen   lived

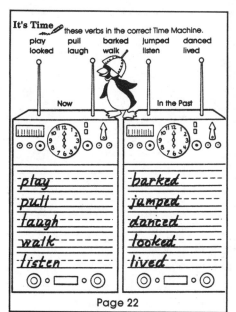

Now

In the Past

play	barked
pull	jumped
laugh	danced
walk	looked
listen	lived

Page 22

I Was. Were You?

Use "was" and "were" to tell about something that happened in the past. Use "was" to tell about one person or thing. Use "were" to tell about more than one person or thing. Always use "were" with the word "you."

✏ "was" or "were" in each sentence below.

1. Lois **was** in the second grade last year.
2. She **was** eight years old.
3. Carmen and Judy **were** friends.
4. They **were** on the same soccer team.
5. I **was** on the team, too.
6. You **were** too young to play.

Page 23

Playing in the Summer Sun

Look at the picture. Read the sentence. Circle the missing word. Then write it on the line.

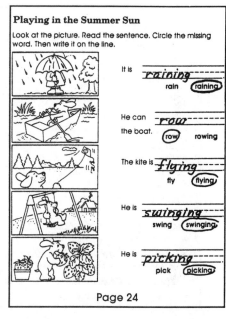

It is **raining**
rain (raining)

He can **row** the boat.
(row) rowing

The kite is **flying**
fly (flying)

He is **swinging**
swing (swinging)

He is **picking**
pick (picking)

Page 24

An Owlish Activity

Write the words where they belong.

Word Bank
bite   school   children   skip   donkey   house
jump   lunchbox   kitten   write   hop   run

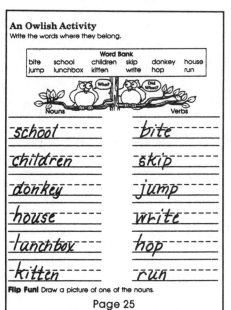

Nouns   Verbs

school	bite
children	skip
donkey	jump
house	write
lunchbox	hop
kitten	run

Flip Fun! Draw a picture of one of the nouns.

Page 25

Tic-Tac-Toe

Circle all of the naming words (nouns).
Put an X on all of the doing words (verbs).
Under each game, write the X words that scored a tic-tac-toe.

boy	well	tell
mother	wished	ladder
ran	man	cake

ran
wished
fell

fished	water	book
told	stone	lamp
pumped	people	ghost

fished
told
pumped

child	sent	house
tree	ate	China
China	raked	body

sent
ate
raced

paper	bear	bridge
nickel	table	flower
read	yelled	jump

read
yelled
jump

Page 26

Picking Pronouns

The words *he, she, it,* and *they* can be used in place of a noun.

Read the sentence pairs. Write the correct pronoun in each blank.

1. John won first place.
   He got a blue ribbon.

2. Janet and Gail rode on a bus.
   They went to visit their grandmother.

3. Sarah had a birthday party.
   She invited six friends to the party.

4. The kitten likes to play.
   It likes to tug on shoelaces.

5. Ed is seven years old.
   He is in the second grade.

Page 27

Daily Learning Drills Grade 2

Marvelous Me!

You know that you are a very special person for many reasons. Some of these reasons include your body!

Draw hair and eyes on the body below to make it look like you. Then, use the describing words listed in the box with the names of your beautiful body parts to label yourself. Be sure both words start with the same sound. Write a story about your body and how each part is special!

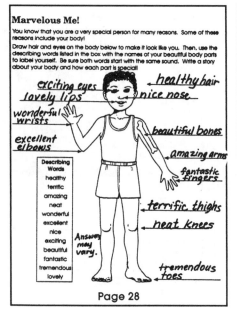

exciting eyes — healthy hair
lovely lips — nice nose
wonderful wrists
excellent elbows — beautiful bones
— amazing arms
— fantastic fingers
— terrific thighs
— neat knees
— tremendous toes

Describing Words
healthy
terrific
amazing
neat
wonderful
excellent
nice
exciting
beautiful
fantastic
tremendous
lovely

Answers may vary.

Page 28

Add the Adjectives

Read each sentence. Write a describing word on each line. Draw a picture to match each sentence. **Answers will vary.**

The _____ flag waved over the _____ building.

A _____ lion searched for food in the _____ jungle.

We saw _____ fish in the _____ aquarium.

Her _____ car was parked by the _____ van.

The _____ dog barked and chased the _____ truck.

The _____ building was filled with _____ packages.

Page 29

Wordy Treats

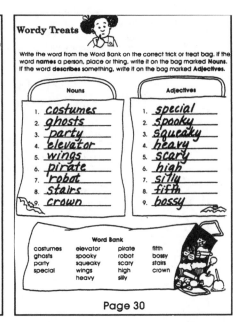

Write the word from the Word Bank on the correct trick or treat bag. If the word **names** a person, place or thing, write it on the bag marked **Nouns**. If the word **describes** something, write it on the bag marked **Adjectives**.

Nouns
1. costumes
2. ghosts
3. party
4. elevator
5. wings
6. pirate
7. robot
8. stairs
9. crown

Adjectives
1. special
2. spooky
3. squeaky
4. heavy
5. scary
6. high
7. silly
8. fifth
9. bossy

Word Bank
costumes elevator pirate fifth
ghosts spooky robot bossy
party squeaky scary stairs
special wings high crown
heavy silly

Page 30

Summer Camp

A telling sentence begins with a capital letter and ends with a period. Write each telling sentence correctly on the lines.

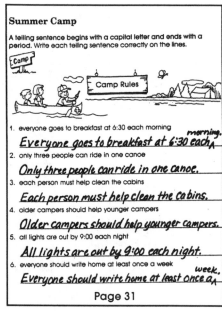

Camp Rules

1. everyone goes to breakfast at 6:30 each morning
   Everyone goes to breakfast at 6:30 each morning.
2. only three people can ride in one canoe
   Only three people can ride in one canoe.
3. each person must help clean the cabins
   Each person must help clean the cabins.
4. older campers should help younger campers
   Older campers should help younger campers.
5. all lights are out by 9:00 each night
   All lights are out by 9:00 each night.
6. everyone should write home at least once a week
   Everyone should write home at least once a week.

Page 31

Tell-a-vision

Look at each TV picture. Write a telling sentence about each program. **Answers will vary.**

Page 32

Telephone Talk

An asking sentence is called a question. A question begins with a capital letter and ends with a question mark.

_____ these questions correctly.

1. how old are you
   How old are you?
2. are you in second grade
   Are you in second grade?
3. who is your teacher
   Who is your teacher?
4. did you read that book
   Did you read that book?
5. where do you live
   Where do you live?

Page 33

Asking Questions

Look at the picture. Write five asking sentences about the picture. **Answers will vary.**

Page 34

That Doesn't Make Sense!

A sentence must make sense. Read each sentence. Put an X on the two words which do not belong. Write the corrected sentence on the lines below.

Yard Sale My neighbor is ~~orange~~ having a yard ~~very~~ sale.
1. My neighbor is having a yard sale.

She is ~~slow~~ selling lots of old things ~~phone~~.
2. She is selling lots of old things.

A man ~~until~~ is buying five ~~candle~~ old books.
3. A man is buying five old books.

My brother is buying an ~~salt~~ old checkers ~~X~~ game.
4. My brother is buying an old checkers game.

Two ladies ~~pull~~ are buying an old ~~teach~~ toy chest.
5. Two ladies are buying an old toy chest.

Page 35

Flight to Fun

Would you like to fly away for a fun trip? Write words about a trip on the plane. Use the words to write five sentences about the trip.

TICKET

1. Answers will vary.
2. _____
3. _____
4. _____
5. _____

Page 36

About Me

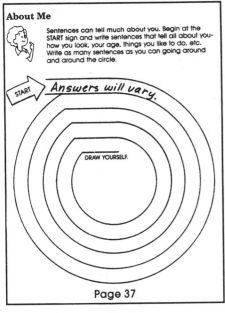

Sentences can tell much about you. Begin at the START sign and write sentences that tell all about you—how you look, your age, things you like to do, etc. Write as many sentences as you can going around and around the circle.

START → Answers will vary.

DRAW YOURSELF.

Page 37

A Sensational Scent

Circle the letters that should be capital letters. Then write them in the matching numbered blanks to answer the question.

1. (E)ddie, Homer's friend, lives on (E)lm Street.
2. Homer's aunt lives in (K)ansas City, (K)ansas.
3. (A)re you sure Aunt (A)ggie is coming?
4. (O)ld Rip Van Winkle came to town.
5. The doughnuts were made by (H)omer Price.
6. Miss (T)erwilliger and Uncle (T)elly saved yam.
7. Homer (P)rice was written by (R)obert McCloskey.
8. Uncle (U)lysses owned a lunch room.
9. The (S)uper–Duper was a comic book hero.
10. Doc (P)elly lived in Homer's town.
11. (M)oney was stolen by the robbers.
12. (N)ow you have the answer to the question.

Who is hiding in the suitcase?
A r o m a   t h e   p e t   s k u n k
3 7 4 11 3   6 5 1   10 1 6   9 2 8 12 2

Page 38

Now, How Does That Go?

Write the sentences correctly. Be sure to put capital letters, periods and exclamation marks where they belong.

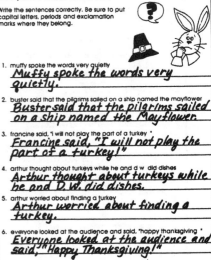

1. muffy spoke the words very quietly
   Muffy spoke the words very quietly.

2. buster said that the pilgrims sailed on a ship named the mayflower
   Buster said that the pilgrims sailed on a ship named the Mayflower.

3. francine said, "i will not play the part of a turkey"
   Francine said, "I will not play the part of a turkey!"

4. arthur thought about turkeys while he and d w did dishes
   Arthur thought about turkeys while he and D. W. did dishes.

5. arthur worried about finding a turkey
   Arthur worried about finding a turkey.

6. everyone looked at the audience and said, "happy thanksgiving"
   Everyone looked at the audience and said, "Happy Thanksgiving!"

Page 39

Punctuation Magic

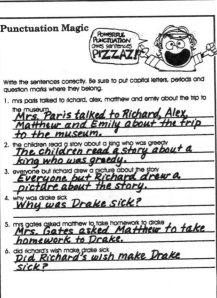

POWERFUL PUNCTUATION GIVES SENTENCES PIZZAZZ!

Write the sentences correctly. Be sure to put capital letters, periods and question marks where they belong.

1. mrs paris talked to richard, alex, matthew and emily about the trip to the museum
   Mrs. Paris talked to Richard, Alex, Matthew and Emily about the trip to the museum.

2. the children read a story about a king who was greedy
   The children read a story about a king who was greedy.

3. everyone but richard drew a picture about the story
   Everyone but Richard drew a picture about the story.

4. why was drake sick
   Why was Drake sick?

5. mrs gates asked matthew to take homework to drake
   Mrs. Gates asked Matthew to take homework to Drake.

6. did richard's wish make drake sick
   Did Richard's wish make Drake sick?

Page 40

An Excellent Exercise

The words a and an help point out a noun. Use a before a word that begins with a consonant. Use an before a word that begins with a vowel.

1. Our class visited _a_ farm.
2. We could only stay _an_ hour.
3. A man let us pick eggs out of _a_ nest.
4. We saw _an_ egg that was cracked.
5. We watched _a_ lady milk a cow.
6. We got to eat _an_ ice cream cone.

Page 41

Add an Apostrophe

Add 's to a noun to show who or what **owns** something.

✎ the correct word under each picture.

The ___ nose is big.
clown   clowns   (clown's)

This is ___ coat.
Bettys   (Betty's)   Betty

I know ___ brother.
(Burt's)   Burt   Burts

The ___ hat is pretty.
girls   girl   (girl's)

That is the ___ ball.
(kitten's)   kitten   kittens

My ___ shoe is missing.
sisters   sister   (sister's)

The ___ coach is Mr. Hall.
teams   (team's)   team

The ___ cover is torn.
(book's)   books   book

Page 42

Fish for Plurals

Write the words on the fish in the correct tank.

kites   mitten   star   cats   chick   matches   foxes   lunch

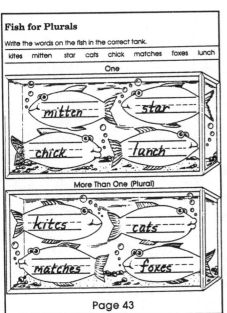

One
mitten   star   chick   lunch

More Than One (Plural)
kites   cats   matches   foxes

Page 43

Who Is Hungrier?

Use the pictures to help you complete each sentence with the correct word.

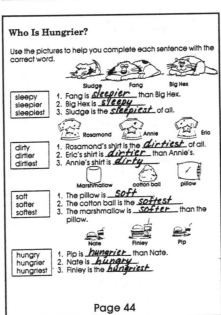

Sludge   Fang   Big Hex

sleepy / sleepier / sleepiest
1. Fang is _sleepier_ than Big Hex.
2. Big Hex is _sleepy_.
3. Sludge is the _sleepiest_ of all.

Rosamond   Annie   Eric

dirty / dirtier / dirtiest
1. Rosamond's shirt is the _dirtiest_ of all.
2. Eric's shirt is _dirtier_ than Annie's.
3. Annie's shirt is _dirty_.

Marshmallow   cotton ball   pillow

soft / softer / softest
1. The pillow is _soft_.
2. The cotton ball is the _softest_.
3. The marshmallow is _softer_ than the pillow.

Nate   Finley   Pip

hungry / hungrier / hungriest
1. Pip is _hungrier_ than Nate.
2. Nate is _hungry_.
3. Finley is the _hungriest_.

Page 44

Is It a World Record?

Read each sentence. Choose the correct word and write it on the line.

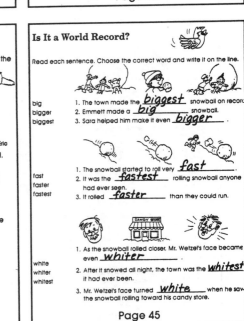

big / bigger / biggest
1. The town made the _biggest_ snowball on record.
2. Emmett made a _big_ snowball.
3. Sara helped him make it even _bigger_.

fast / faster / fastest
1. The snowball started to roll very _fast_.
2. It was the _fastest_ rolling snowball anyone had ever seen.
3. It rolled _faster_ than they could run.

white / whiter / whitest
1. As the snowball rolled closer, Mr. Wetzel's face became even _whiter_.
2. After it snowed all night, the town was the _whitest_ it had ever been.
3. Mr. Wetzel's face turned _white_ when he saw the snowball rolling toward his candy store.

Page 45

Daily Learning Drills Grade 2

Can I, or Can't I?

Read each sentence. Write **can** or **can't** on the line.

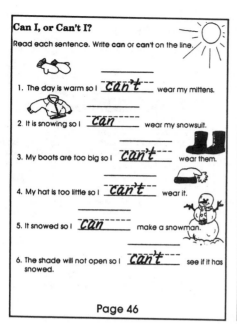

1. The day is warm so I **can't** wear my mittens.
2. It is snowing so I **can** wear my snowsuit.
3. My boots are too big so I **can't** wear them.
4. My hat is too little so I **can't** wear it.
5. It snowed so I **can** make a snowman.
6. The shade will not open so I **can't** see if it has snowed.

Page 46

Bunny Bunch

There are ten bunnies in this family. Each one is special.

Read the clues and fill in the blank with the word that rhymes and makes sense.

1. I like to hop and drink **pop**
2. I can run fast, but still I am always **last**
3. I like to run and jump, but sometimes I fall and get a **bump**
4. I like to help Mom and Pop by scrubbing the floor with a **mop**
5. After I feed the cat, I take out my baseball and **bat**
6. I like to go on a hike or ride my **bike**
7. I like to dig in the sand and play the drums in a **band**
8. I like to play with a toy car while I eat a candy **bar**
9. I can walk in the fog and also chop a **log**
10. I can fly my kite but not during the **night**

Word list: band, bar, bat, bike, bump, cast, daylight, far, fat, fog, hand, last, like, log, mop, night, pop, pump, stop, top

Page 47

Loosey Goosey

Find the names of the birds at the bottom of the page that will rhyme with the words given. For example: Loose goose

narrow **sparrow**
hairy **canary**
men **wren**
pork **stork**
love **dove**
pleasant **pheasant**
perky **turkey**
soon **loon**
luck **duck**
darling **starling**

bobbin **robin**
dark **lark**
pinch **finch**
muffin **puffin**
beagle **eagle**
frail **quail**
hull **gull**
lay **jay**
howl **owl**

dove stork canary wren robin jay

starling sparrow pheasant eagle turkey owl gull

quail loon puffin duck lark finch

Page 48

Do You Know a Boa?

Print a rhyming word under each word on the boa's body. Slither down from the head to the tail. Ssssssssssss.

words will vary.

pet **set**   Jim **slim**
snake **rake**   throw **know**
kid **hid**
class **lass**
kick **stick**   farm **charm**   cow **hour**
hen **pen**   eat **feet**
mother **brother**   boy **toy**   school **rule**
day **say**   corn **horn**   end **lend**

Page 49

What an Act!

Read about each act. Read the titles in the Word Bank. Write the best title for each act.

1. The lady climbed on the horse's back. The horse galloped around the ring as she stood up on its back.
Lady on a Galloping Horse

2. Four seals stood up on their flippers. They spun and tossed a ball to each other. The biggest seal threw it to his trainer, Mac, who threw it back.
Mac and His Ball-Playing Seals

3. The trainer led the five bears into the ring. Each bear had its own bike. They rode up and down ramps as they raced each other around the ring.
The Bike-Riding Bears

4. The clowns tumbled as they came into the ring. They did forward rolls, backward rolls and even walked on their hands.
The Tumbling Clowns

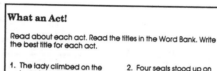

Word Bank

Three Brown Bears
Mac and His Ball-Playing Seals
A Horse Rider
The Tumbling Clowns

Mac and His Seals
The Bike-Riding Bears
Lady on a Galloping Horse
The Lazy Clowns

Page 50

High-Flying Acts

Read each sentence. Look at the underlined words. Write who, what, when, where or why to show what the underlined words tell.

1. Clifford and Emily Elizabeth spent the day at the circus. **where**
2. The biggest elephant couldn't lead the parade because he had a cold. **why**
3. The circus owner was afraid there would not be a show. **who**
4. Clifford shot a tent pole at the hot air balloon. **what**
5. Clifford caught the diver before he landed in the empty tank. **when**
6. The clowns needed help because some had quit. **why**
7. Clifford liked the cotton candy. **what**
8. The poster said there would be a circus today. **When**
9. The human cannon ball landed on top of a haystack. **where**
10. The lions and tigers didn't listen to the lion tamer. **who**

Page 51

Donuts, Anyone?

Wanna Buy a Donut?

Write who, what, when, where or why to show what the underlined words tell you in each sentence.

1. The Pee Wee Scouts went to Mrs. Peter's house on Tuesday. **where**
2. The Scouts turned in the money they had received for selling the boxes of donuts. **who**
3. Roger and Rachel sold the most boxes of donuts. **what**
4. Sonny's mother sold many boxes at work. **where**
5. Rachel sold the donuts to her relatives. **who**
6. Rachel was angry at Molly because she was making fun of her relatives. **why**
7. Sonny and Rachel would win badges because they sold the most boxes of donuts. **why**
8. If people eat a lot of donuts, they might get fat. **what**
9. Everyone was happy that they had earned enough money to go to camp in two weeks. **when**
10. The scout meeting started after three o'clock. **when**

Page 52

It's a Surprise!

Read the clues. Find the answers in the Word Bank.

1. You need snow to do this. You can go fast or slow. You can turn corners. You need a pair of something to do this. What is it?
skiing
2. This can be soft or hard. It can be made of paper or metal. You need it when you want to buy something. What is it?
money
3. It is a place where you can buy sweet treats to eat. Many of the treats that can be bought there have to be baked in an oven. What is it?
bakery
4. In larger cities these come out every day. It can have a few pages or many pages. It tells you what is happening in the world. What is it?
newspaper
5. It can be large or small. It smells very good. It is green. It is very special and people like to decorate it at one time of the year. What is it?
Christmas tree
6. It needs gas. It is very big. Its driver stops a lot at people's houses to pick up things. What is it?
garbage truck

Word Bank

book
coins
money
skiing

magazine
paper bag
gas station
sledding

newspaper
holly plant
candy store
bakery

garbage truck
Christmas tree
snowballing

Page 53

Reflect on the Riddles

Read each riddle. Find the answer in the Word Bank and write it on the line.

1. There are two of me. We can blink. We can see. We can wink. We can weep. What are we? **eyes**
2. There is one of me. I can sing. I can form words. I can eat. I can even blow a big bubble. I can eat ice cream, too. What am I? **mouth**
3. There is one of me. If I tickle, I will sneeze. I like to sniff flowers. I like the whiff of hot dogs, also. What am I? **nose**
4. We need to bend and stretch. We need rest. We need to work and we need to play. We are all different. What are we? **bodies**
5. I can be almost any color. I can be long or short. I can be curled and I can be spiked. What am I? **hair**
6. We can change. We can be happy or sad. We can be worried or excited. We can even be scared. What are we? **feelings**
7. I cover a lot. I have muscles, bones, and blood inside your body. I let you know if it is hot or cold. I tell you if something is wet or dry. What am I? **skin**
8. We all have feelings. We all have bodies. We all like to do many of the same things. But, we also are all very different. Who are we? **people**

Word Bank

bodies   eyes
people   feelings
hair   mouth
nose   skin

Page 54

It's a Fact!

Read each sentence. If it states a fact, write the word fact on the line. If it states an opinion, write the word opinion on the line.

1. An opera is a play that is sung. — *fact*
2. Many operas are terribly boring. — *opinion*
3. Opera stars wear costumes on stage. — *fact*
4. People who have trunks filled with jewels are robbers. — *opinion*
5. In many cities people dial 911 for emergency help. — *fact*
6. It is fun to check the mailbox every day. — *opinion*
7. Seventy is a very old age. — *opinion*
8. Second and third grade are about the same. — *opinion*
9. Many operas are recorded on records. — *fact*
10. It is all right to snoop in other people's things if you have a reason. — *opinion*

Page 55

Is This for Real?

Read each sentence. If it tells something that could really happen, draw a pumpkin on the line.

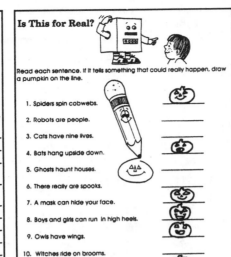

1. Spiders spin cobwebs.
2. Robots are people.
3. Cats have nine lives.
4. Bats hang upside down.
5. Ghosts haunt houses.
6. There really are spooks.
7. A mask can hide your face.
8. Boys and girls can run in high heels.
9. Owls have wings.
10. Witches ride on brooms.
11. Some people buy costumes.
12. Pirates sail on ships.

Page 56

Elephant Dressing

Mrs. Marsh's kids need your help dressing. First color all of the elephants' skin gray. Then follow the directions to color their clothes.

1. Color Robbie's pants brown and his shirt yellow. His shoes are brown.
2. Color Mollie's dress pink polka dots. Put a pink bow in her hair. Her shoes are black.
3. Color Lisa's dress blue, green and purple stripes. Her bow and shoes are purple.
4. Color Jason's jeans blue and his shirt red. His shoes are red.
5. Color Gary's pants orange. His shirt is orange and white stripes. His shoes are black.
6. Color Megan's dress red with pink flowers. Her shoes are red.

Page 57

Top or Bottom?

Read and follow the directions.

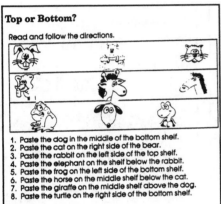

1. Paste the dog in the middle of the bottom shelf.
2. Paste the cat on the right side of the bear.
3. Paste the rabbit on the left side of the top shelf.
4. Paste the elephant on the shelf below the rabbit.
5. Paste the frog on the left side of the bottom shelf.
6. Paste the horse on the middle shelf below the cat.
7. Paste the giraffe on the middle shelf above the dog.
8. Paste the turtle on the right side of the bottom shelf.

Page 58

Where Is It?

Follow the directions. **Hint:** Read through all of the directions before starting.

Pictures will vary.

1. Draw a brown mound in the middle of the box.
2. Draw a red car on top of the mound.
3. Draw apartments behind and to the left of the mound.
4. Draw a bird nest, with four blue eggs inside, on top of the car.
5. Draw three yellow birds flying away from the nest.
6. Draw two tin cans at the bottom of the mound.
7. Put an X on one of the tin cans.
8. Draw you and your friend looking at the car.

Page 59

I'll Try Another Way

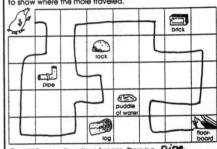

Help the little mole find his way to Percy's hut. Read and follow the directions. Write each word that tells what blocks his path as he looks for the loose floorboard. Then draw a line to show where the mole traveled.

Go right 1 space, then down 1 space. There is a *pipe*
Go left 1 space, down 3 spaces,
then right 2 spaces. There is a *log*
Go up 1 space, right 1 space, then up 1. There is a *rock*
Go left 1 space, up 2, then right 3 spaces. There is a *brick*
Go down 1 space, right 2 spaces,
down 2, then left 2 spaces. There is a *puddle of water*
Go down 1 space, then right 1 space. Hooray! It's the *floorboard*

Page 60

What Did I Say?

Unscramble the words in each ⬜. each sentence on the line.

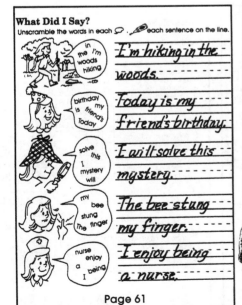

I'm hiking in the woods.

Today is my friend's birthday.

I will solve this mystery.

The bee stung my finger.

I enjoy being a nurse.

Page 61

The One in the Middle

Print the words in order to make a sentence. The word in the middle is there to help you. Print the sentences.

1. good Dissel jumper Freddy a — *Freddy Dissel was a good jumper.*
2. was Gumber teacher Ms. — *Ms. Gumber was Freddy's teacher.*
3. and one sister had Freddy one — *Freddy had one brother and one sister.*
4. Freddy play going in was to a — *Freddy was going to be in a play.*
5. green They face on painted his — *They painted green dots on his face.*
6. break Gumber to a told leg Ms. — *Ms. Gumber told Freddy to break a leg.*

Now color this picture.

Page 62

What Do I Do First?

Look at the pictures. Number them in the correct order. Then read and number the sentences in the correct order.

3 Cut along the line.
1 Fold a piece of paper in half.
2 Draw one half of a heart on the paper.
4 Open the heart.

3 Draw two antennas on the first heart.
2 Paste the hearts in a line.
4 Then draw two eyes and a mouth on the first heart.
1 Cut out seven small hearts.
What did you make? *caterpillar*

4 Draw two eyes and a nose. Paste a cotton ball on the big heart.
1 Paste a big heart upside down on a piece of paper.
3 Glue a smaller heart upside down on top of the big heart.
2 Paste two long skinny hearts upside down on the smaller heart.
What did you make? *rabbit*

Page 63

Daily Learning Drills Grade 2

Terrific Toast

Lionel said he made the best toast in the world! Number the sentences to show the best order to make terrific toast. The first two are done. *Order may vary.*

- **13** Close the jar of jam.
- **6** Close the package of bread.
- **5** Push down on the toaster button.
- **11** Put butter on the hot toast.
- **14** Place the plate of toast on the table and enjoy.
- **2** Open the package of bread.
- **1** Plug in the toaster.
- **10** Put the toast on a plate.
- **3** Take out two slices of bread.
- **4** Place the two slices of bread in the toaster.
- **7** Open the jar of jam.
- **8** Wait for the toast to pop up.
- **12** Put jam on the toast.
- **9** Take the toast out of the toaster.

What do you like to put on your toast? _____

What is your favorite flavor of jam? _____

Page 64

What's What?

Write the words from the Word Bank in the correct category.

Living	Non-Living
1. hen	1. car
2. bird	2. nest
3. kitten	3. boat
4. cow	4. rocks
5. dog	5. plane
6. tree	6. truck

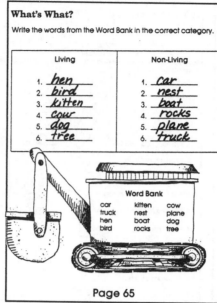

Word Bank

car kitten cow
truck nest plane
hen boat dog
bird rocks tree

Page 65

Tidying Up

Write the words from the Word Bank in the correct category.

wash dishes scrub floors parlor dining room
dust mop bedroom kitchen

Household Chores — **Rooms in a House**

chair table
desk couch

Furniture

Word Bank

parlor dust
chair mop
bedroom couch
wash dishes kitchen
table scrub floors
desk dining room

Page 66

Cookie Jar

Read the categories on the jars. Cut and paste the cookies in the correct jar.

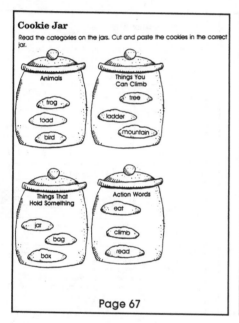

Animals: frog, toad, bird
Things You Can Climb: tree, ladder, mountain
Things That Hold Something: jar, bag, box
Action Words: eat, climb, read

Page 67

Sense-ational!

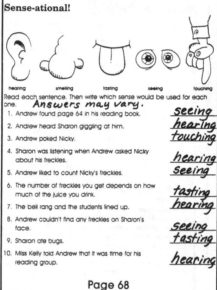

hearing   smelling   tasting   seeing   touching

Read each sentence. Then write which sense would be used for each one. *Answers may vary.*

1. Andrew found page 64 in his reading book. — seeing
2. Andrew heard Sharon giggling at him. — hearing
3. Andrew poked Nicky. — touching
4. Sharon was listening when Andrew asked Nicky about his freckles. — hearing
5. Andrew liked to count Nicky's freckles. — seeing
6. The number of freckles you get depends on how much of the juice you drink. — tasting
7. The bell rang and the students lined up. — hearing
8. Andrew couldn't find any freckles on Sharon's face. — seeing
9. Sharon ate bugs. — tasting
10. Miss Kelly told Andrew that it was time for his reading group. — hearing

Page 68

What's Going On?

Look at the pictures. Find the sentence in the Word Bank that explains each one. Write it on the lines.

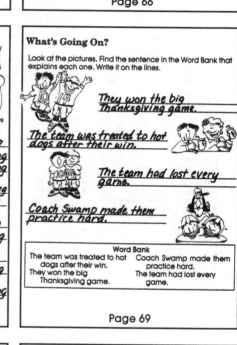

They won the big Thanksgiving game.

The team was treated to hot dogs after their win.

The team had lost every game.

Coach Swamp made them practice hard.

Word Bank

The team was treated to hot dogs after their win.
Coach Swamp made them practice hard.
They won the big Thanksgiving game.
The team had lost every game.

Page 69

Just Rolling Along!

Help Emmett roll the snowball down the hill. Read the clues. Then find the words in the Word Bank and write them in the correct spaces. Hint: The last letter of each answer is the first letter of the next answer.

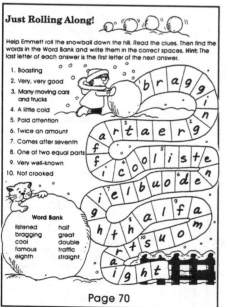

1. Boasting
2. Very, very good
3. Many moving cars and trucks
4. A little cold
5. Paid attention
6. Twice an amount
7. Comes after seventh
8. One of two equal parts
9. Very well-known
10. Not crooked

Word Bank

listened half
bragging great
cool double
famous traffic
eighth straight

Page 70

A-maze-ing

Draw a line through the maze in the order of the clues to help baby bird find his way back to his nest.

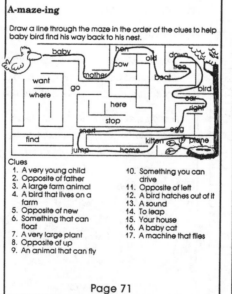

Clues

1. A very young child
2. Opposite of father
3. A large farm animal
4. A bird that lives on a farm
5. Opposite of new
6. Something that can float
7. A very large plant
8. Opposite of up
9. An animal that can fly
10. Something you can drive
11. Opposite of left
12. A bird hatches out of it
13. A sound
14. To leap
15. Your house
16. A baby cat
17. A machine that flies

Page 71

Circus Sights

Find the answers to the puzzle in the Word Bank.

Across
1. To save from danger
4. The last act
6. A silly person
8. Your mistake
10. To give an order
11. A poster

Down
2. A large weapon
3. A show with clowns and animal acts
5. You dress up in these
7. Great
9. A person who trains animals
11. A trick

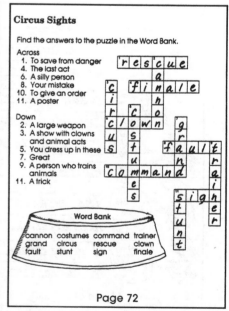

Across/Down answers (crossword): rescue, finale, clown, fault, command, sign, stunt, circus, grand, trainer, costumes, cannon

Word Bank

cannon costumes command trainer
grand circus rescue clown
fault stunt sign finale

Page 72

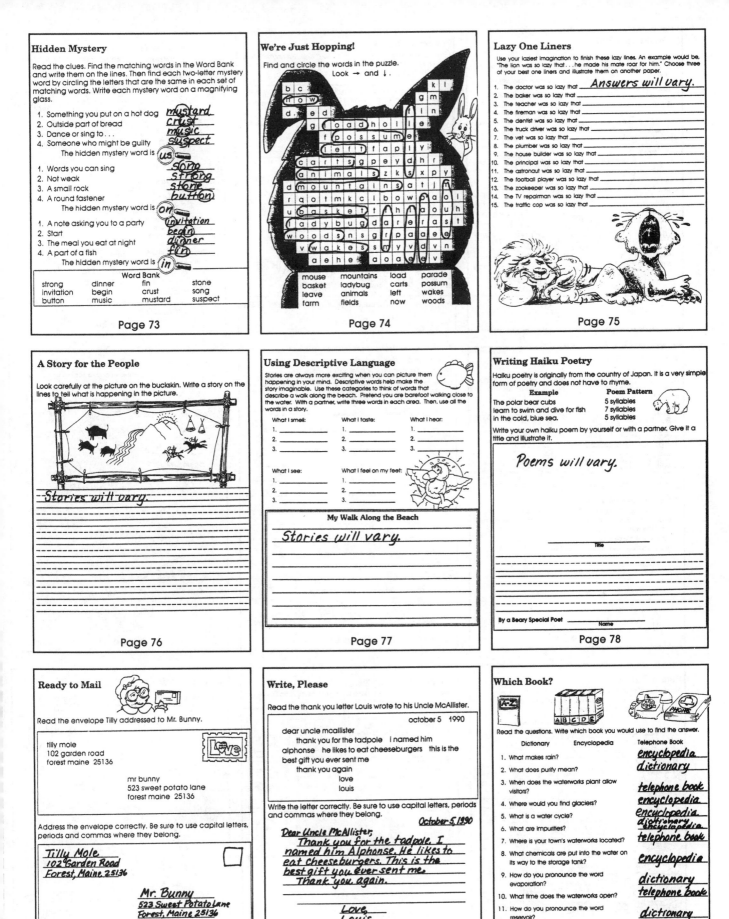

Hidden Mystery

Read the clues. Find the matching words in the Word Bank and write them on the lines. Then find each two-letter mystery word by circling the letters that are the same in each set of matching words. Write each mystery word on a magnifying glass.

1. Something you put on a hot dog — mustard
2. Outside part of bread — crust
3. Dance or sing to . . . — music
4. Someone who might be guilty — suspect
   The hidden mystery word is (us)

1. Words you can sing — song
2. Not weak — strong
3. A small rock — stone
4. A round fastener — button
   The hidden mystery word is (on)

1. A note asking you to a party — invitation
2. Start — begin
3. The meal you eat at night — dinner
4. A part of a fish — fin
   The hidden mystery word is (in)

Word Bank
strong	dinner	fin	stone
invitation	begin	crust	song
button	music	mustard	suspect

Page 73

We're Just Hopping!

Find and circle the words in the puzzle.
Look → and ↓.

mouse, basket, leave, farm, mountains, ladybug, animals, fields, load, carts, left, now, parade, possum, wakes, woods

Page 74

Lazy One Liners

Use your laziest imagination to finish these lazy lines. An example would be, "The lion was so lazy that . . . he made his mate roar for him." Choose three of your best one liners and illustrate them on another paper.

Answers will vary.

1. The doctor was so lazy that ____
2. The baker was so lazy that ____
3. The teacher was so lazy that ____
4. The fireman was so lazy that ____
5. The dentist was so lazy that ____
6. The truck driver was so lazy that ____
7. The vet was so lazy that ____
8. The plumber was so lazy that ____
9. The house builder was so lazy that ____
10. The principal was so lazy that ____
11. The astronaut was so lazy that ____
12. The football player was so lazy that ____
13. The zookeeper was so lazy that ____
14. The TV repairman was so lazy that ____
15. The traffic cop was so lazy that ____

Page 75

A Story for the People

Look carefully at the picture on the buckskin. Write a story on the lines to tell what is happening in the picture.

Stories will vary.

Page 76

Using Descriptive Language

Stories are always more exciting when you can picture them happening in your mind. Descriptive words help make the story imaginable. Use these categories to think of words that describe a walk along the beach. Pretend you are barefoot walking close to the water. With a partner, write three words in each area. Then, use all the words in a story.

What I smell:
1. ____
2. ____
3. ____

What I taste:
1. ____
2. ____
3. ____

What I hear:
1. ____
2. ____
3. ____

What I see:
1. ____
2. ____
3. ____

What I feel on my feet:
1. ____
2. ____
3. ____

My Walk Along the Beach

Stories will vary.

Page 77

Writing Haiku Poetry

Haiku poetry is originally from the country of Japan. It is a very simple form of poetry and does not have to rhyme.

Example	Poem Pattern
The polar bear cubs	5 syllables
learn to swim and dive for fish	7 syllables
in the cold, blue sea.	5 syllables

Write your own haiku poem by yourself or with a partner. Give it a title and illustrate it.

Poems will vary.

____ Title

By a Beary Special Poet ____ Name

Page 78

Ready to Mail

Read the envelope Tilly addressed to Mr. Bunny.

tilly mole
102 garden road
forest maine 25136

mr bunny
523 sweet potato lane
forest maine 25136

Address the envelope correctly. Be sure to use capital letters, periods and commas where they belong.

Tilly Mole
102 Garden Road
Forest, Maine 25136

Mr. Bunny
523 Sweet Potato Lane
Forest, Maine 25136

Draw and color a stamp on the envelope.

Page 79

Write, Please

Read the thank you letter Louis wrote to his Uncle McAllister.

october 5 1990
dear uncle mcallister
    thank you for the tadpole   i named him alphonse   he likes to eat cheeseburgers   this is the best gift you ever sent me
        thank you again
            love
            louis

Write the letter correctly. Be sure to use capital letters, periods and commas where they belong.

October 5, 1990
Dear Uncle McAllister;
    Thank you for the tadpole. I named him Alphonse. He likes to eat cheeseburgers. This is the best gift you ever sent me.
    Thank you again.

        Love,
        Louis

Page 80

Which Book?

Read the questions. Write which book you would use to find the answer.

Dictionary   Encyclopedia   Telephone Book

1. What makes rain? — encyclopedia
2. What does purify mean? — dictionary
3. When does the waterworks plant allow visitors? — telephone book
4. Where would you find glaciers? — encyclopedia
5. What is a water cycle? — encyclopedia
6. What are impurities? — dictionary / encyclopedia
7. Where is your town's waterworks located? — telephone book
8. What chemicals are put into the water on its way to the storage tank? — encyclopedia
9. How do you pronounce the word evaporation? — dictionary
10. What time does the waterworks open? — telephone book
11. How do you pronounce the word reservoir? — dictionary
12. How are clouds formed? — encyclopedia

Page 81

Let's Get Cooking!

Read each phrase.
If you would need a dictionary to find the information, color the space yellow.
If you would need an encyclopedia to find the information, color the space white.
If you would need a cookbook to find the information, color the space brown.

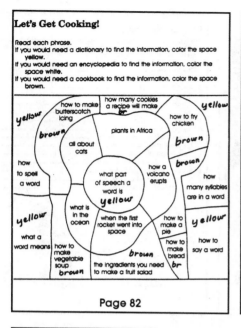

yellow how to make butterscotch icing — how many cookies a recipe will make *br*
brown plants in Africa — how to fry chicken *yellow*
all about cats — *brown*
how to spell a word — what part of speech a word is *yellow* — how a volcano erupts — *brown* — how many syllables are in a word
yellow — what is in the ocean — when the first rocket went into space — how to make a pie — how to make bread *br* — *yellow*
what a word means — how to make vegetable soup *brown* — the ingredients you need to make a fruit salad *brown* — how to say a word

Page 82

Pottery Patterns

Before beginning a project, an artist who makes pottery must think about how the piece will be used, what type of clay to use, and what color and patterns to use.

This talented artist does something special with all the pottery he makes. Here are some examples of his pottery.

The pottery here is not his. Something is different.

Circle the pottery below that the talented artist might have made.

What is special about his pottery? *Divided in three sections*

Page 83

Dressing the Part

People who act in plays are called actors and actresses. For each play, costumes are chosen that make the characters in the story seem more realistic.

Below is the inside of a costume closet.

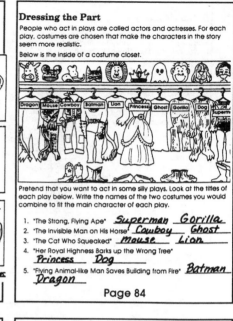

Dragon Mouse Cowboy Batman Lion Princess Ghost Gorilla Dog Superm...

Pretend that you want to act in some silly plays. Look at the titles of each play below. Write the names of the two costumes you would combine to fit the main character of each play.

1. "The Strong, Flying Ape" — *Superman Gorilla*
2. "The Invisible Man on His Horse" — *Cowboy Ghost*
3. "The Cat Who Squeaked" — *Mouse Lion*
4. "Her Royal Highness Barks up the Wrong Tree" — *Princess Dog*
5. "Flying Animal-like Man Saves Building from Fire" — *Batman Dragon*

Page 84

Everyone Is Welcome

Cut out the pictures of the people at the bottom of the page. Read the clues carefully. Paste the people where they belong at the table.

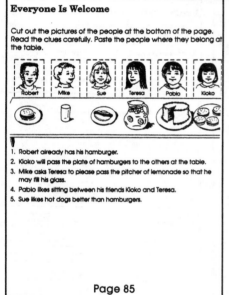

Robert   Mike   Sue   Teresa   Pablo   Kioko

1. Robert already has his hamburger.
2. Kioko will pass the plate of hamburgers to the others at the table.
3. Mike asks Teresa to please pass the pitcher of lemonade so that he may fill his glass.
4. Pablo likes sitting between his friends Kioko and Teresa.
5. Sue likes hot dogs better than hamburgers.

Page 85

Comparing the Seasons

Each of the four seasons (winter, spring, summer, autumn) has certain characteristics. Choose two of the seasons and write their names on the lines above each shape below. Then, complete the other lines with words that describe the season. In the center area, write words that describe both seasons. This is called a Venn diagram.

name of season   Both Seasons   name of season

Answers will vary.

different   same   different

Page 86

Just Napping

Count. Write the correct number of cats in the box on each cat bed.

5   9
3
12   6
10
4   2
11
8
1   7

Page 87

Plump Piglets

Pigs like to eat corn. These little pigs just ate lunch.

Read the clues to find out how many ears of corn each pig ate. Write the number on the line below each pig.

I ate the number that comes before 26. (Patsy) — *25*
I ate the number that comes between 87 and 89. (Horace) — *88*
I ate the number that comes after 92. (Portly) — *93*
I ate the number that comes before 57. (Hilda) — *56*
I ate the number that comes between 39 and 41. (Pesky) — *40*

Who ate the most and was really piggy? *Portly*
Who ate the least? *Patsy*

Page 88

Unpack the Teddy Bears

Cut out the bears at the bottom of the page. Paste them where they belong in numbered order.

39 40 41   29 30 31
10 11 12   78 79 80
84 85 86   64 65 66

Page 89

Air Bear Addition

Help Buddy off the ground. Solve the problems. Then color the clouds with sums of 9 to find the right path.

5+5=10   7+4=11   3+7=10   4+4=8
6+9   8+1
2+7=9
5+7   2+9   4+4=10
10+1=11
5+9   6+5=11   3+4   3+2=5
2+5=7   4+5=9   0+9   3+9
2+6=9   8+2=10   3+6=9

Page 90

Math-Minded Mermaids

Each mermaid sits upon her own special rock.
Look at the number on each shell. Then look → and ↓ in the number boxes. Circle each pair of numbers that can be added together to equal the number in the shell the mermaid is holding.

Page 91

Domino Math

Write the number that tells how many dots are on the greater side of each domino. Then, "count on" to find the sum of both sides.

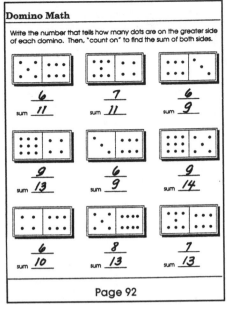

6   sum *11*   *7*   sum *11*   *6*   sum *9*

9   sum *13*   *6*   sum *9*   *9*   sum *14*

6   sum *10*   *8*   sum *13*   *7*   sum *13*

Page 92

Ride the Rapids

Write each problem on the life jacket with the correct answer.

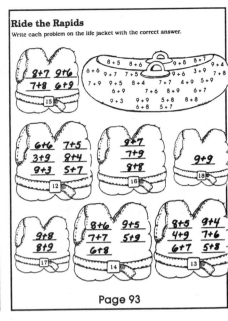

Page 93

Story Problems

The key words in all tell you to add. Circle the key words in all and solve the problems.

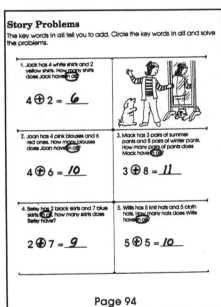

1. Jack has 4 white shirts and 2 yellow shirts. How many shirts does Jack have in all?

$4 \oplus 2 = $ *6*

2. Joan has 4 pink blouses and 6 red ones. How many blouses does Joan have in all?

$4 \oplus 6 = $ *10*

3. Mack has 3 pairs of summer pants and 8 pairs of winter pants. How many pairs of pants does Mack have in all?

$3 \oplus 8 = $ *11*

4. Betsy has 2 black skirts and 7 blue skirts. In all, how many skirts does Betsy have?

$2 \oplus 7 = $ *9*

5. Willis has 5 knit hats and 5 cloth hats. How many hats does Willis have in all?

$5 \oplus 5 = $ *10*

Page 94

Additional Story Problems

Circle the addition key words in all and solve the problems.

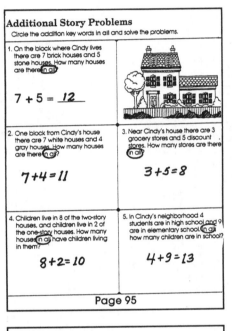

1. On the block where Cindy lives there are 7 brick houses and 5 stone houses. How many houses are there in all?

$7 + 5 = $ *12*

2. One block from Cindy's house there are 7 white houses and 4 gray houses. How many houses are there in all?

$7 + 4 = 11$

3. Near Cindy's house there are 3 grocery stores and 5 discount stores. How many stores are there in all?

$3 + 5 = 8$

4. Children live in 8 of the two-story houses, and children live in 2 of the one-story houses. How many houses in all have children living in them?

$8 + 2 = 10$

5. In Cindy's neighborhood 4 students are in high school and 9 are in elementary school. In all, how many children are in school?

$4 + 9 = 13$

Page 95

Problems in the Park

Circle the addition key words in all and solve the problems.

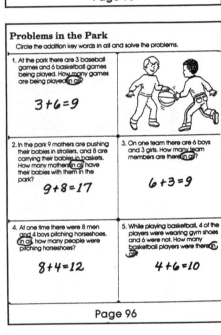

1. At the park there are 3 baseball games and 6 basketball games being played. How many games are being played in all?

$3 + 6 = 9$

2. In the park 9 mothers are pushing their babies in strollers, and 8 are carrying their babies in baskets. How many mothers in all have their babies with them in the park?

$9 + 8 = 17$

3. On one team there are 6 boys and 3 girls. How many team members are there in all?

$6 + 3 = 9$

4. At one time there were 8 men and 4 boys pitching horseshoes. In all, how many people were pitching horseshoes?

$8 + 4 = 12$

5. While playing basketball, 4 of the players were wearing gym shoes and 6 were not. How many basketball players were there in all?

$4 + 6 = 10$

Page 96

Solving Stories

Write a number sentence to solve each problem.

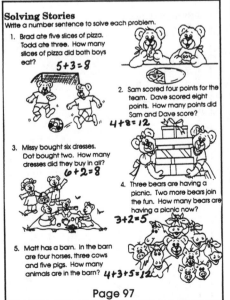

1. Brad ate five slices of pizza. Todd ate three. How many slices of pizza did both boys eat?

$5 + 3 = 8$

2. Sam scored four points for the team. Dave scored eight points. How many points did Sam and Dave score?

$4 + 8 = 12$

3. Missy bought six dresses. Dot bought two. How many dresses did they buy in all?

$6 + 2 = 8$

4. Three bears are having a picnic. Two more bears join the fun. How many bears are having a picnic now?

$3 + 2 = 5$

5. Matt has a barn. In the barn are four horses, three cows and five pigs. How many animals are in the barn?

$4 + 3 + 5 = 12$

Page 97

Daisy Subtraction

Work problems.
Use code to color.

2—green	7—orange	10—pink
3—blue	8—red	11—red
4—yellow	9—purple	12—purple

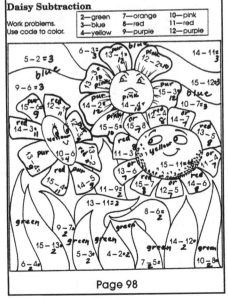

Page 98

Pick a Picnic

Subtract. Write each answer. Then draw a line to show where three answers are the same in a row.

Page 99

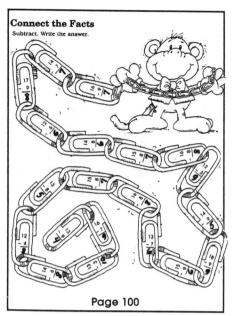

Connect the Facts
Subtract. Write the answer.

Page 100

How Many Animals Are Left?
The key word *left* tells you to subtract. Circle the key word *left* and solve the problems.

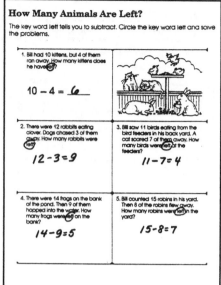

1. Bill had 10 kittens, but 4 of them ran away. How many kittens does he have left?

$10 - 4 = 6$

2. There were 12 rabbits eating clover. Dogs chased 3 of them away. How many rabbits were left?

$12 - 3 = 9$

3. Bill saw 11 birds eating from the bird feeders in his back yard. A cat scared 7 of them away. How many birds were left at the feeders?

$11 - 7 = 4$

4. There were 14 frogs on the bank of the pond. Then 9 of them hopped into the water. How many frogs were left on the bank?

$14 - 9 = 5$

5. Bill counted 15 robins in his yard. Then 8 of the robins flew away. How many robins were left in the yard?

$15 - 8 = 7$

Page 101

Maggy at School
Circle the subtraction key word *left* and solve the problems.

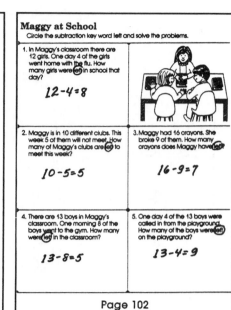

1. In Maggy's classroom there are 12 girls. One day 4 of the girls went home with the flu. How many girls were left in school that day?

$12 - 4 = 8$

2. Maggy is in 10 different clubs. This week 5 of them will not meet. How many of Maggy's clubs are left to meet this week?

$10 - 5 = 5$

3. Maggy had 16 crayons. She broke 9 of them. How many crayons does Maggy have left?

$16 - 9 = 7$

4. There are 13 boys in Maggy's classroom. One morning 8 of the boys went to the gym. How many were left in the classroom?

$13 - 8 = 5$

5. One day 4 of the 13 boys were called in from the playground. How many of the boys were left on the playground?

$13 - 4 = 9$

Page 102

A Hidden Message
Add or subtract. Use the code to find out your new motto!

Code:

9	18	6	15	13	12	16	11	8	7	14	17
H	Y	D	E	V	T	S	O	A	M	N	I

9 +8		16 -7	14 -6	8 +5	6 +9		14 -7	9 +9
17		9	8	13	15		7	18
I		h	a	v	e		m	y

17 -8	15 -7	9 +5	13 -7	8 +8
9	8	14	6	16
h	a	n	d	s

4 +7	6 +8		12 -5	17 -9	6 +6	15 -6
11	14		7	8	12	9
O	n		m	a	t	h

Page 103

All Aboard!
Add or subtract. Match the related facts.

$5 + 9 = 14$

$8 + 7 = 15$

$15 - 9 = 6$

$17 - 8 = 9$

$7 + 7 = 14$

$6 + 9 = 15$

$14 - 9 = 5$

$15 - 7 = 8$

$14 - 7 = 7$

$9 + 8 = 17$

Add or subtract. Color spaces with answers greater than 12 brown. Color the rest green.

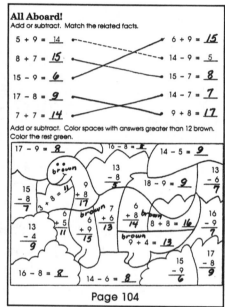

$17 - 9 = 8$ $16 - 8 = 8$ $14 - 5 = 9$

$16 - 8 = 8$ $14 - 6 = 8$

Page 104

Add or Subtract?
The key words *in all* tell you to add. The key word *left* tells you to subtract. Circle the key words and solve the problems.

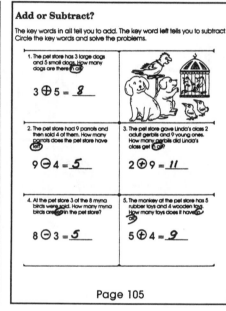

1. The pet store has 3 large dogs and 5 small dogs. How many dogs are there in all?

$3 \oplus 5 = 8$

2. The pet store had 9 parrots and then sold 4 of them. How many parrots does the pet store have left?

$9 \ominus 4 = 5$

3. The pet store gave Linda's class 2 adult gerbils and 9 young ones. How many gerbils did Linda's class get in all?

$2 \oplus 9 = 11$

4. At the pet store 3 of the 8 myna birds were sold. How many myna birds are left in the pet store?

$8 \ominus 3 = 5$

5. The monkey at the pet store has 5 rubber toys and 4 wooden toys. How many toys does it have in all?

$5 \oplus 4 = 9$

Page 105

Training with Facts
Use the numbers on each train to write the fact families.

8 6 14

$8 + 6 = 14$

$6 + 8 = 14$

$14 - 6 = 8$

$14 - 8 = 6$

6 15 9

$6 + 9 = 15$

$9 + 6 = 15$

$15 - 9 = 6$

$15 - 6 = 9$

17 8 9

$8 + 9 = 17$

$9 + 8 = 17$

$17 - 8 = 9$

$17 - 9 = 8$

9 5 14

$9 + 5 = 14$

$5 + 9 = 14$

$14 - 9 = 5$

$14 - 5 = 9$

Page 106

Adding Strategies
When adding three numbers, add two numbers first, then add the third to that sum. To decide which two numbers to add first, try one of these strategies.

Look for doubles.

8 3 +3	4 4 +5	2 9 +2
14	13	13

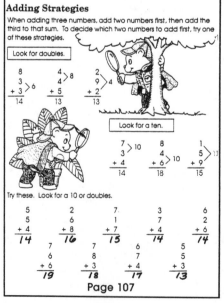

Look for a ten.

7 3 +4	8 4 +6	1 5 +9
14	18	15

Try these. Look for a 10 or doubles.

5 5 +4	2 6 +8	7 1 +7	3 7 +4	6 2 +6
14	16	15	14	14

7 6 +6	8 7 +3	7 6 +4	5 5 +3
19	18	17	13

Page 107

Sum Ice Cream
Add. If the sum is 11 or more, color the cone brown. If the sum is less than 11, color the cone yellow.

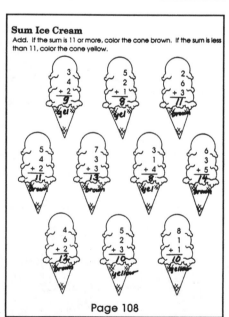

Page 108

Path Problems
Add. Show the detective the correct path. Color the path with sums of 13.

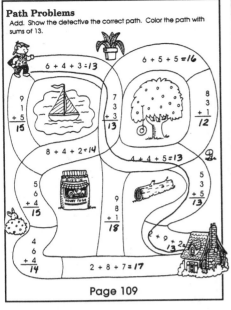

$6 + 4 + 3 = 13$
$6 + 5 + 5 = 16$

$8 + 4 + 2 = 14$
$4 + 4 + 5 = 13$

$2 + 8 + 7 = 17$
$9 + 2 + 3 = ...$

$\begin{array}{r} 9 \\ 1 \\ + 5 \\ \hline 15 \end{array}$
$\begin{array}{r} 8 \\ 3 \\ + 1 \\ \hline 12 \end{array}$

$\begin{array}{r} 7 \\ 3 \\ + 3 \\ \hline 13 \end{array}$

$\begin{array}{r} 5 \\ + 6 \\ \hline 4 \\ \hline 15 \end{array}$
$\begin{array}{r} 5 \\ 3 \\ + 5 \\ \hline 13 \end{array}$

$\begin{array}{r} 9 \\ 8 \\ + 1 \\ \hline 18 \end{array}$

$\begin{array}{r} 4 \\ 6 \\ + 4 \\ \hline 14 \end{array}$

Page 109

Something's Missing

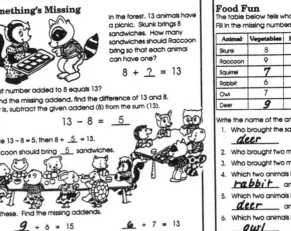

In the forest, 13 animals have a picnic. Skunk brings 8 sandwiches. How many sandwiches should Raccoon bring so that each animal can have one?

$8 + \underline{?} = 13$

What number added to 8 equals 13?
To find the missing addend, find the difference of 13 and 8. That is, subtract the given addend (8) from the sum (13).

$13 - 8 = \underline{5}$

Since $13 - 8 = 5$, then $8 + \underline{5} = 13$.
Raccoon should bring $\underline{5}$ sandwiches.

Try these. Find the missing addends.

$\underline{9} + 6 = 15$ $\underline{6} + 7 = 13$

$9 + \underline{5} = 14$ $8 + \underline{6} = 14$

$\underline{8} + 8 = 16$ $9 + \underline{9} = 18$

Page 110

Food Fun
The table below tells what each animal brought to the picnic. Fill in the missing numbers.

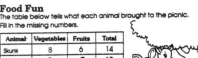

Animal	Vegetables	Fruits	Total
Skunk	8	6	14
Raccoon	9	8	17
Squirrel	7	8	15
Rabbit	6	7	13
Owl	7	9	16
Deer	9	9	18

Write the name of the animal that answers each question.
1. Who brought the same number of vegetables as fruits? _deer_
2. Who brought two more fruits than vegetables? _owl_
3. Who brought two more vegetables than fruits? _skunk_
4. Which two animals brought one more fruit than vegetables? _rabbit_ and _squirrel_
5. Which two animals brought the most vegetables? _deer_ and _racoon_
6. Which two animals brought the most fruit? _deer_ and _owl_
7. Which animal brought the least vegetables? _rabbit_
8. Which animal brought the least fruit? _skunk_
9. Who brought more fruit, Skunk and Squirrel, or Raccoon and Rabbit? _racoon & rabbit_

Page 111

Circus Fun
Add. Remember to add the ones first.

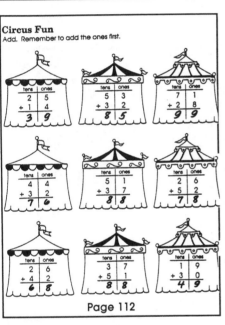

$\begin{array}{c|c} tens & ones \\ 2 & 5 \\ +1 & 4 \\ \hline 3 & 9 \end{array}$
$\begin{array}{c|c} tens & ones \\ 5 & 3 \\ +3 & 2 \\ \hline 8 & 5 \end{array}$
$\begin{array}{c|c} tens & ones \\ 7 & 1 \\ +2 & 8 \\ \hline 9 & 9 \end{array}$

$\begin{array}{c|c} tens & ones \\ 4 & 4 \\ +3 & 2 \\ \hline 7 & 6 \end{array}$
$\begin{array}{c|c} tens & ones \\ 5 & 1 \\ +3 & 7 \\ \hline 8 & 8 \end{array}$
$\begin{array}{c|c} tens & ones \\ 2 & 6 \\ +5 & 2 \\ \hline 7 & 8 \end{array}$

$\begin{array}{c|c} tens & ones \\ 2 & 6 \\ +4 & 2 \\ \hline 6 & 8 \end{array}$
$\begin{array}{c|c} tens & ones \\ 3 & 7 \\ +5 & 1 \\ \hline 8 & 8 \end{array}$
$\begin{array}{c|c} tens & ones \\ 1 & 9 \\ +3 & 0 \\ \hline 4 & 9 \end{array}$

Page 112

Anchors Away
Add. Use the code to find the answer to this riddle:
What did the pirate have to do before every trip out to sea?

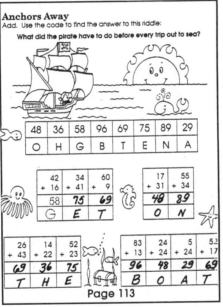

48	36	58	96	69	75	89	29
O	H	G	B	T	E	N	A

42	34	60		17	55
+ 16	+ 41	+ 9		+ 31	+ 34
58	75	69		48	89
G	E	T		O	N

26	14	52		83	24	5	52
+ 43	+ 22	+ 23		+ 13	+ 24	+ 24	+ 17
69	36	75		96	48	29	69
T	H	E		B	O	A	T

Page 113

Digital Addition

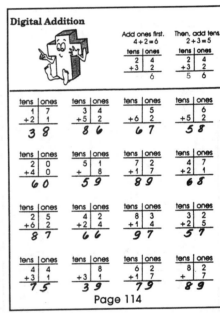

Add ones first.   Then, add tens.
$4 + 2 = 6$ $2 + 3 = 5$

$\begin{array}{c|c} tens & ones \\ 2 & 4 \\ +3 & 2 \\ \hline & 6 \end{array}$
$\begin{array}{c|c} tens & ones \\ 2 & 4 \\ +3 & 2 \\ \hline 5 & 6 \end{array}$

$\begin{array}{c|c} tens & ones \\ 1 & 7 \\ +2 & 1 \\ \hline 3 & 8 \end{array}$
$\begin{array}{c|c} tens & ones \\ 3 & 4 \\ +5 & 2 \\ \hline 8 & 6 \end{array}$
$\begin{array}{c|c} tens & ones \\ & 5 \\ +6 & 2 \\ \hline 6 & 7 \end{array}$
$\begin{array}{c|c} tens & ones \\ & 6 \\ +5 & 2 \\ \hline 5 & 8 \end{array}$

$\begin{array}{c|c} tens & ones \\ 2 & 0 \\ +4 & 0 \\ \hline 6 & 0 \end{array}$
$\begin{array}{c|c} tens & ones \\ 5 & 1 \\ + & 8 \\ \hline 5 & 9 \end{array}$
$\begin{array}{c|c} tens & ones \\ 7 & 2 \\ +1 & 7 \\ \hline 8 & 9 \end{array}$
$\begin{array}{c|c} tens & ones \\ 4 & 7 \\ +2 & 1 \\ \hline 6 & 8 \end{array}$

$\begin{array}{c|c} tens & ones \\ 2 & 5 \\ +6 & 2 \\ \hline 8 & 7 \end{array}$
$\begin{array}{c|c} tens & ones \\ 4 & 2 \\ +2 & 4 \\ \hline 6 & 6 \end{array}$
$\begin{array}{c|c} tens & ones \\ 8 & 3 \\ +1 & 4 \\ \hline 9 & 7 \end{array}$
$\begin{array}{c|c} tens & ones \\ 3 & 2 \\ +2 & 5 \\ \hline 5 & 7 \end{array}$

$\begin{array}{c|c} tens & ones \\ 4 & 4 \\ +3 & 1 \\ \hline 7 & 5 \end{array}$
$\begin{array}{c|c} tens & ones \\ & 8 \\ +3 & 1 \\ \hline 3 & 9 \end{array}$
$\begin{array}{c|c} tens & ones \\ 6 & 2 \\ +1 & 7 \\ \hline 7 & 9 \end{array}$
$\begin{array}{c|c} tens & ones \\ 8 & 2 \\ + & 7 \\ \hline 8 & 9 \end{array}$

Page 114

Nutty Addition
Sam Squirrel and his friend Wendy were gathering acorns. When they got 10 acorns, they put them in a bucket. The picture shows how many acorns Sam and Wendy each gathered. Write the number that tells how many.

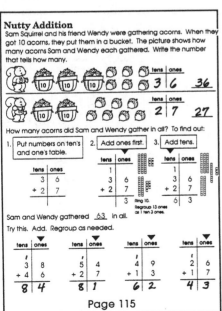

$\begin{array}{c|c} tens & ones \\ 3 & 6 \end{array}$ 36

$\begin{array}{c|c} tens & ones \\ 2 & 7 \end{array}$ 27

How many acorns did Sam and Wendy gather in all? To find out:
1. Put numbers on ten's and one's table.

$\begin{array}{c|c} tens & ones \\ 3 & 6 \\ +2 & 7 \end{array}$

2. Add ones first.

$\begin{array}{c|c} tens & ones \\ & 1 \\ 3 & 6 \\ +2 & 7 \\ \hline & 3 \end{array}$

Ring 10.
Regroup 13 ones as 1 ten 3 ones.

3. Add tens.

$\begin{array}{c|c} tens & ones \\ & 1 \\ 3 & 6 \\ +2 & 7 \\ \hline 6 & 3 \end{array}$

Sam and Wendy gathered _63_ in all.

Try this. Add. Regroup as needed.

$\begin{array}{c|c} tens & ones \\ 1 & \\ 3 & 8 \\ +4 & 6 \\ \hline 8 & 4 \end{array}$
$\begin{array}{c|c} tens & ones \\ 1 & \\ 5 & 4 \\ +2 & 7 \\ \hline 8 & 1 \end{array}$
$\begin{array}{c|c} tens & ones \\ 1 & \\ 4 & 9 \\ +1 & 3 \\ \hline 6 & 2 \end{array}$
$\begin{array}{c|c} tens & ones \\ 1 & \\ 2 & 6 \\ +1 & 7 \\ \hline 4 & 3 \end{array}$

Page 115

Keep On Truckin'
Write each sum. Connect the sums of 83 to make a road for the truck.

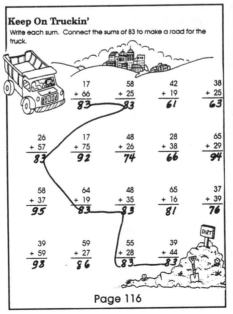

$\begin{array}{r} 17 \\ + 66 \\ \hline 83 \end{array}$
$\begin{array}{r} 58 \\ + 25 \\ \hline 83 \end{array}$
$\begin{array}{r} 42 \\ + 19 \\ \hline 61 \end{array}$
$\begin{array}{r} 38 \\ + 25 \\ \hline 63 \end{array}$

$\begin{array}{r} 26 \\ + 57 \\ \hline 83 \end{array}$
$\begin{array}{r} 17 \\ + 75 \\ \hline 92 \end{array}$
$\begin{array}{r} 48 \\ + 26 \\ \hline 74 \end{array}$
$\begin{array}{r} 28 \\ + 38 \\ \hline 66 \end{array}$
$\begin{array}{r} 65 \\ + 29 \\ \hline 94 \end{array}$

$\begin{array}{r} 58 \\ + 37 \\ \hline 95 \end{array}$
$\begin{array}{r} 64 \\ + 19 \\ \hline 83 \end{array}$
$\begin{array}{r} 48 \\ + 35 \\ \hline 83 \end{array}$
$\begin{array}{r} 65 \\ + 16 \\ \hline 81 \end{array}$
$\begin{array}{r} 37 \\ + 39 \\ \hline 76 \end{array}$

$\begin{array}{r} 39 \\ + 59 \\ \hline 98 \end{array}$
$\begin{array}{r} 59 \\ + 27 \\ \hline 86 \end{array}$
$\begin{array}{r} 55 \\ + 28 \\ \hline 83 \end{array}$
$\begin{array}{r} 39 \\ + 44 \\ \hline 83 \end{array}$

Page 116

Just Like Magic

Add. Write each answer.

Use the answers and the letter on each lamp to solve the code.

May all your wishes come true!
71 74 88 88 74 88 50 55   91 80 61 76 34 61 96 75 71 34 53 55 50 34

Page 117

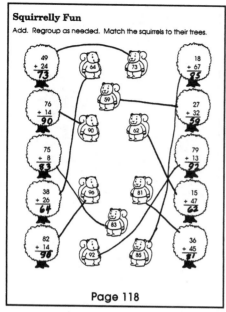

Squirrelly Fun
Add. Regroup as needed. Match the squirrels to their trees.

Page 118

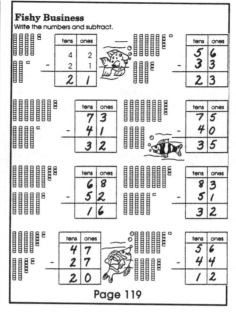

Fishy Business
Write the numbers and subtract.

Page 119

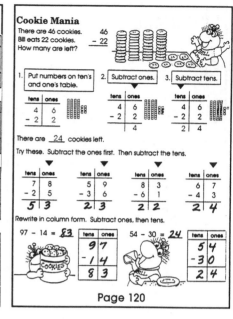

Cookie Mania
There are 46 cookies. Bill eats 22 cookies. How many are left?

Page 120

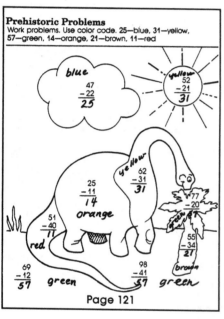

Prehistoric Problems
Work problems. Use color code. 25—blue, 31—yellow, 57—green, 14—orange, 21—brown, 11—red

Page 121

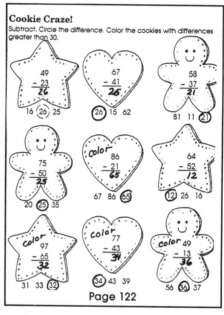

Cookie Craze!
Subtract. Circle the difference. Color the cookies with differences greater than 30.

Page 122

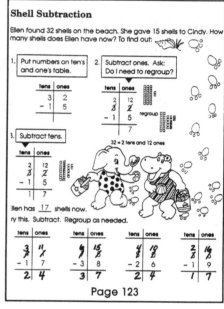

Shell Subtraction
Ellen found 32 shells on the beach. She gave 15 shells to Cindy. How many shells does Ellen have now? To find out:

Page 123

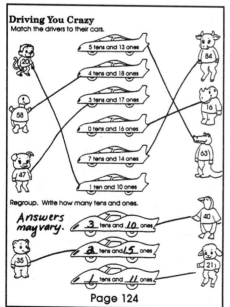

Driving You Crazy
Match the drivers to their cars.

Page 124

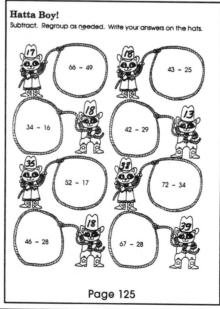

Hatta Boy!
Subtract. Regroup as needed. Write your answers on the hats.

Page 125

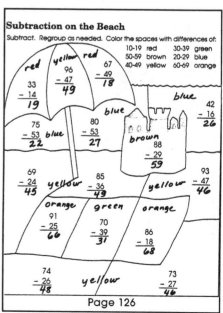

Subtraction on the Beach
Subtract. Regroup as needed. Color the spaces with differences of:
10-19 red   30-39 green
50-59 brown   20-29 blue
40-49 yellow   60-69 orange

Page 126

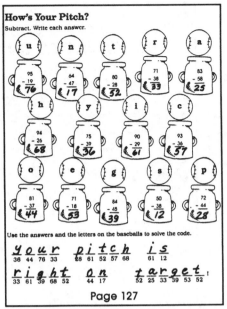

How's Your Pitch?

Subtract. Write each answer.

u: 95 − 19 = 76
n: 64 − 47 = 17
t: 80 − 28 = 52
r: 71 − 38 = 33
a: 83 − 58 = 25

h: 94 − 26 = 68
y: 75 − 39 = 36
i: 90 − 29 = 61
c: 93 − 36 = 57

o: 81 − 37 = 44
e: 71 − 18 = 53
g: 84 − 45 = 39
s: 50 − 38 = 12
p: 72 − 44 = 28

Use the answers and the letters on the baseballs to solve the code.

y o u r   p i t c h   i s
36 44 76 33   28 61 52 57 68   61 12

r i g h t   o n   t a r g e t !
33 61 39 68 52   44 17   52 25 33 39 53 52

Page 127

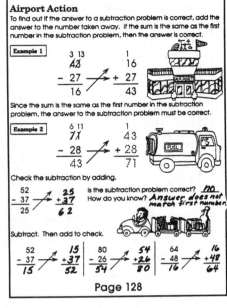

Airport Action

To find out if the answer to a subtraction problem is correct, add the answer to the number taken away. If the sum is the same as the first number in the subtraction problem, then the answer is correct.

Example 1

$$\begin{array}{r} 3\ 13 \\ 4\cancel{3} \\ -27 \\ \hline 16 \end{array} \qquad \begin{array}{r} 1 \\ 16 \\ +27 \\ \hline 43 \end{array}$$

Since the sum is the same as the first number in the subtraction problem, the answer to the subtraction problem must be correct.

Example 2

$$\begin{array}{r} 6\ 11 \\ 7\cancel{1} \\ -28 \\ \hline 43 \end{array} \qquad \begin{array}{r} 1 \\ 43 \\ +28 \\ \hline 71 \end{array}$$

Check the subtraction by adding.

$$\begin{array}{r} 52 \\ -37 \\ \hline 25 \end{array} \qquad \begin{array}{r} 25 \\ +37 \\ \hline 62 \end{array}$$

Is the subtraction problem correct? **no**
How do you know? *Answer does not match first number.*

Subtract. Then add to check.

$$\begin{array}{r} 52 \\ -37 \\ \hline 15 \end{array} \quad \begin{array}{r} 15 \\ +37 \\ \hline 52 \end{array} \quad \bigg| \quad \begin{array}{r} 80 \\ -26 \\ \hline 54 \end{array} \quad \begin{array}{r} 54 \\ +26 \\ \hline 80 \end{array} \quad \bigg| \quad \begin{array}{r} 64 \\ -48 \\ \hline 16 \end{array} \quad \begin{array}{r} 16 \\ +48 \\ \hline 64 \end{array}$$

Page 128

Playing in the Park

Circle **Add** or **Subtract**. Then, write a number sentence to solve each problem. Think and check to see if your answer makes sense.

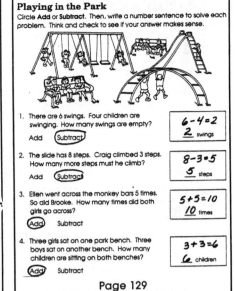

1. There are 6 swings. Four children are swinging. How many swings are empty?
   Add   (Subtract)
   6 − 4 = 2
   2 swings

2. The slide has 8 steps. Craig climbed 3 steps. How many more steps must he climb?
   Add   (Subtract)
   8 − 3 = 5
   5 steps

3. Ellen went across the monkey bars 5 times. So did Brooke. How many times did both girls go across?
   (Add)   Subtract
   5 + 5 = 10
   10 times

4. Three girls sat on one park bench. Three boys sat on another bench. How many children are sitting on both benches?
   (Add)   Subtract
   3 + 3 = 6
   6 children

Page 129

Superstar Students

Fill in the table using the information given. Then answer the questions.

Second Grade Students at Superstar School

Class	Boys	Girls	Total
A	11	17	28
B	12	15	27
C	9	14	23
Total	32	46	78

1. Which class has the most students? **A**
2. Which class has the least students? **C**
3. How many more girls than boys are in second grade? **14**
4. Which class has the most boys? **B**
5. Which class has the least girls? **C**
6. If each boy in class A gave his teacher an apple, how many apples would she get? **11**
7. How many students are in second grade at Superstar School? **78** Outline in red the box that tells this.
8. How many more students are in class A than class C? **5**
9. If each boy in class B gave a girl in class A an apple, how many girls would not get an apple? **5**
10. If 9 students move away, how many students would be in second grade then? **69**

Page 130

Tree Troubles

Help the squirrels get to their trees. Add or subtract in your head. Write the final answer on the tree.

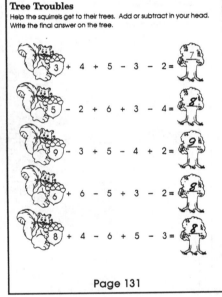

3 + 4 + 5 − 3 − 2 = **7**

5 − 2 + 6 + 3 − 4 = **8**

9 − 3 + 5 − 4 + 2 = **9**

6 + 6 − 5 + 3 − 2 = **8**

8 + 4 − 6 + 5 − 3 = **8**

Page 131

Roll Call

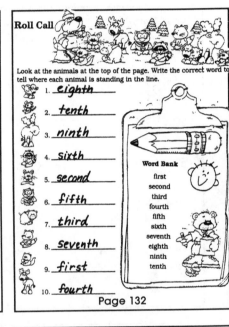

Look at the animals at the top of the page. Write the correct word to tell where each animal is standing in the line.

1. eighth
2. tenth
3. ninth
4. sixth
5. second
6. fifth
7. third
8. seventh
9. first
10. fourth

Word Bank
first
second
third
fourth
fifth
sixth
seventh
eighth
ninth
tenth

Page 132

My First Treat Will Be . . .

Circle the ordinal number word for each treat.

16. third, sixteenth, (fifth)
    fifteenth, (fourth), first
    (twelfth), second, seventh
15. third, eleventh, (fifteenth)
14. eighth, first, (tenth)
    (sixteenth), thirteenth, third
13. ninth, second, (thirteenth)
    sixth, (seventh), ninth

Page 133

Two by Two

Finish counting.

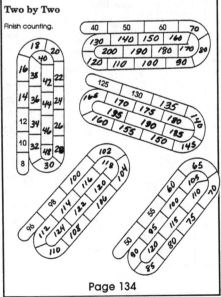

40 50 60 70
130 140 150 160
200 190 180 170 80
120 110 100 90

18 20
16 40 22
14 36 42 24
12 34 44 26
10 32 46 28
8 30 48

125 130
165 170 175 135
195 190 180 140
160 155 150 145

102
100 118
98 116 120 104
96 114 122 106
112 124 108
110

65
60 105
55 100 110 70
50 115 75
80 90
85

Page 134

Critter Count

Number of turtles found. = 5

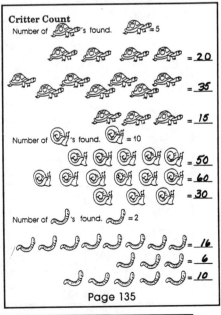

(4 turtles) = 20
(7 turtles) = 35
(3 turtles) = 15

Number of snails found. = 10

(5 snails) = 50
(6 snails) = 60
(3 snails) = 30

Number of worms found. = 2

(8 worms) = 16
(3 worms) = 6
(5 worms) = 10

Page 135

Daily Learning Drills Grade 2

Who Has the Most?
Circle the right answer.

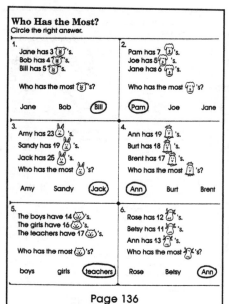

1. Jane has 3 🐑's.
   Bob has 4 🐑's.
   Bill has 5 🐑's.
   Who has the most 🐑's?
   Jane   Bob   (Bill)

2. Pam has 7 🐶's.
   Joe has 5 🐶's.
   Jane has 6 🐶's.
   Who has the most 🐶's?
   (Pam)   Joe   Jane

3. Amy has 23 🐰's.
   Sandy has 19 🐰's.
   Jack has 25 🐰's.
   Who has the most 🐰's?
   Amy   Sandy   (Jack)

4. Ann has 19 🧂's.
   Burt has 18 🧂's.
   Brent has 17 🧂's.
   Who has the most 🧂's?
   (Ann)   Burt   Brent

5. The boys have 14 🐱's.
   The girls have 16 🐱's.
   The teachers have 17 🐱's.
   Who has the most 🐱's?
   boys   girls   (teachers)

6. Rose has 12 🐤's.
   Betsy has 11 🐤's.
   Ann has 13 🐤's.
   Who has the most 🐤's?
   Rose   Betsy   (Ann)

Page 136

Who Has the Least?
Circle the right answer.

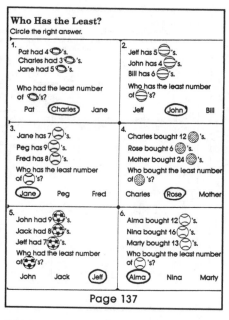

1. Pat had 4 🥚's.
   Charles had 3 🥚's.
   Jane had 5 🥚's.
   Who had the least number of 🥚's?
   Pat   (Charles)   Jane

2. Jeff has 5 🥚's.
   John has 4 🥚's.
   Bill has 6 🥚's.
   Who has the least number of 🥚's?
   Jeff   (John)   Bill

3. Jane has 7 ⚾'s.
   Peg has 9 ⚾'s.
   Fred has 8 ⚾'s.
   Who has the least number of ⚾'s?
   (Jane)   Peg   Fred

4. Charles bought 12 🍪's.
   Rose bought 6 🍪's.
   Mother bought 24 🍪's.
   Who bought the least number of 🍪's?
   Charles   (Rose)   Mother

5. John had 9 ⚽'s.
   Jack had 8 ⚽'s.
   Jeff had 7 ⚽'s.
   Who had the least number of ⚽'s?
   John   Jack   (Jeff)

6. Alma bought 12 🎾's.
   Nina bought 16 🎾's.
   Marty bought 13 🎾's.
   Who bought the least number of 🎾's?
   (Alma)   Nina   Marty

Page 137

Munch a Bunch
Gertrude Goat and her friends Ginger, George, and Gus are making special popcorn balls. Each piece of popcorn has a number on it.
Read the clues to find out which pieces of popcorn each goat will use for his/her popcorn ball. Write the numbers on the popcorn.

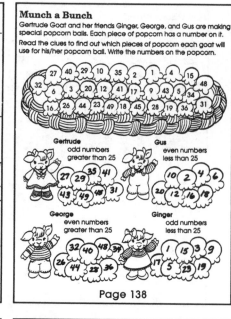

Gertrude — odd numbers greater than 25
27 29 35 41 43 49 47 31

Gus — even numbers less than 25
10 2 4 6 20 12 16 18

George — even numbers greater than 25
32 40 48 26 44 28 36

Ginger — odd numbers less than 25
1 15 3 17 5 23 19

Page 138

"Mouth" Math
Write < or > in each circle. Make sure the "mouth" is open toward the greater number!

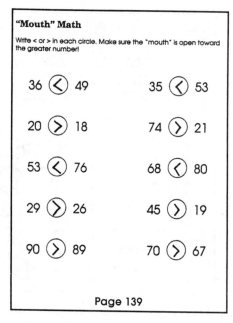

36 (<) 49   35 (<) 53

20 (>) 18   74 (>) 21

53 (<) 76   68 (<) 80

29 (>) 26   45 (>) 19

90 (>) 89   70 (>) 67

Page 139

Right on Time
Cut out the time signs at the bottom of the page. Paste each sign on the engine next to the correct clock.

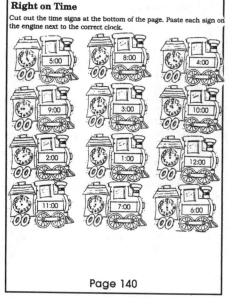

5:00   8:00   4:00
9:00   3:00   10:00
2:00   1:00   12:00
11:00 7:00   6:00

Page 140

Space Time
What time is it?

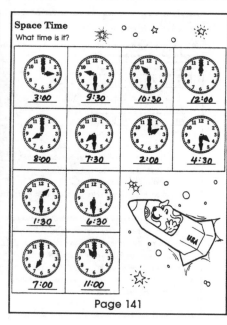

3:00   9:30   10:30   12:00
8:00   7:30   2:00   4:30
1:30   6:30
7:00   11:00

Page 141

Turtle Time
What time is it?

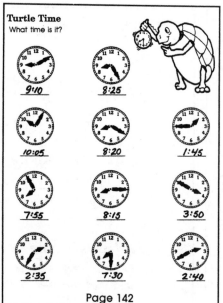

9:10   8:25
10:05   8:20   1:45
7:55   8:15   3:50
2:35   7:30   2:40

Page 142

My Family Time Tree
Write the time.
Draw the hands on each clock.

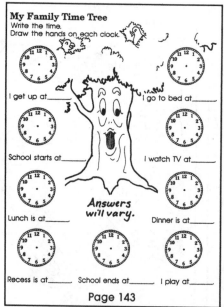

I get up at_____

I go to bed at_____

School starts at_____

I watch TV at_____

Answers will vary.

Lunch is at_____

Dinner is at_____

Recess is at_____   School ends at_____   I play at_____

Page 143

Time to Clean Up
Match the digital time with each clock face by cutting and pasting each lid on the correct trash can.

9:05   12:25   5:40   11:20
4:15   7:35   8:00   2:55
1:30   10:50   3:10   6:45

Page 144

It's About Time!

Trace each 🐭 with red if it has a time word.

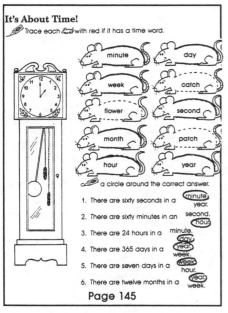

minute	day
week	catch
flower	second
month	patch
hour	year

Draw a circle around the correct answer.

1. There are sixty seconds in a **minute** / year.
2. There are sixty minutes in an **hour** / second.
3. There are 24 hours in a **day** / minute.
4. There are 365 days in a **year** / week.
5. There are seven days in a **week** / hour.
6. There are twelve months in a **year** / week.

Page 145

Postage Stamp, Please

Add up the coins on each envelope. Write the total on the stamp.

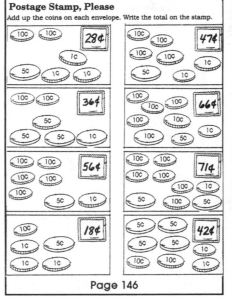

Page 146

Pencil Topper Purchases

Peggy wants to buy three different pencil toppers. Look at the cost of each topper.

bear 5¢ · penguin 3¢ · mouse 6¢ · elephant 2¢ · pig 1¢ · duck 8¢ · cat 4¢ · monkey 7¢

Peggy has 12¢ to spend. Write the names of the different pencil topper combinations she might pick.

1. bear	1. monkey	1. bear
2. penguin	2. cat	2. mouse
3. cat	3. pig	3. pig
1. cat	1. duck	1. monkey
2. mouse	2. pig	2. penguin
3. elephant	3. penguin	3. elephant

Page 147

Mall Mania

Count the coins in each purse. Then draw a line from each coin purse to the store where that amount is given.

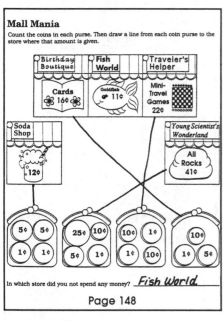

In which store did you not spend any money? **Fish World**

Page 148

So Many Choices!

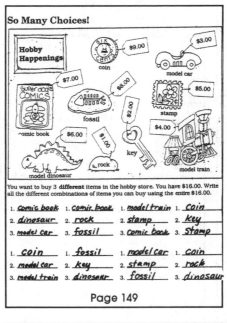

You want to buy 3 **different** items in the hobby store. You have $16.00. Write all the different combinations of items you can buy using the entire $16.00.

1. comic book	1. comic book	1. model train	1. coin
2. dinosaur	2. rock	2. stamp	2. key
3. model car	3. fossil	3. comic book	3. stamp
1. coin	1. fossil	1. model car	1. coin
2. model car	2. key	2. stamp	2. rock
3. model train	3. dinosaur	3. fossil	3. dinosaur

Page 149

Earnings Add Up!

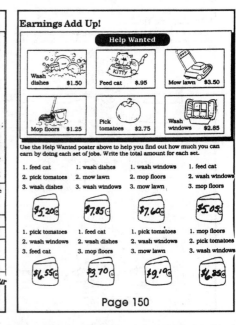

Help Wanted

Wash dishes $1.50 · Feed cat .95 · Mow lawn $3.50 · Mop floors $1.25 · Pick tomatoes $2.75 · Wash windows $2.85

Use the Help Wanted poster above to help you find out how much you can earn by doing each set of jobs. Write the total amount for each set.

1. feed cat	1. wash dishes	1. wash windows	1. feed cat
2. pick tomatoes	2. mow lawn	2. mop floors	2. wash windows
3. wash dishes	3. wash windows	3. mow lawn	3. mop floors
$5.20	**$7.85**	**$7.60**	**$5.05**

1. pick tomatoes	1. feed cat	1. wash windows	1. mop floors
2. wash windows	2. wash dishes	2. wash windows	2. pick tomatoes
3. feed cat	3. mop floors	3. mow lawn	3. wash windows
$6.55	**$3.70**	**$9.10**	**$6.85**

Page 150

Here's Your Order

Count the money on each tray. Write the name of the food that costs that amount.

hamburger ..$2.45	milk ....$.64	cake $2.85
hot dog $1.77	soda pop $1.26	pie $2.25
sandwich $1.55	milkshake ...$1.89	sundae ......$.95

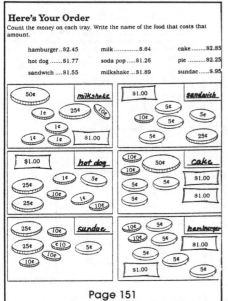

milkshake · sandwich · hot dog · cake · sundae · hamburger

Page 151

Flowers That "Measure" Up

Cut out the centimeter ruler at the bottom of the page. Use the ruler to measure how tall each flower is from the bottom of the stem to the top of the flower. Write the answer below the bee.

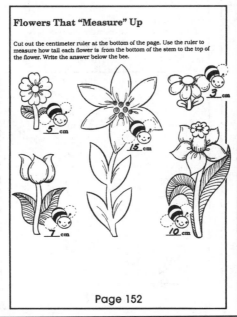

5 cm · 15 cm · 3 cm · 7 cm · 10 cm

Page 152

Brush Up on Measuring!

Use your centimeter ruler to measure these brushes to the nearest centimeter.

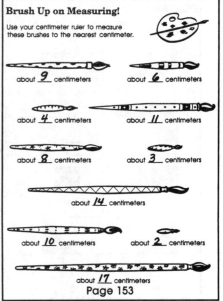

about **9** centimeters · about **6** centimeters
about **4** centimeters · about **11** centimeters
about **8** centimeters · about **3** centimeters
about **14** centimeters
about **10** centimeters · about **2** centimeters
about **17** centimeters

Page 153

Daily Learning Drills Grade 2

Jungle Journey

Use a centimeter ruler to measure the line segments. Write the total length on each hut.

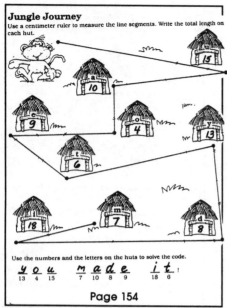

Use the numbers and the letters on the huts to solve the code.

y o u   m a d e   i t !
13 4 15 7 10 8 9 18 6

Page 154

Jumping Jellybeans

Use an inch ruler to measure the line segments. Write the total length on each candy jar.

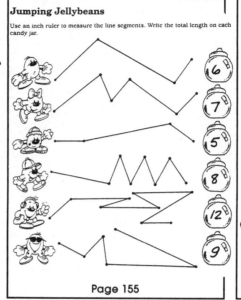

Page 155

The Inch Worm

Measure these worms to the nearest inch.

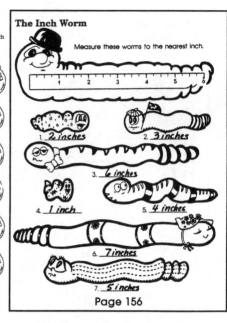

1. 2 inches
2. 3 inches
3. 6 inches
4. 1 inch
5. 4 inches
6. 7 inches
7. 5 inches

Page 156

How Big Are You?

You are getting so big! Every day, you grow a little more. Estimate how long some of your body parts are. Then, using a ruler, work with a friend to find the actual measurements.

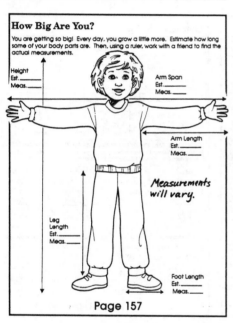

Height Est. ___ Meas. ___

Arm Span Est. ___ Meas. ___

Arm Length Est. ___ Meas. ___

Leg Length Est. ___ Meas. ___

Foot Length Est. ___ Meas. ___

Measurements will vary.

Page 157

How Far Is It?

Use your ruler to measure each distance on the map. Then use the letters on the tires and your answers to solve the message at the bottom of the page.

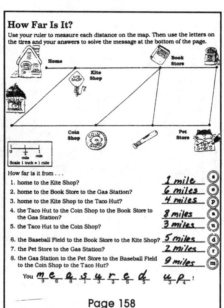

Scale 1 inch = 1 mile

How far is it from . . .
1. home to the Kite Shop? — 1 mile (s)
2. home to the Book Store to the Gas Station? — 6 miles (e)
3. home to the Kite Shop to the Taco Hut? — 4 miles (p)
4. the Taco Hut to the Coin Shop to the Book Store to the Gas Station? — 8 miles (u)
5. the Taco Hut to the Coin Shop? — 3 miles (a)
6. the Baseball Field to the Book Store to the Kite Shop? — 5 miles (d)
7. the Pet Store to the Gas Station? — 2 miles (r)
8. the Gas Station to the Pet Store to the Baseball Field to the Coin Shop to the Taco Hut? — 9 miles (m)

You m e a s u r e d u p !
        9 5 3 4 8 7 2 6 3 5 4

Page 158

Liquid Limits

Draw a line from the containers on the left to the containers on the right that will hold the same amount of liquid. **Hint: 2 pints = 1 quart.**

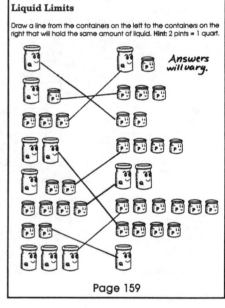

Answers will vary.

Page 159

Shape Sort

Color the ones in each row that are the same size and shape. Write T for triangle, R for rectangle and S for square.

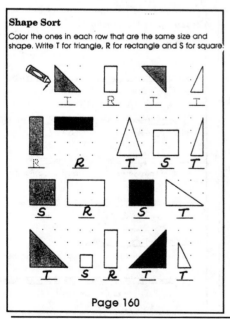

T   R   T   T

R   R   T   S   T

S   R   S   T

T   S   R   T   T

Page 160

Sea Shapes

Find the shapes and color them using the code.

△ red   ○ blue   ◇ yellow
⬭ green   ▭ orange   ▭ black

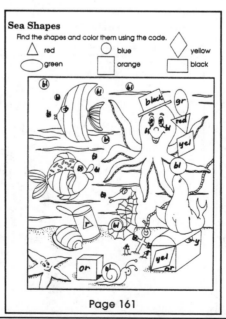

Page 161

Equal and Unequal Parts

Cut out each shape below along the solid lines. Then fold the shape on the dotted lines. Do you get equal or unequal parts? Sort the shapes into two piles: those with equal parts and those with unequal parts.

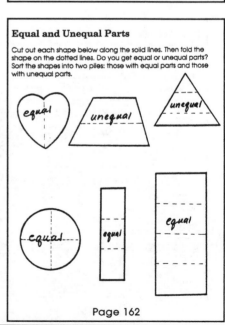

equal   unequal   unequal

equal   equal   equal

Page 162

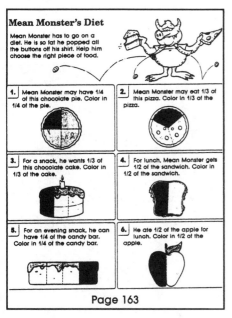

Mean Monster's Diet

Mean Monster has to go on a diet. He is so fat he popped all the buttons off his shirt. Help him choose the right piece of food.

1. Mean Monster may have 1/4 of this chocolate pie. Color in 1/4 of the pie.

2. Mean Monster may eat 1/3 of this pizza. Color in 1/3 of the pizza.

3. For a snack, he wants 1/3 of this chocolate cake. Color in 1/3 of the cake.

4. For lunch, Mean Monster gets 1/2 of the sandwich. Color in 1/2 of the sandwich.

5. For an evening snack, he can have 1/4 of the candy bar. Color in 1/4 of the candy bar.

6. He ate 1/2 of the apple for lunch. Color in 1/2 of the apple.

Page 163

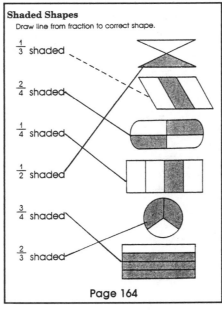

Shaded Shapes

Draw line from fraction to correct shape.

$\frac{1}{3}$ shaded

$\frac{2}{4}$ shaded

$\frac{1}{4}$ shaded

$\frac{1}{2}$ shaded

$\frac{3}{4}$ shaded

$\frac{2}{3}$ shaded

Page 164

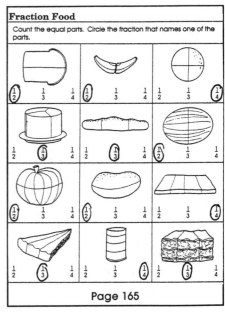

Fraction Food

Count the equal parts. Circle the fraction that names one of the parts.

Page 165

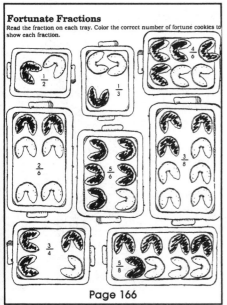

Fortunate Fractions

Read the fraction on each tray. Color the correct number of fortune cookies to show each fraction.

$\frac{1}{2}$ $\frac{1}{3}$ $\frac{4}{6}$

$\frac{2}{6}$ $\frac{5}{6}$ $\frac{3}{8}$

$\frac{3}{4}$ $\frac{5}{8}$

Page 166

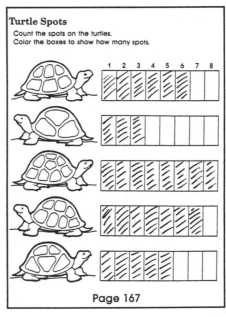

Turtle Spots

Count the spots on the turtles.
Color the boxes to show how many spots.

Page 167

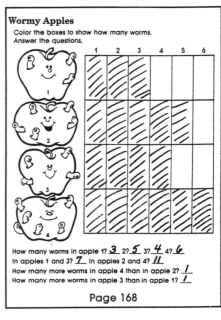

Wormy Apples

Color the boxes to show how many worms. Answer the questions.

How many worms in apple 1? **3** 2? **5** 3? **4** 4? **6**
In apples 1 and 3? **7** In apples 2 and 4? **11**
How many more worms in apple 4 than in apple 2? **1**
How many more worms in apple 3 than in apple 1? **1**

Page 168

Pat's Fish

I go fishing every Saturday!

This picture graph shows how many fish Pat caught.

First Saturday
Second Saturday
Third Saturday
Fourth Saturday

Color the fish Pat caught on the third Saturday red.
Color the fish he caught on the first Saturday blue,
the second Saturday yellow, and the fourth Saturday green.
How many fish did he catch on the first Saturday? **3**
second Saturday? **6** third Saturday? **4** fourth Saturday? **2**

Page 169

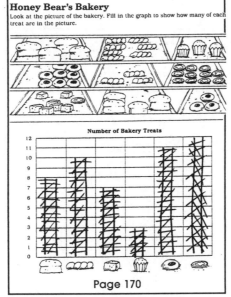

Honey Bear's Bakery

Look at the picture of the bakery. Fill in the graph to show how many of each treat are in the picture.

Number of Bakery Treats

Page 170

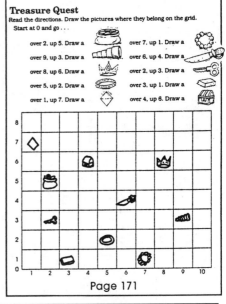

Treasure Quest

Read the directions. Draw the pictures where they belong on the grid. Start at 0 and go . . .

over 5, up 5. Draw a
over 9, up 3. Draw a
over 8, up 6. Draw a
over 5, up 2. Draw a
over 1, up 7. Draw a

over 7, up 1. Draw a
over 6, up 4. Draw a
over 2, up 3. Draw a
over 3, up 1. Draw a
over 4, up 6. Draw a

Page 171

Multiplying Rabbits

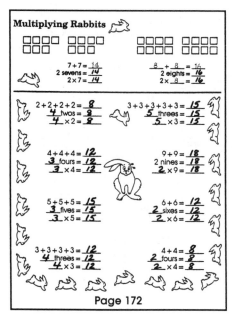

$7 + 7 = 14$
2 sevens = 14
$2 \times 7 = 14$

$8 + 8 = 16$
2 eights = 16
$2 \times 8 = 16$

$2 + 2 + 2 + 2 = 8$
4 twos = 8
$4 \times 2 = 8$

$3 + 3 + 3 + 3 + 3 = 15$
5 threes = 15
$5 \times 3 = 15$

$4 + 4 + 4 = 12$
3 fours = 12
$3 \times 4 = 12$

$9 + 9 = 18$
2 nines = 18
$2 \times 9 = 18$

$5 + 5 + 5 = 15$
3 fives = 15
$3 \times 5 = 15$

$6 + 6 = 12$
2 sixes = 12
$2 \times 6 = 12$

$3 + 3 + 3 + 3 = 12$
4 threes = 12
$4 \times 3 = 12$

$4 + 4 = 8$
2 fours = 8
$2 \times 4 = 8$

Page 172

Mr. X and His Cookies

Draw a line from each picture to its matching problem.

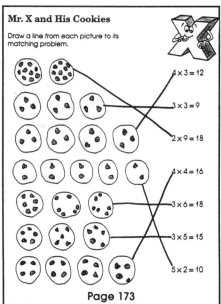

$4 \times 3 = 12$

$3 \times 3 = 9$

$2 \times 9 = 18$

$4 \times 4 = 16$

$3 \times 6 = 18$

$3 \times 5 = 15$

$5 \times 2 = 10$

Page 173

Move That Body

Read a task on the chart. Color the spaces on the chart which show the parts of the body that would be used for the task.

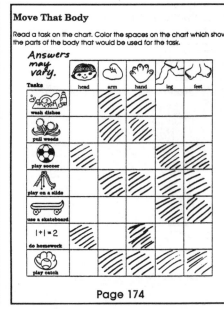

Answers may vary.

Tasks	head	arm	hand	leg	feet
wash dishes					
pull weeds					
play soccer					
play on a slide					
use a skateboard					
do homework ($1+1=2$)					
play catch					

Page 174

Body Works

Read the clues. Write the words in the puzzle.

Across:
2. You use these to breathe.
4. You need to do this when you're tired.
5. This breaks down food.
7. This tells your body what to do.
9. A gas you breathe.
10. It pumps blood.

Down:
1. It carries oxygen to your body.
3. Microscopic living things that can make you sick.
6. This helps when you are sick.
8. These support and shape your body.

bones   rest
germs
brain   lungs
oxygen   medicine
heart   blood
stomach

Page 175

My Bones

Bones give your body shape. They let you stand up tall. You cannot see your bones. But you can feel many of your bones under your skin

Draw a line from each bone to the part of the body where it is found. Write the name of the bone(s).

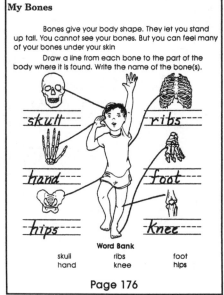

skull

ribs

hand

foot

hips

knee

Word Bank

skull   ribs   foot
hand   knee   hips

Page 176

Name That Bone

Name these bones of your skeleton.

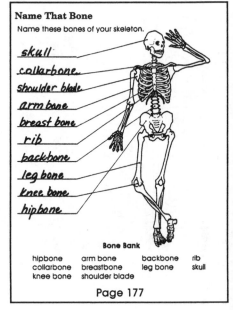

skull
collarbone
shoulder blade
arm bone
breast bone
rib
backbone
leg bone
knee bone
hipbone

Bone Bank

hipbone	arm bone	backbone	rib
collarbone	breastbone	leg bone	skull
knee bone	shoulder blade		

Page 177

Crossbones

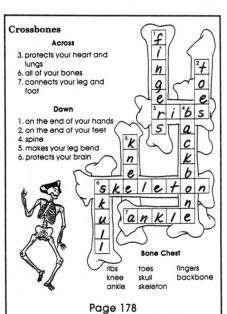

Across
3. protects your heart and lungs
6. all of your bones
7. connects your leg and foot

Down
1. on the end of your hands
2. on the end of your feet
4. spine
5. makes your leg bend
6. protects your brain

finger
toes
ribs
knee
skeleton
skull
ankle
backbone

Bone Chest

ribs   toes   fingers
knee   skull   backbone
ankle   skeleton

Page 178

Outfitted for Health

Read the phrases in the Word Bank. Write only the **good** health habits on the lines.

Word Bank	Take a bath.	Eat a lot of sweets	Stay up all night.
	Drink water.	Get plenty of sleep.	Keep cuts clean.
	Sit all day.	Never wash your hands.	Brush your teeth.
	Exercise.	Eat healthy foods.	

1. Take a bath.
2. Drink water.
3. Exercise.
4. Eat healthy foods.
5. Get plenty of rest.
6. Keep cuts clean.
7. Brush your teeth.

Page 179

Solving the Pyramid's Mystery
Use with page 181.

Pyramid Food Chart

Fats, Oils, and Sweets— very few servings

Milk Group— 2 or 3 servings

Meat Group— 2 servings

Vegetable Group— 4 servings

Fruit Group— 3 servings

Bread Group— 9 servings

Amy and Bob's Food Graph

Number of Servings

Amy Bob Bread | Amy Bob Vegetable | Amy Bob Fruit | Amy Bob Milk | Amy Bob Meat | Amy Bob Fats, Oils, and Sweets

Page 180

Solving the Pyramid's Mystery (cont.)

Use the graph and Pyramid Food Chart on page 180 to help you answer the questions. Then use your answers and the circled letters to solve the code at the bottom of the page.

1. How many servings of bread did Amy eat? __4__ (O)
2. How many servings of bread did Bob eat? __6__ (I)
3. How many more servings of vegetables did Amy eat than Bob? __1__ (A)
4. Which person ate less servings of fruit? __Bob__ (F)
5. Did Bob drink more or less servings of milk than Amy? __less__ (G)
6. Which person ate the most servings of meat? __Amy__ (T)
7. Did Bob eat more or less servings of fats, oils, and sweets than Amy? __more__ (M)
8. How many less servings of fruit did Bob eat than Amy? __2__ (S)
9. Did Amy and Bob eat the needed number of servings of food in the bread group? __no__
10. Did they eat at least the needed number of servings of food in the meat group? __yes__ (U)

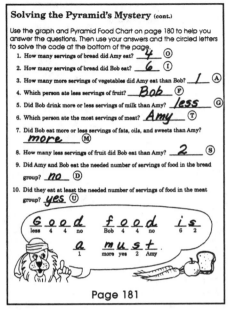

Good food is
less 4 4 no Bob 4 4 no 6 2

a must.
1 more yes 2 Amy

Page 181

A "Sense"-ible Arrangement

Cut out the flowers at the bottom of the page. Pick one flower and look at the object on it. Paste the flower on the vase that tells which sense you would mainly use with the object on that flower.

Page 182

Identifying Prints

Cut out the fingerprints at the bottom of the page. Use a magnifying glass to match the cut-out fingerprints to those on the page. Paste each fingerprint next to the one it matches.

Exhibit D, Exhibit C, Exhibit B, Exhibit A, Exhibit F, Exhibit E

Page 183

Interesting Invertebrates

Invertebrates are animals that have no backbone or inside skeleton. Some have soft bodies protected by shells. Others have soft bodies that are not protected. Some invertebrates are so small that they can only be seen with a microscope.

Below are some examples of invertebrates. Use the clues to name each one.

c e n t IPEDE   s t a r f i s h

j e l l y

E a r t h w o r m   f i s h

s a n d

D o l l a r   s n a i l

s e a   c u c u m b e r

Page 184

A "Class"-y Group

Read a word. If it names a mammal, write M above the word. If it names a reptile, write R above the word. If it names an amphibian, write A above the word. If it names an insect, write I above the word. If it names a bird, write B above the word. If it names a fish, write F above the word. Then draw a line to show where three of these letters are the same in a row.

F	I	B
eel	dragonfly	penguin
R	A	R
turtle	frog	snake
M	M	M
camel	moose	hippopotamus

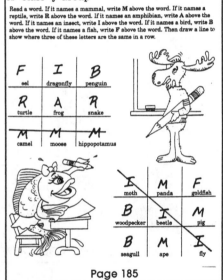

I	M	F
moth	panda	goldfish
B	I	M
woodpecker	beetle	pig
B	M	I
seagull	ape	fly

Page 185

From the Inside Out

Animals whose skeletons have backbones are called **vertebrates**. The backbone, or spine, is made up of bones called **vertebrae**.

Look at the skeletons below. Use the riddle and the Word Bank to write the name of each vertebrate.

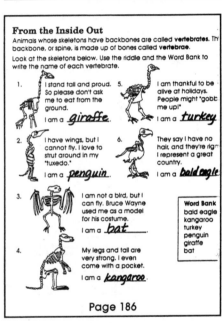

1. I stand tall and proud. So please don't ask me to eat from the ground.
   I am a __giraffe__.

2. I have wings, but I cannot fly. I love to strut around in my "tuxedo."
   I am a __penguin__.

3. I am not a bird, but I can fly. Bruce Wayne used me as a model for his costume.
   I am a __bat__.

4. My legs and tail are very strong. I even come with a pocket.
   I am a __kangaroo__.

5. I am thankful to be alive at holidays. People might "gobb me up!"
   I am a __turkey__.

6. They say I have no hair, and they're right. I represent a great country.
   I am a __bald eagle__.

Word Bank
bald eagle
kangaroo
turkey
penguin
giraffe
bat

Page 186

Fine, Feathered Friends

Do the puzzle about birds.
Color only the birds.

Down
1. _____ keep a bird's body warm and dry.
4. A bird uses its _____ to pick up food.

Across
2. A bird is a _____ -blooded animal.
3. Baby birds are hatched from _____.
5. Birds breathe with their _____.

Word Bank				
feathers	bill	lungs	eggs	warm

Page 187

Birds of a Feather

Birds are the only animals that have feathers. All birds have wings, but not all can fly. They all hatch from eggs, have backbones, and are warm-blooded.

The eggs in the nest contain names of different birds. When filling in the puzzle, the last letter of one name becomes the first letter of the next name. Write the names of the birds in the puzzle in the correct order. Start at the outside edge and spiral in toward the center. The first three names are written for you.

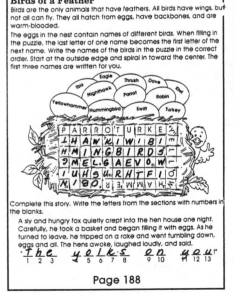

Complete this story. Write the letters from the sections with numbers in the blanks.

A sly and hungry fox quietly crept into the hen house one night. Carefully, he took a basket and began filling it with eggs. As he turned to leave, he tripped on a rake and went tumbling down, eggs and all. The hens awoke, laughed loudly, and said,
"The yolks on you!"
1 2 3   4 5 6 7 8   9 10 11 12 13

Page 188

A Fish Story

Fish live almost anywhere there is water. Although fish come in many different shapes, colors, and sizes, they are alike in many ways.

- All fish have backbones.
- Fish breathe with gills.
- Most fish are cold-blooded.
- Most fish have fins.
- Many fish have scales and fairly tough skin.

Professor Fish teaches a school of fish in the ocean. He decided that he would make name tags for everyone. But, he decided to have some fun, and he jumbled the fish' names on their name tags.

Use the clues to unscramble the fish names. Write each name correctly at the top of the name tag. Then use your imagination to draw each fish.

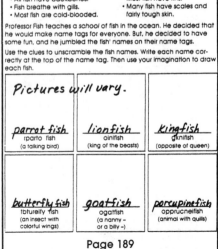

Pictures will vary.

__parrot fish__
rparto fish
(a talking bird)

__lionfish__
oinifish
(king of the beasts)

__kingfish__
gknifish
(opposite of queen)

__butterfly fish__
tbtureify fish
(an insect with colorful wings)

__goatfish__
ogatfish
(a nanny – or a billy –)

__porcupinefish__
opprucneifish
(animal with quills)

Page 189

Daily Learning Drills Grade 2

A Mixture of Mammals

Mammals live in many different places. They are a special group because they . . .

- can give milk to their babies.
- protect and guide their young.
- are warm-blooded.
- have hair at some time during their lives.
- have a large, well-developed brain.

Below are some silly pictures made from two mammals put together. Write the names of the two real mammals on the lines. The last letter(s) in the name of the first animal is the first letter(s) in the name of the second animal. The first one is done for you.

1. whale — leopard
2. porpoise — seal
3. zebra — racoon
4. bear — armadillo
5. elephant — anteater
6. skunk — kangaroo
7. tiger — rabbit
8. camel — elephant

Page 190

The Reptile House

There are about 6,000 different kinds of reptiles. They come in all sorts of shapes and colors. Their sizes in length range from 2 inches to almost 30 feet. Reptiles can be found on every continent except Antarctica. Even though reptiles can seem quite different, they all . . .

- breathe with lungs.
- are cold-blooded.
- have dry, scaly skin.
- have a backbone.

In the Reptile House at the zoo, each animal needs to be placed in the correct area. Read the information about each reptile. Then use the clues and the pictures to write the name of each reptile in its area.

Giant Tortoise can live over 100 years. It can hide under its shell for protection.

Reticulated Python is the longest snake. One was almost 33 feet long.

Saltwater Crocodile is one of the largest reptiles. It can weigh almost 1,000 lbs.

Komodo Dragon is a dragon-like reptile. It is the largest living lizard.

Tuatara is closely related to the extinct dinosaur.

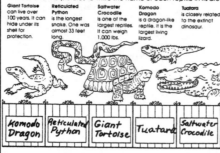

| Komodo Dragon | Reticulated Python | Giant Tortoise | Tuatara | Saltwater Crocodile |

Clues:
- The snake is between the largest lizard and the largest member of the turtle family.
- A relative of the alligator is on the far right side.
- The reptile who carries its "house" is in the middle.

Page 191

Amazing Amphibians

Amphibians are cold-blooded vertebrates (animals with backbones). They have no scales on their skin. Most amphibians hatch from eggs laid in water or on damp ground. Many amphibians grow legs as they develop into adults. Some live on land and have both lungs and gills for breathing. Frogs and toads are examples of amphibians.

Santjie, a South African sharp-nosed frog, holds the record for the longest triple jump. He jumped a total of more than 33 feet!

The frogs below won 1st, 2nd, and 3rd place in a recent triple-jump contest. Each jump after each frog's first jump was two feet shorter than the jump before. How many total feet did each frog jump? Fill in the answers on the trophies.

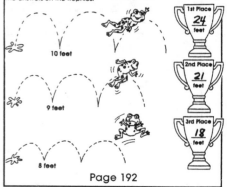

10 feet
9 feet
8 feet

1st Place 24 feet
2nd Place 21 feet
3rd Place 18 feet

Page 192

Plotting Plants

Follow Rupert Rabbit as he learns about plants. Use the words in the Word Bank to help you.

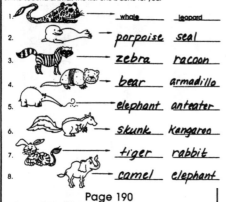

Word Bank
flower
root
leaf
stem
seed

Read and follow the directions. Start at Rupert Rabbit.

1. Go right 5 spaces. Then go down 3 spaces and left 5 spaces. Write the word that names what grows into a new plant here.
2. Now go up 2 spaces. Then go right 6 spaces and down 3 spaces. Write the word that names the part of the plant that is underground here.
3. Now go up 3 spaces. Then go left 3 spaces and down 1 space. Write the word that names the part of the plant that makes the food here.
4. Now go right 2 spaces. Then go up 1 space and left 4 spaces. Write the word that names the part of the plant that carries food and water to the rest of the plant here.
5. Now go down 2 spaces. Then go right 5 spaces and up 3 spaces. Write the word that names the part of the plant that makes the seeds here.

Page 193

Those Nutty Seeds

Seeds are found in different parts of the flower. Some seeds are found in the flower. Some seeds are found in the fruit or the nut.

Circle the part of the plant that has the seed. Write the name of the seed.

Word Bank
pine   maple
apple   acorn
corn   dandelion

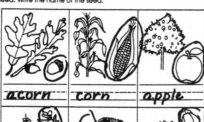

| acorn | corn | apple |
| pine | dandelion | maple |

Page 194

Traveling Seeds

Seeds travel from one place to another. Sometimes people move the seeds. Sometimes they are moved in other ways.

Finish the sentences to tell how seeds travel.

Word Bank
people
animals
animals
wind
water

Seeds travel with _people_
Seeds travel in _water_
Seeds travel on _animals_
Seeds travel in _animals_
Seeds travel in the _wind_

Page 195

Eyes in the Dark

What has eyes, but cannot see? A potato! The little white bumps that grow on a potato's skin are called "eyes." An eye can grow into a new potato plant.

You will need:
potato
potting soil
flowerpot or plastic glass

1. Put the potato in a dark cupboard or closet. Check it daily for small bumps called "eyes."

2. When the eyes appear ask an adult to cut them off the potato.

3. Fill a flowerpot half full of potting soil and lay the piece of potato on it with the "eyes" facing up.

Record what happened after . . .

1 week

Answers will vary.

2 weeks

4. Cover the "eyes" with 1 inch of soil. Water. Keep moist–but not wet. Watch closely for about two weeks.

What happened?
A potato is a tuber. A tuber is a fat underground stem with little buds that can grow into new plants. The "eye" that you planted was really a potato bud that grew into a new plant.

Page 196

Dynamic Dinosaurs

Dinosaurs were reptiles that lived millions of years ago. Some of them were the biggest animals to ever live on land. Some were as small as chickens. Some dinosaurs ate plants, while other ate meat-eaters.

Scientists have given names to the dinosaurs that often describe their special bodies, sizes, and habits.

Look at the object(s) placed in the picture with each dinosaur. Use the objects as clues to fill in the blanks and finish each dinosaur's name.

TRICERA _TOPS_
LAMB EOSAURUS
DIME TRODON
SALT ASAURUS
PLATE OSAURUS

Page 197

Dial a Dinosaur

Danny loves dinosaurs. In fact, he loves them so much that everyone calls him Dinosaur Danny! Find out what Dinosaur Danny's favorite dinosaur is by decoding the message below. To do this, use the numbers on the telephone and the directional markers.

For example: 3 points to the letter D.

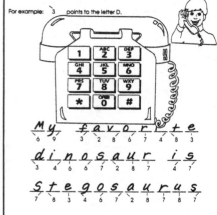

_My_ _favorite_
6 9   3 4 2 8 7 4 8 3

dinosaur _is_
3 4 6 6 7 2 8 7   4 7

Stegosaurus
7 8 3 4 6 7 2 8 7 8 7

Write your own message and share it with a classmate.

Page 198

Magic Square Mania

Did you know that the word dinosaur comes from two Greek words meaning terrible lizard? Dinosaurs were not lizards at all! To further improve your dinosaur vocabulary, read Column A. Choose an answer from Column B. Write the number of the answer in the Magic Square. The first one has been done for you.

Column A	
A.	Person who studies fossils
B.	Petrified remains of animals and plants
C.	Meat-eating dinosaurs
D.	Plant-eating dinosaurs
E.	Movement of animals over long distances
F.	Large bony plates on dinosaur's neck
G.	Bones on the top of a dinosaur's head
H.	The Age of Dinosaurs
I.	Large groups of animals that live together

Column B	
1.	skeleton
2.	Mesozoic Age
3.	carnivores
4.	herbivores
5.	paleontologist
6.	migration
7.	herds
8.	frills
9.	crest
10.	fossils

A 5	B 10	C 3
D 4	E 6	F 8
G 9	H 2	I 7

Add the numbers across, down, and diagonally. What answer do you get? _18_
Why do you think this is called a magic square? _____

Page 199

Weather Watch

Weather is the condition of the air around the earth for a period of time. The weatherman's job is to predict the weather.

There were some very unusual weather patterns recorded for a recent month. Use the key to draw the correct weather symbols for each day.

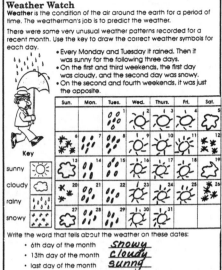

- Every Monday and Tuesday it rained. Then it was sunny for the following three days.
- On the first and third day was cloudy, and the second day was snowy.
- On the second and fourth weekends, it was just the opposite.

Key

sunny	☀
cloudy	☁
rainy	🌧
snowy	❄

Write the word that tells about the weather on these dates:
- 6th day of the month _snowy_
- 13th day of the month _cloudy_
- last day of the month _sunny_

Page 200

Gauging the Weather

Cut out the centimeter ruler at the bottom of the page. Use the ruler to measure the amount of rainfall from the bottom of the gauge to the top of the water. Write the measurement on the raindrop.

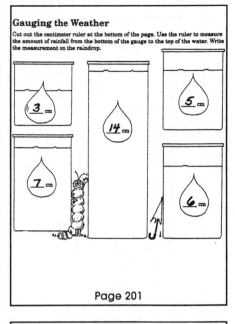

3 cm
14 cm
5 cm
7 cm
6 cm

Page 201

A Cloudy Day

Clouds bring us many kinds of weather. Some clouds give us fair weather. Other clouds bring rain.

Paste the picture of the cloud next to its description.

	How the Clouds Look	Weather
Cumulus	Big, puffy clouds	Nice day, but there might be a small shower.
Cumulo-nimbus	Tall, dark, piles of clouds.	Thunderstorm
Cirrus	Whispy clouds that look like feathers.	Fair
Stratus	Layers of gray clouds that cover the whole sky.	Steady drizzle.

Page 202

Lacy Patterns

Kim likes to look at the lacy patterns of snowflakes with her magnifying glass. Most of them have six sides or six points. But she has never seen two snowflakes that are alike. Kim catches them on small pieces of dark paper so that she can see them better. Some of the snowflakes are broken because they bump into each other as they fall from the clouds.

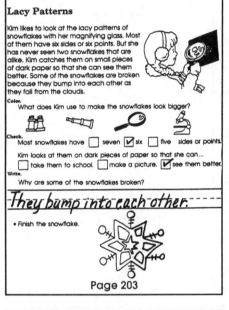

Color.
What does Kim use to make the snowflakes look bigger?

Check.
Most snowflakes have ☐ seven ☑ six ☐ five sides or points.

Kim looks at them on dark pieces of paper so that she can...
☐ take them to school. ☐ make a picture. ☑ see them better.

Write.
Why are some of the snowflakes broken?

They bump into each other.

- Finish the snowflake.

Page 203

Sink or Float?

Why do some objects float? Why do other objects sink? Is it because of their shape? Is it because of their color? Let's find out!

You will need:
large bowl of water
test objects such as –
apple, nail, orange, eraser, wood, stone, egg, penny, crayon

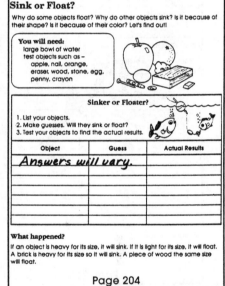

Sinker or Floater?

1. List your objects.
2. Make guesses. Will they sink or float?
3. Test your objects to find the actual results.

Object	Guess	Actual Results
Answers will vary.		

What happened?
If an object is heavy for its size, it will sink. If it is light for its size, it will float. A brick is heavy for its size so it will sink. A piece of wood the same size will float.

Page 204

Salty Water Evaporation

1. With a partner, decide which of you will be responsible for each job below.
   Experimenter—responsible for following the given directions, gathering materials, and cleaning up.
   Recorder—responsible for reading the directions and questions out loud and for recording the answers.

2. Gather the following materials:
   spoon
   salt
   paper cup
   1/4 cup water

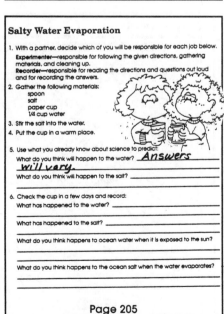

3. Stir the salt into the water.
4. Put the cup in a warm place.
5. Use what you already know about science to predict:
   What do you think will happen to the water? _Answers will vary._
   What do you think will happen to the salt? _____

6. Check the cup in a few days and record:
   What has happened to the water? _____
   _____
   What has happened to the salt? _____

   What do you think happens to ocean water when it is exposed to the sun?
   _____

   What do you think happens to the ocean salt when the water evaporates?
   _____
   _____

Page 205

Anti-Freeze

Water turns into a solid at a temperature of 32°F. This is called the freezing point. Does all water freeze at 32°F? Let's find out!

You will need:
2 small paper cups
4 teaspoons of salt
water
marking pen
freezer

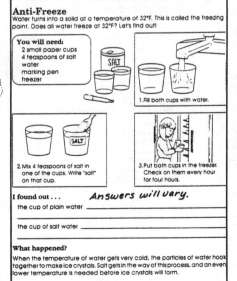

1. Fill both cups with water.
2. Mix 4 teaspoons of salt in one of the cups. Write "salt" on that cup.
3. Put both cups in the freezer. Check on them every hour for four hours.

I found out . . . _Answers will vary._
the cup of plain water _____

the cup of salt water _____

What happened?
When the temperature of water gets very cold, the particles of water hook together to make ice crystals. Salt gets in the way of this process, and an even lower temperature is needed before ice crystals will form.

Page 206

Layers of the Ocean Floor

Have you ever wondered what is under the sand on a beach? Some beaches are really layers of rock, pebbles, shells, and sand. Work in a group of four students and choose one of these materials to bring to school for your group. Write your name next to the material that you will bring.

sand _____ shells _____
rock _____ pebbles _____

Your teacher will provide a glass jar and water.

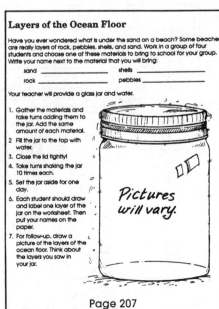

1. Gather the materials and take turns adding them to the jar. Add the same amount of each material.
2. Fill the jar to the top with water.
3. Close the lid tightly!
4. Take turns shaking the jar 10 times each.
5. Set the jar aside for one day.
6. Each student should draw and label one layer of the jar on the worksheet. Then put your names on the paper.
7. For follow-up, draw a picture of the layers of the ocean floor. Think about the layers you saw in your jar.

Pictures will vary.

Page 207

Ocean Temperatures

Where do you think the ocean temperatures are the warmest? Do you think the salt makes the ocean warmer or cooler? Do you think the sun makes the ocean warmer or cooler? Try this experiment to find out!

1. Get 4 clear glasses of water.
2. Add salt to 2 of the glasses and stir well.
3. Set one freshwater glass and one saltwater glass in the shade outside.
4. Set the other 2 glasses in the sun outside.
5. Set thermometers in each of the 4 glasses.
6. Divide into 4 equal groups and start at a different glass.
7. Wait 15 minutes, then read the thermometer and record below.
8. On signal, rotate to the next glass.

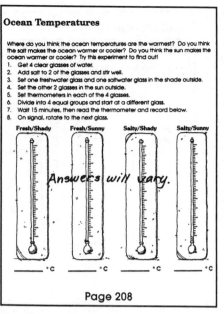

Fresh/Shady   Fresh/Sunny   Salty/Shady   Salty/Sunny

Answers will vary.

°C   °C   °C   °C

Page 208

The Dancing Coin

You can make a coin dance on the top of a bottle as if a ghost were pushing on it. Let's try!

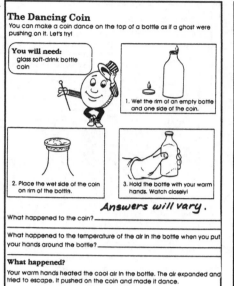

You will need:
glass soft-drink bottle
coin

1. Wet the rim of an empty bottle and one side of the coin.

2. Place the wet side of the coin on rim of the bottle.

3. Hold the bottle with your warm hands. Watch closely!

Answers will vary.

What happened to the coin? _____

What happened to the temperature of the air in the bottle when you put your hands around the bottle? _____

What happened?

Your warm hands heated the cool air in the bottle. The air expanded and tried to escape. It pushed on the coin and made it dance.

Page 209

The Crusher

I'll bet you can crush a plastic soft-drink bottle without even touching it. Of course there is a little trick. Let's try it!

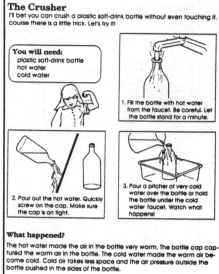

You will need:
plastic soft-drink bottle
hot water
cold water

1. Fill the bottle with hot water from the faucet. Be careful. Let the bottle stand for a minute.

2. Pour out the hot water. Quickly screw on the cap. Make sure the cap is on tight.

3. Pour a pitcher of very cold water over the bottle or hold the bottle under the cold water faucet. Watch what happens!

What happened?

The hot water made the air in the bottle very warm. The bottle cap captured the warm air in the bottle. The cold water made the warm air become cold. Cold air takes less space and the air pressure outside the bottle pushed in the sides of the bottle.

Page 210

Powerful Push-Up

Can air hold up water? It can with a little help from you. Let's find out how!

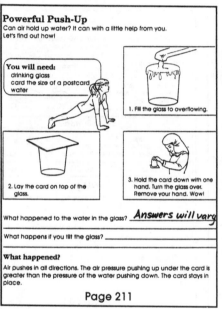

You will need:
drinking glass
card the size of a postcard
water

1. Fill the glass to overflowing.

2. Lay the card on top of the glass.

3. Hold the card down with one hand. Turn the glass over. Remove your hand. Wow!

What happened to the water in the glass? *Answers will vary.*

What happens if you tilt the glass? _____

What happened?

Air pushes in all directions. The air pressure pushing up under the card is greater than the pressure of the water pushing down. The card stays in place.

Page 211

High and Dry

Can you put a piece of paper under water without getting it wet? You can do it with a little help from air pressure. Let's try!

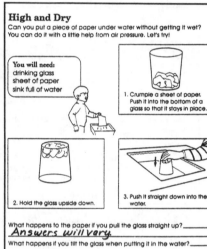

You will need:
drinking glass
sheet of paper
sink full of water

1. Crumple a sheet of paper. Push it into the bottom of a glass so that it stays in place.

2. Hold the glass upside down.

3. Push it straight down into the water.

What happens to the paper if you pull the glass straight up? _____
Answers will vary.
What happens if you tilt the glass when putting it in the water? _____

What happened?

The glass is full of air. The air cannot come out because it is lighter than the water. If you tilt the glass, the air escapes and water enters.

Page 212

The Last Straw

Sodas, milkshakes and root beer are all fun to sip through a straw. It would be fun to sip them through two straws. Could you sip liquid through three straws? four straws? What is the most you could use? Let's find out!

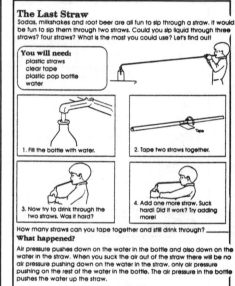

You will need:
plastic straws
clear tape
plastic pop bottle
water

1. Fill the bottle with water.

2. Tape two straws together.

3. Now try to drink through the two straws. Was it hard?

4. Add one more straw. Suck hard! Did it work? Try adding more!

How many straws can you tape together and still drink through? _____

What happened?

Air pressure pushes down on the water in the bottle and also down on the water in the straw. When you suck the air out of the straw there will be no air pressure pushing down on the water in the straw, only air pressure pushing on the rest of the water in the bottle. The air pressure in the bottle pushes the water up the straw.

Page 213

What's the Matter?

All things are made of **matter**. Matter takes up space. It can take three forms – solid, liquid or gas.

Solids have shape and volume. They do not change shape easily.

Liquids have volume, but they have no shape of their own. They take the shape of the container they are in.

Gases have no shape or volume. Most gases are invisible.

Find and circle the words in each wordsearch that are examples of each kind of matter. Then write the words on the lines.

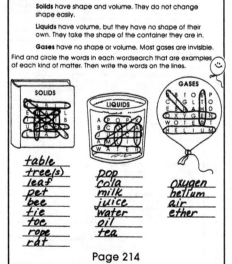

SOLIDS
table
tree(s)
leaf
pet
bee
tie
toe
rope
rat

LIQUIDS
pop
cola
milk
juice
water
oil
tea

GASES
oxygen
helium
air
ether

Page 214

"Shadowing" Shadows

Cut out the pictures at the bottom of the page. Read the directions and paste the objects where they belong.

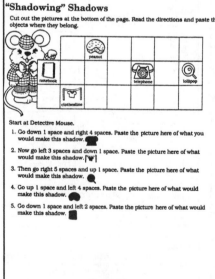

peanut
notebook
telephone
lollipop
clothesline

Start at Detective Mouse.

1. Go down 1 space and right 4 spaces. Paste the picture here of what you would make this shadow.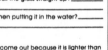

2. Now go left 3 spaces and down 1 space. Paste the picture here of what would make this shadow.

3. Then go right 5 spaces and up 1 space. Paste the picture here of what would make this shadow.

4. Go up 1 space and left 4 spaces. Paste the picture here of what would make this shadow.

5. Go down 1 space and left 2 spaces. Paste the picture here of what would make this shadow.

Page 215

Volume Control

If the words name something that makes a loud sound, color the space gray.
If the words name something that makes a soft sound, color the space red.

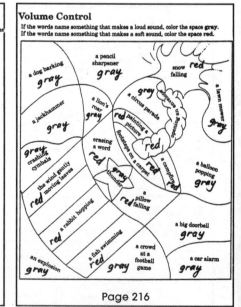

a dog barking — gray
a pencil sharpener — gray
snow falling — red
a lawn mower — gray
a lion's roar — gray
a circus parade — gray
Painting a picture — red
a jackhammer — gray
crashing cymbals — gray
erasing a word — red
a balloon popping — gray
the wind gently moving leaves — red
thunder — gray
a campfire — red
a pillow falling — red
a rabbit hopping — red
a big doorbell — gray
an explosion — gray
a fish swimming — red
a crowd at a football game — gray
a car alarm — gray

Page 216

Energetic "Source"-ry

Write the sources of energy from the Word Bank above the correct cauldron.

furnace
camp stove
curling iron

heat

buzzer
alarm
trumpet

sound

lamp
candle
flashlight

light

Page 217

Keep It Clean!

Have you ever cleaned a penny? Let's try it!

Materials:

4 dirty pennies	soap	window cleaner
salt	water	steel wool pad
vinegar	taco sauce	paper towels

Directions:

1. In the "I predict . . ." section on the chart, explain what you think each penny will look like after you clean it with one of the materials.
2. Your teacher will place a small amount of each material in the center of each table.
3. Try cleaning one penny using window cleaner. Explain what it looks like in the "I observed . . ." section.
4. Now try cleaning another penny using soap, water, and the steel wool pad. Explain what it looks like.
5. Clean a different penny in salt and vinegar. Explain what it looks like.
6. Now clean the last penny in taco sauce. Explain what it looks like.

Materials	I predict . . .	I observed . . .
window cleaner	Answers will vary.	
soap, water, and steel wool pad		
salt and vinegar		
taco sauce		

Page 218

Magnetic Attraction

The word **magnet** begins with the same three letters as the word magic, and sometimes magnets do seem a little magical.

Every magnet has two poles — north and south. The north pole of one magnet attracts and pulls toward the south pole of another magnet. Two poles that are the same (two north poles or two south poles) do not attract each other. Instead, they push away from each other.

Using the information above, continue labeling the horseshoe and bar magnets below with **N** (for north) and **S** (for south).

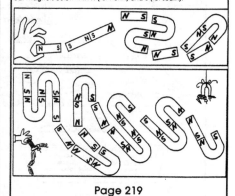

Page 219

"Attractive" Magnets

Cut out each object and paste it on the chart where it belongs. Use a crayon to graph the results.

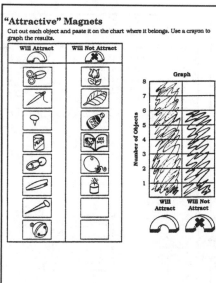

Page 220

Lifting with Levers

A lever is a simple machine used to lift or move things. It has two parts. The **arm** is the part that moves. The **fulcrum** supports the arm and does not move.

Name the parts of this lever.

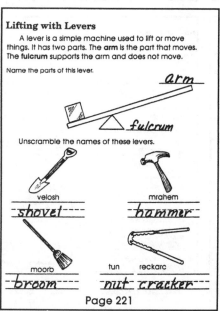

arm

fulcrum

Unscramble the names of these levers.

velosh
shovel

mrahem
hammer

moorb
broom

tun   reckarc
nut cracker

Page 221

Levers at Work

Levers help make our work easier. Circle all the levers. Then find their names in the wordsearch.

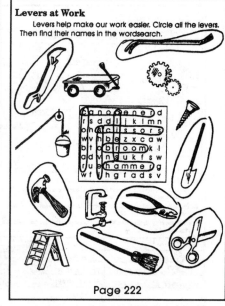

Page 222

The Right Tool for the Job

Mother gave Tyrone and Kim a list of jobs. Help them pick the right tool for each job. Draw a line from the job to the tool.

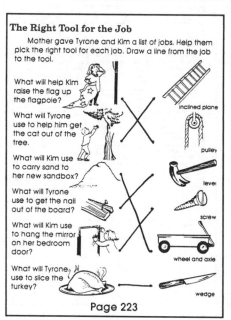

What will help Kim raise the flag up the flagpole?

What will Tyrone use to help him get the cat out of the tree.

What will Kim use to carry sand to her new sandbox?

What will Tyrone use to get the nail out of the board?

What will Kim use to hang the mirror on her bedroom door?

What will Tyrone use to slice the turkey?

inclined plane

pulley

lever

screw

wheel and axle

wedge

Page 223

Slanted Machines

An inclined plane has a slanted surface. It is used to move things from a low place to a high place. Some inclined planes are smooth. Others have steps.

Color the inclined planes in the picture.

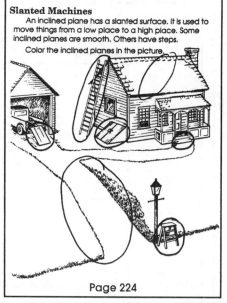

Page 224

The Wedge

A wedge is a type of inclined plane. It is made up of two inclined planes joined together to make a sharp edge. A wedge can be used to cut things. Some wedges are pointed.

Color only the pictures of wedges.

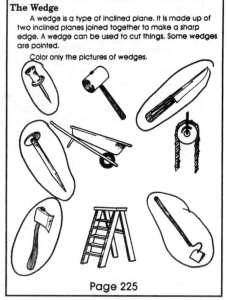

Page 225

Daily Learning Drills Grade 2

Ready for Work!

Read the names of the objects in the Word Bank. Write the objects under the correct kind of simple machine.

Inclined Plane
sloped sidewalk
truck ramp
slide

Wheel and Axle
car
mixer
skateboard

Wedge
doorstop
ax

Lever
bottle opener
shovel
light switch
screwdriver

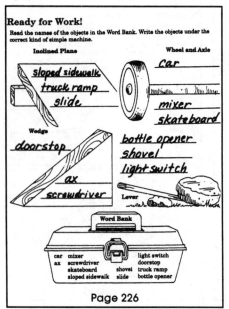

Word Bank
car   mixer   light switch
ax   screwdriver   doorstop
skateboard   shovel   truck ramp
sloped sidewalk slide   bottle opener

Faraway and Close Up

Kim's favorite subject is science. She has a telescope and a microscope in her bedroom. At night, she looks through her telescope. Things that are far away, like the moon, stars and planets, look bigger. When she looks through her microscope, she can see tiny things close up, like a drop of water or a bit of salt.

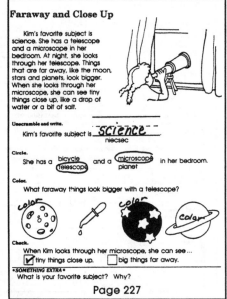

Unscramble and write.
Kim's favorite subject is _science_
niecsec

Circle.
She has a ~~bicycle~~ (telescope) and a (microscope) ~~planet~~ in her bedroom.

Color.
What faraway things look bigger with a telescope?

color   color   color

Check.
When Kim looks through her microscope, she can see ...
☑ tiny things close up.   ☐ big things far away.

• SOMETHING EXTRA •
What is your favorite subject? Why?

Planets

There are nine planets that move around the sun. Our planet is Earth. Earth is closest to Mars and Venus. Jupiter is the largest planet. It is many times larger than Earth. Saturn is the planet with seven rings around it. The smallest planet is called Mercury!

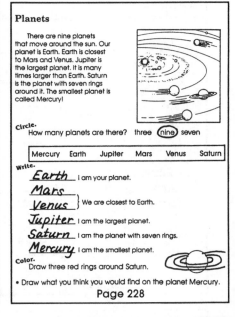

Circle.
How many planets are there?   three   (nine)   seven

Mercury	Earth	Jupiter	Mars	Venus	Saturn

Write.
Earth I am your planet.
Mars
Venus } We are closest to Earth.
Jupiter I am the largest planet.
Saturn I am the planet with seven rings.
Mercury I am the smallest planet.

Color.
Draw three red rings around Saturn.

• Draw what you think you would find on the planet Mercury.

Position the Planets

Write the names of the planets on the lines according to their distance from the sun. Use the Word Bank to help you spell the words correctly.

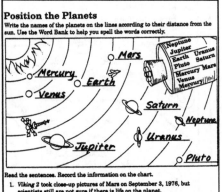

Mars
Mercury   Earth
Venus   Saturn
          Neptune
          Uranus
Jupiter   Pluto

Word Bank
Neptune Jupiter Earth Uranus Pluto Saturn Mars Venus Mercury

Read the sentences. Record the information on the chart.

1. *Viking 2* took close-up pictures of Mars on September 3, 1976, but scientists still are not sure if there is life on the planet.

2. Two of Saturn's outer rings were very clear in pictures taken by *Pioneer-Saturn* on September 1, 1979.

3. In March of 1979, the probe *Voyager 1* discovered that Jupiter has a thin ring around it.

Name of Probe	Planet Destination	Date	Results or Discoveries
Viking 2	Mars	Sept. 3 1976	took pictures still not sure of life
Pioneer-Saturn	Saturn	Sept. 1, 1979	pictures clearly showed Saturn's rings
Voyager 1	Jupiter	March 1979	discovered Jupiter has a thin ring

---

Spacing Out

Read a clue. Find the matching word in the puzzle and write it on the line. Then connect the puzzle dots in the same order as your answers.

Clues

1. The planet we live on _Earth_
2. The closest star _sun_
3. They shine in the sky at night _stars_
4. Earth is a _planet_
5. Planets, stars, and moons are in _space_
6. Time when the sun shines _day_
7. A group of stars _constellation_
8. A person who travels in space _astronaut_
9. The path a planet follows to travel around the sun _orbit_
10. It gives us light at night _moon_
11. People who study the stars _astronomers_
12. You use this to see the stars close up _telescope_
13. Time when the sun does not shine _night_
14. We feel this from the sun _heat_

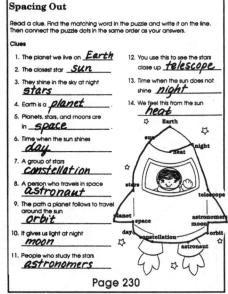

Birthday Surprise!

1. Complete sentences 1 and 2.
2. Connect the numbers in the dot-to-dot.
3. Color 2 presents red and 3 presents blue.
4. Draw candles on the dot-to-dot picture to show how old you are.
5. Color the dot-to-dot.

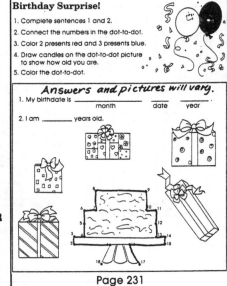

Answers and pictures will vary.

1. My birthdate is _____ _____ _____
   month   date   year

2. I am _____ years old.

I Like Me!

Complete the sentences below to tell about you.

Most people like the way I _Answers will vary._

I feel happy when _____

The thing I like best about me is _____

I feel sad when _____

I feel special when _____

At home I _____

At school I _____

Featuring the One and Only Me

In each box write about a different event in your life. Draw a picture to go with each event. *Answers will vary.*

I was born.		

My Body Homework

You know how special your body is! To keep your body working and looking its best, you should start developing good habits now and keep them as you grow older. Use this check list to keep yourself on track for the next week. Keep it on your bathroom mirror or next to your bed where it will remind you to do your 'homework!'

	Sun.	Mon.	Tues.	Wed.	Thurs.	Fri.	Sat.
I slept at least 8 hours.							
I ate a healthy breakfast.							
I brushed my teeth this morning.							
I ate a healthy lunch.							
I washed my hands after using the bathroom.							
I exercised at least 30 minutes today.							
I drank at least 6 glasses of water.							
I stood and sat up straight.							
I ate a healthy dinner.							
I bathed.							
I brushed my teeth this evening.							

People Scavenger Hunt

Get to know the kids in your class. Find someone to fit each description. Try not to use the same name twice!

How We Look

1. _____ has freckles on his/her arms.
2. _____ is wearing a watch, ring or necklace.
3. _____ has red on his/her socks.
4. _____ has 3 buttons on his/her shirt.
5. _____ is missing 3 baby teeth.

How We Feel

1. _____ likes green beans.
2. _____ wants a baby brother or sister.
3. _____ is scared during thunderstorms.
4. _____ would like a snake as a pet.
5. _____ would like his/her room painted blue.

What We Do

1. _____ ate cereal for breakfast.
2. _____ played a sport last weekend.
3. _____ can dive into a swimming pool.
4. _____ made his/her bed today.
5. _____ is taking lessons to learn how to do something.

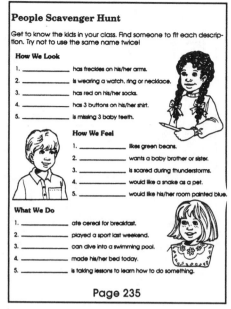

Page 235

Shooting for My Goals

What is something new you want to do? Maybe you want to improve at something you already do. Fill in the sentences below.

There are two goals I have for the rest of the school year.

One is

Goals will vary.

Two is _____

I will do this by

day _____

month _____

year _____

_____
signed

Page 236

My Personal Shield

Let your friends learn more about how special you are. Complete each sentence and draw a picture to go with it.

Answers and pictures will vary.

My proudest moment is _____ | I am good at _____

I helped _____ | I try very hard at _____

Page 237

Interview a Friend

Interview your friend and then fill out the information below.
My friend is _Answers will vary._

Favorite Colors

Favorite Book

Favorite Activities

Favorite Foods

Page 238

Create a Comrade!

Imagine that you could create a perfect friend. Describe your "creation" on the lines below.

Name _____
Age _____

Favorite Pastime _____

Personal Qualities | Special Interests/Hobbies

Answers will vary.

Talents

What we could do together

Page 239

Friendly Favorites

Think of the names of favorite animals, food and places that begin with the letters in the word FRIENDS. Write the names in the correct boxes below. One word in each column has already been done for you. For extra fun, play with a friend. The one who can think of the most names is the winner.

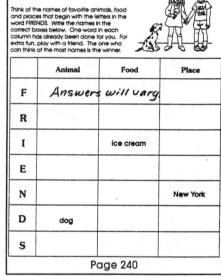

	Animal	Food	Place
F	_Answers will vary._		
R			
I		ice cream	
E			
N			New York
D	dog		
S			

Page 240

Buddy's Lists

Buddy likes to make lists. Yesterday, he wrote a list of his favorite things to do with friends. Today, he wants to divide this list into three more lists. Help Buddy by filling in these three lists with one-syllable, two-syllable and three-syllable words from his word list. The first word has been done for you.

One-syllable words
1. golf
2. _swim_
3. _camp_
4. _skate_
5. _swing_

Buddy's Word List Things to Do with Friends

golf | basketball
Ping-Pong | camp
swim | snorkeling
backpacking | biking
volleyball | skate
baseball | canoeing
fishing | soccer
swing

Two-syllable words
1. _Ping-Pong_
2. _baseball_
3. _fishing_
4. _biking_
5. _soccer_

Three-syllable words
1. _backpacking_
2. _volleyball_
3. _basketball_
4. _snorkeling_
5. _canoeing_

Page 241

Cars and Colors

Answers will vary.

What is the color of your family car? _____
If you have more than one car, what are the other colors? _____

Record the colors of all the cars in your class on the bar graph below. If a color is not shown, include it in "Other."

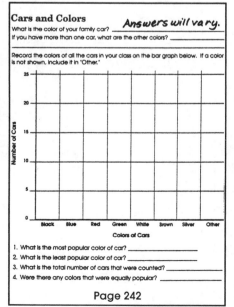

Number of Cars (y-axis: 0, 5, 10, 15, 20, 25)

Colors of Cars (x-axis: Black, Blue, Red, Green, White, Brown, Silver, Other)

1. What is the most popular color of car? _____
2. What is the least popular color of car? _____
3. What is the total number of cars that were counted? _____
4. Were there any colors that were equally popular? _____

Page 242

Comparing a Car and a Truck

In some ways, cars and trucks are alike. In other ways, they are different. On the car, write words and phrases that are true about it but are not true about the truck. Do the same with the truck. Where the car and the truck overlap, write words and phrases that are common to both of them.

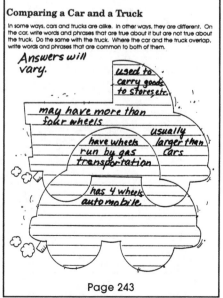

Answers will vary.

used to carry goods to store, etc.

may have more than four wheels

have wheels run by gas

usually larger than cars

transportation

has 4 wheels

automobile

Page 243

Sightseeing by Train

Follow the train as it travels through the countryside. Identify by number the places where the train:

goes through a forest	14
comes to a stop	16
crosses a high bridge	1
passes a water tower	12
exits a tunnel	3
crosses a low bridge	7
passes a school	13
enters a tunnel	2

goes through a covered bridge	8
passes through a plowed field	11
comes down the mountain	4
passes a volcano	10
goes through rocks	6
crosses a lake	5
goes by a small town	9
passes cows	15

Page 244

Sights and Sounds of Travel

Look at the numbered pictures below. Write the numbers of the pictures by each question.

What can carry more than one person?	1,2,3,4,5,6,7,8,11
What moves on wheels?	3,4,6,7,9,10,12
What moves on just two wheels?	3,9
What makes a very loud noise?	1,2,3,5,8,12 Answers may vary.
What moves through water?	1,2,11
What has a motor to make it run?	3,1,2,4,5,7,8,12
What can hold large, heavy objects?	1,2,4
What can travel very fast?	1,2,3,4,5,7,8
What has to be pushed or pulled?	6,10

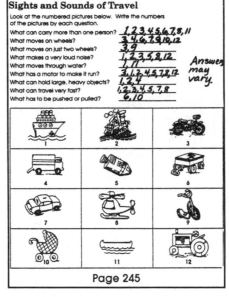

Page 245

Transportation Sort

Study the examples of transportation below. Sort the objects into three groups. Think how each type travels.

Draw a ○ around objects in group one.
Draw a △ around objects in group two.
Draw a □ around objects in group three.

Answers will vary.

Page 246

How Many Wheels?

Cut out the pictures of the vehicles at the bottom of the page.

Paste the vehicles with no wheels in section 1.
Paste the vehicles with two wheels in section 2.
Paste the vehicles with three wheels in section 3.
Paste the vehicles with four wheels in section 4.
Paste the vehicles with more than four wheels in section 5.

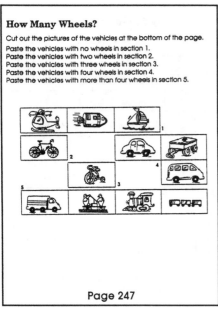

Page 247

Transportation Magic Square

1. Read Column A. Choose an answer from Column B. Write the number of the answer in the correct square. The first one has been done for you.

Column A	Column B
A. Filled with helium	1. jet plane
B. Runs on gasoline	2. rowboat
C. Powered by wind	3. sailboat
D. Burns coal or wood	4. steam locomotive
E. Runs on nuclear energy	5. blimp
F. Moves on snow or ice	6. submarine
G. Moves by pedals	7. wagon
H. Powered by oars	8. sled
I. Pulled by horses or oxen	9. bicycle
	10. car

A 5	B 10	C 3
D 4	E 6	F 8
G 9	H 2	I 7

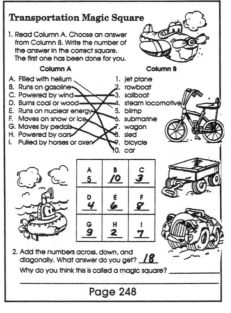

2. Add the numbers across, down, and diagonally. What answer do you get? 18

Why do you think this is called a magic square? _____

Page 248

Traveling to a Large City

1. Circle the correct answer. Then follow the directions.

A large truck used for moving furniture is called a:
a. dump truck - Mark out all letter M's below.
b. van - Mark out all letter C's below.
c. pickup truck - Mark out all letter F's below.

A large vehicle for transporting children to school is called a:
a. bus - Mark out all letter B's below.
b. yacht - Mark out all letter A's below.
c. jet - Mark out all letter F's below.

A vehicle pulled by horses or oxen is called a:
a. hot air balloon - Mark out all letter D's below.
b. tricycle - Mark out all letter O's below.
c. wagon - Mark out all letter P's below.

A long line of boxcars that runs on a track is called a:
a. submarine - Mark out all letter L's below.
b. train - Mark out all letter N's below.
c. bicycle - Mark out all letter R's below.

A vehicle that sails through water is called a:
a. ship - Mark out all letter E's below.
b. tank - Mark out all letter M's below.
c. sled - Mark out all letter A's below.

2. Start at the top. Write the name of the remaining letters in the spaces below.
I will travel to what city? Miami Florida

Page 249

By Land, by Sea, and by Air

Write the first letter of the names of the objects below. The letters form words.
Underline the word in red if it travels "By Land."
Underline the word in green if it travels "By Sea."
Underline the word in orange if it travels "By Air."

air H O T A I R

B A L L O O N

sea R A F T

land S U B W A Y

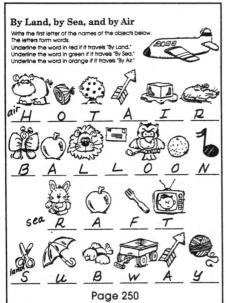

Page 250

Follow That Sign!

Look at the road sign symbols below. Each sign is matched to a letter. Use the road sign code to find the names of four vehicles that travel on roads.

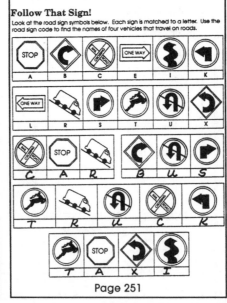

C A R

B U S

T R U C K

T A X I

Page 251

The Subway

Some big cities have a subway. A subway is a railroad that is under the ground. The trains carry people from one part of the city to another. The trains stop often to let people off and on. Many people ride to work on a subway. Others ride to school or to go shopping. Subways are nice because they do not take up space in a city.

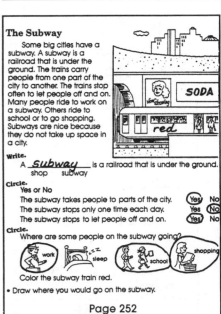

Write.
A __subway__ is a railroad that is under the ground.
    shop   subway

Circle.
Yes or No
The subway takes people to parts of the city.   **Yes**   No
The subway stops only one time each day.   Yes   **No**
The subway stops to let people off and on.   **Yes**   No

Circle.
Where are some people on the subway going?

work   sleep   school   shopping

Color the subway train red.

• Draw where you would go on the subway.

Page 252

A Helicopter

Would you like to ride in a helicopter? A helicopter flies in the air. It can fly up and **down**. It can fly forward and **backward**. It can fly **sideways**. A helicopter can even stay in one spot in the air! Helicopters can be many sizes. Some helicopters carry just one person. Some carry 30 people. Helicopters can be used for many jobs.

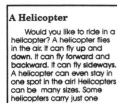

Crossword:
1 - sideways
2 - backward
3 - down
4 - up
5 - forward

Write.
A _helicopter_ flies in the air.
　trailer　　Helicopter

Write.
Which way can a helicopter fly? (Look at story.)

4→u _p_　3→d_own_　5→f _orward_
2→b _ackward_　1→s _ideways_

Write the answers in the puzzle above.

Circle.
Yes or No
A helicopter can stay in one spot in the air.　(Yes)　No
Helicopters come in many sizes.　(Yes)　No
All helicopters can carry 10 people.　Yes　(No)

• Draw a big green helicopter.

Page 253

Hot Air Balloons

Would you like to fly in a hot air balloon? A hot air balloon can fly when it is filled with hot air or a gas, called helium. Most hot air balloons use helium to fly. People can ride in a basket that is tied to the balloon. The wind moves the balloon in the sky. To come down, the people must let some of the air or gas out of the balloon.

Circle.
What does a hot air balloon need to fly?
(hot air)　music　(gas)

Write.
Most hot air balloons use _helium_ to fly.
　　helmets　helium

Circle.
What do people ride in?
　　cart　(basket)

Circle.
The (wind) ~~moon~~ moves the balloon in the sky.

Color.
1 - red　2 - purple　3 - green

• Draw a hot air balloon with two people in the basket.

Page 254

What's New?

Inventions help to make life easier. Various inventors from all around the world try to come up with ways to improve upon things presently used.

Below are pictures of inventions that have changed as inventors improved them. Number them in the correct order each version appeared by writing 1, 2, and 3 in the boxes.

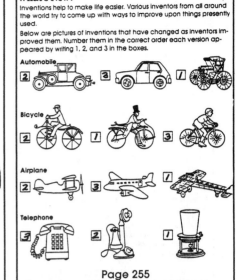

Automobile: 2　3　1
Bicycle: 2　1　3
Airplane: 2　3　1
Telephone: 3　2　1

Page 255

Selecting Supplies

Read each word in the Word Bank. If a word names a **need**, write it on the sack of flour. If a word names a **want**, write it on the pickle barrel.

Word Bank
videotape　milk　bracelet
kite　soda pop　bed　candy bar
soccer ball　home　backpack
vegetables　balloon　fruit
bread　coat　hat

Want
Videotape
bracelet
kite soda pop
candy bar
soccer ball
backpack
balloon

Need
milk　bed
home　vegetables
fruit　bread
coat　hat

Page 256

"Good Service" Delivery

Read each word. If it names an occupation that provides goods, mark **G** on the word. If it names an occupation that provides a service, mark **S** on the word. Then draw a line to show where three answers are the same in a row.

television salesperson	veterinarian	zookeeper
S	S	S
receptionist	pizza parlor owner	lawyer
S	G	S
crossing guard	school bus driver	kite manufacturer
S	S	G

actor	plumber	toy maker
S	S	G
firefighter	music store owner	principal
S	G	S
shoe salesperson	cook	babysitter
G	G	S

Page 257

Brought to You from . . .

Look at each picture. If the picture shows something that comes from a farm, mark **X** on the picture. If it shows something that comes from a factory, mark **O** on the picture. Then draw a line to show where three answers are the same in a row.

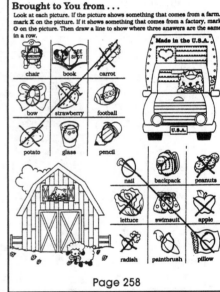

chair　book　carrot
bow　strawberry　football
potato　glass　pencil

nail　backpack　peanuts
lettuce　swimsuit　apple
radish　paintbrush　pillow

Page 258

"Time"-ly Toy Gifts

Use the time line to answer the questions.

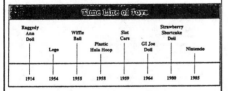

Time Line of Toy

Raggedy Ann Doll (1914)　Lego (1954)　Wiffle Ball (1955)　Plastic Hula Hoop (1958)　Slot Cars (1959)　GI Joe Doll (1964)　Strawberry Shortcake Doll (1980)　Nintendo (1985)

1. When was Nintendo first sold? _1985_
2. Could you play a game with a Wiffle Ball in 1940? _no_
3. What new toy was sold in 1964? _G.I. Joe Doll_
4. In what year were plastic Hula Hoops first sold? _1958_
5. How many years passed between the first Raggedy Ann Doll and the first GI Joe Doll? _50 years_
6. What toys were invented during the 1950s? _Lego, Wiffle Ball, Hula Hoop, Slot Cars_
7. How many toys on the time line were invented in the 1970s? _0_
8. Could you have played with a plastic Hula Hoop in 1960? _yes_
9. In what year was the Strawberry Shortcake Doll first sold? _1980_
10. What new toy was first sold in 1954? _Lego_

Page 259

It's Time to Eat

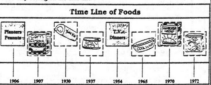

Cut out the pictures at the bottom of this page. Follow the clues to paste them where they belong on the time line.

Time Line of Foods

Planters Peanuts 1906　Corn Flakes 1907　Twinkies 1930　Spam 1937　T.V. Dinners 1954　1965　Cool Whip 1970　1972

1. You could begin to eat Corn Flakes for breakfast 1 year after you could munch on Planters Peanuts.
2. Twinkies were first sold 23 years after Corn Flakes and 7 years before Spam.
3. You could top your favorite piece of pie with Cool Whip 35 years after you first tasted Twinkies.
4. A quick dinner could be made with Hamburger Helper two years before one could be made with Tuna Helper.

Page 260

Build a Community

Cut out the pictures at the bottom of this page. Read the directions. Paste the pictures where they belong.

1. Place the **school** west of the house and **east** of the row of trees.
2. Place the **train** at the **southwest** edge of the railroad tracks.
3. Place the **Police Station** west of the Train Station and **east** of the train.
4. Place the **Grocery Store** east of the house and **south** of the rising sun.
5. Place the **Bank** north of the train.
6. Place the **Fire House** south of the Grocery Store and **east** of the Train Station.

Page 261

Just Being Neighborly

Go along with Percival Porcupine as he delivers the Welcome basket.

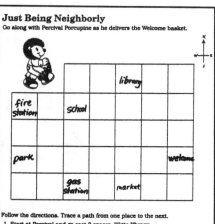

			library	
fire station	school			
				welcome
park				
	gas station	market		

Follow the directions. Trace a path from one place to the next.
1. Start at Percival and go east 3 spaces. Write library.
2. Then go south 4 spaces. Write market.
3. Next go west 2 spaces. Write gas station.
4. Now go north 3 spaces. Write school.
5. Go west 2 spaces. Write fire station.
6. Go south 2 spaces. Write park.
7. Go east 6 spaces. Write welcome.

Page 262

Find the Ring

Look at the map. Read each clue and write the correct word on the line. Then draw a line from one place to the next to show where each clue takes you.

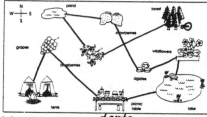

1. Begin where campers sleep. _tents_
2. Go north to a fruit that makes a purple-colored juice. _grapes_
3. Go southeast to a place where you can sit and eat. _picnic table_
4. Then go east where you can row a boat. _lake_
5. Turn north to the small plants with colored petals. _wildflowers_
6. Go southwest to find some special rocks. _agates_
7. Now go northwest to pick some sweet, red berries. _strawberries_
8. Go west to a place where you can swim. _pond_
9. Then go southeast and pick some round, blue-colored fruit. _blueberries_
10. At last, go northeast to a place where there are many trees. _forest_
11. Look closely to find the missing ring. Draw a circle around it.

Page 263

Follow the Map

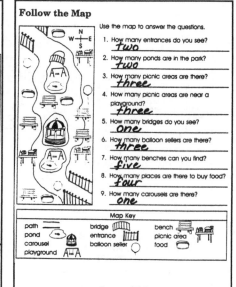

Use the map to answer the questions.
1. How many entrances do you see? _two_
2. How many ponds are in the park? _two_
3. How many picnic areas are there? _three_
4. How many picnic areas are near a playground? _three_
5. How many bridges do you see? _one_
6. How many balloon sellers are there? _three_
7. How many benches can you find? _five_
8. How many places are there to buy food? _four_
9. How many carousels are there? _one_

Map Key		
path	bridge	bench
pond	entrance	picnic area
carousel	balloon seller	food
playground		

Page 264

The Adventure Begins

One rainy Saturday morning, Patrick, Brenda, and Jamie decided they needed something new and exciting to do that morning. They took out the telephone book and turned to the yellow pages. In it they found these advertisements for special places to visit.

Aquarium	Museum of American History
Open weekdays from 10:00 a.m. to 6:00 p.m. Closed weekends. Call 123 - Fish	Open Monday – Saturday from 9:00 a.m. to 5:00 p.m. Closed Sundays. Call HIS-TORY
Planetarium	Zoo
Open Mon. – Friday 12:00 noon to 6:00 p.m. Saturday 3:00 p.m. to 9:00 p.m. Call 835 - TARS	Open daily from 9:00 a.m. to 5:00 p.m. Weather Permitting Call ANI - MALS

The children looked carefully at the ads. Which place did they choose to visit and why?

They chose to go to the _Museum of American History_ because _it is open Saturday morning._

Page 265

Home Sweet Home

At the Museum of American History, Patrick, Brenda, and Jamie saw large exhibits of Native Americans and their homes.
Use the rebuses below to discover the different types of houses various nations of Native Americans lived in. Your answers will sound right, but the spellings won't be right. Get the correct spellings from the Word Box.

 The _Chippewa_ Indians lived in domed bark lodges.

 The _Iroquois_ Indians lived in long houses.

 The _Sioux_ Indians lived in buffalo-hide tepees.

 The _Navajo_ Indians lived in hogans.

 The _Pueblo_ Indians lived in adobes.

Word Box		
Pueblo	Iroquois	Sioux
Navajo	Chippewa	

Page 266

Dinner Time

In the museum, the children saw a display on Eskimos. Eskimos get their name from a Native American word that means eaters of raw meat. Eskimos often ate their meat raw because they didn't have much wood or fuel for fires.

Each of the Eskimos below caught some fish for dinner. Read the clues. Then decide how many fish each person caught and write the number on the line under each one.

I caught twice as many fish as the person on the other end. _12_

I have 4 more fish than the person to the left. _16_

The number of fish I caught is an odd number between 7 and 10. _9_

I caught half as many fish as the 2nd person from the left. _8_

I caught 3 less fish than the person in the middle. _6_

Circle the fisherman who caught the most fish.
Draw boxes around the two whose fish added together equals 14.

Page 267

A Family of Friends

There was a great exhibit at the Museum of American History of figures of Native Americans and Pilgrims sharing the first Thanksgiving feast. When the Pilgrims came to Plymouth, Massachusetts, in 1620, they had a very difficult year. Native Americans helped the Pilgrims hunt and harvest food.

Read each riddle. Use the Word Box to write each food that the Native Americans helped the Pilgrims find or grow.

1. Water doesn't stick –
It rolls off my back;
And when it does,
I loudly say, "Quack, quack!"
I am _a duck_

2. I'm not inside a whale,
But I'm found in a "wheel."
You'll also find me
In a piece of "steel."
I am _an eel_

3. When your roof "leaks,"
You may want to cry.
You'll do the same thing
When I'm near your eye.
I am _a leek_

4. Boil me or pop me
When I am ripe.
Cook me in bread
Or use my cob as a pipe.
I am _corn_

5. I like to "honk,"
And I can fly.
Ask the lady who rode me,
Reciting rhymes in the sky.
I am _a goose_

Word Box		
a goose	a leek	a duck
corn	an eel	

Page 268

Then and Now

The museum had great examples of things the colonists used. Although their lives were different than ours today, many of their needs were the same.

Unscramble the names of objects we use today. (The first letter is underlined.) Then write the correct letter to match similar objects of the past and present.

Present		Past
a. celtreicl nkabelt _electric blanket_		_b._ candles
b. mapl _lamp_		_a._ bed warmer
c. satemhc _matches_		_e._ quill and ink well
d. ttpea _plate_	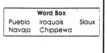	_d._ wooden trencher
e. eqn _pen_		_c._ tinder box

Page 269

Down on the Farm

At the museum the children learned that though the colonists worked very hard, they also took time for some fun. One favorite form of fun was corn-husking competitions.

In the cornfield below, Thomas picked and husked corn from the cornstalks that have circles around the numbers.
Jonathon picked and husked corn from the cornstalks that have squares around the numbers.
James did the same with the cornstalks that have triangles around the numbers.

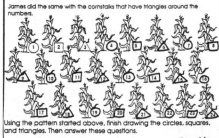

Using the pattern started above, finish drawing the circles, squares, and triangles. Then answer these questions.

1. Who picked and husked corn from cornstalk #20? _Jonathon_
2. Who picked and husked corn from cornstalk #22? _Thomas_
3. If all of the even-numbered cornstalks had two ears of corn, and all of the odd-numbered cornstalks had one ear of corn, how many ears of corn did each boy husk?
Thomas _12_ Jonathon _12_ James _12_

Page 270

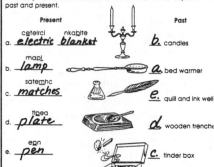

Sew What?

A favorite activity of colonial women and girls was getting together for a quilting bee. The quilts, made from scraps of linen, wool, and cotton, were frequently sewn together in a pattern.

Look carefully at the pattern in the unfinished quilt below. Then continue the pattern by drawing pictures in the blank sections to complete the quilt.

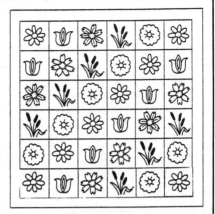

Page 271

Go West, Young Man!

From about 1760 to 1850, pioneers moved westward across the United States. They traveled in big covered wagons called **Conestoga** wagons.

Some of the trails that the pioneers took in their Conestoga wagons are marked on the map below.

Look closely at the trails. Then answer the questions.

1. If the pioneers started at Nauvoo and traveled **west**, how many different trails could they take? __5__
2. If the pioneers began at Independence and traveled **west**, how many choices of trails would they have? __9__

Page 272

A Man of Peace

A large picture of the Lincoln Memorial was on display at the museum. Abraham Lincoln was our 16th president. Shortly after he became President in 1861, America's Civil War began between the people living in the South and the people living in the North.

Abraham Lincoln made a famous speech in which he said that all people are created equal. He wanted all people in our country to live together in peace.

Look carefully at the tall columns around the outside of the building. If you walked around the whole building, how many columns would you pass? __36__

Page 273

What's Your Brand?

The Museum of American History had a great display on cowboys who lived from the 1860's to the 1880's. These cowboys went on cattle drives for two to three months at a time and sometimes traveled 1,000 miles! They were often in danger from rattlesnakes, quicksand, cattle stampedes, and wild horses.

During cattle roundups in the spring and fall, cowboys branded the newborn calves to show what ranch they belonged to.

Look at the brands below. Use the Word Box to write what each brand meant.

Pair of Aces · Too Easy · Big Deal
Twin Snakes · Barbecue · Sunrise
Rocking Chair · Double Z · Extra X
Starlight · Sunset · Tall Hat
Lazy S · Broken Wheel · Two Bees

Word Box				
Twin Snakes	Double Z	Pair of Aces	Sunrise	Too Easy
Rocking Chair	Extra X	Big Deal	Sunset	Barbecue
Broken Wheel	Lazy S	Starlight	Tall Hat	Two Bees

Page 274

News Flash!

One large room in the museum had pages from calendars on its walls, listing events from America's past. Pretend that you were a newspaper reporter in the year 1888. You wrote a story about each event on the day it happened, as shown on the calendar below.

October – 1888

Sunday	Monday	Tuesday	Wednesday	Thursday	Friday	Saturday
	1	2	3	4	5	6
7	8	9 National Monument to George Washington opened	10	11	12	13
14	15	16	17	18 First school for agriculture set up in Minnesota	19	20 American baseball teams go on world tour
21	22	23	24	25 Double-decker ferryboat launched in New York	26	27
28	29	30 J.J. Loud develops ballpoint pen in Plymouth, Mass.	31			

Here are headlines for your newspaper stories. Write the date each story was written.

"Piggyback Ride Across River" __October 25__
"A Hit 'Round The World" __October 20__
"First President Honored" __October 9__
"New Invention Makes Mark" __October 30__
"Learning to Farm Is Fun" __October 18__

Page 275

Help Wanted

America has often been called a "Land of Opportunity." Its people may choose from many types of careers.

Use the Word Box to write two different careers that have the following characteristics in common. *Answers may vary.*

1. Place importance on books	teacher	librarian
2. Consider water an important tool	farmer gardener	fireman
3. Work with needle and thread	seamstress	tailor
4. Work with food	chef	gardener farmer
5. Make sure people follow rules	police	umpire
6. Deliver mail and packages	delivery person	mail carrier
7. Takes care of medical needs	veterinarian	doctor farmer
8. Work with animals	veterinarian	zookeeper
9. Use numbers quite often	mathematician	accountant
10. Provide entertainment	musician	actor

Word Box			
mathematician	veterinarian	teacher	chef
actor	police officer	nurse	doctor
accountant	mail carrier	seamstress	gardener
musician	fireman	librarian	tailor
delivery person	farmer	umpire	zookeeper

Page 276

Geography Magic Square

Read column A and choose an answer from column B. Write the number of the answer in the correct magic square. The first one has been done for you.

Column A
A. Large areas of water
B. A flat area of land that is higher than the land around it
C. One of the seven areas of land on Earth
D. A hot, wetland area of thick trees, plants and animals
E. A sun-dried clay brick used for building
F. A piece of land with water on three sides
G. A cone-shaped mountain made of ash and melted rock
H. A hot, dry area of land covered with sand
I. A group of mountains

Column B
1. peninsula
2. volcano
3. plateau
4. desert
5. continent
6. rain forest
7. ocean
8. adobe
9. range

A 7	B 3	C 5
D 6	**E** 8	**F** 1
G 2	**H** 4	**I** 9

Add the numbers across and down. What answer do you get? __15__

Page 277

Landform Riddles

Use the Word Bank to solve the riddles. Then color the pictures.

Word Bank					
lake	island	plain	river	mountain	peninsula

I have water on three sides. I am a **peninsula**

I have water all around me. I am an **island**

I am wet and have land all around me. I am a **lake**

I am long and narrow and flow through the land. I am a **river**

I am raised land, larger than a hill. I am a **mountain**

I am low and flat. I am a **plain**

Page 278

Seeking the Sights

Read each clue. Use the map to locate the matching state. Write the abbreviation on the line.

1. The Space and Rocket Center is in the state south of Tennessee, **east of** Mississippi and **west of** Georgia. __AL__
2. Buffalo Bill's home is in the state **west of** Iowa and **south of** South Dakota. __NE__
3. Elephant Rock is in the state **southeast of** Oregon and **west of** Utah. __NV__
4. Casey Jones Railroad Museum is in the state **north of** Alabama and **south of** Kentucky. __TN__
5. Fossil National Monument is in the state **east of** Idaho and **south of** Montana. __WY__
6. The Corn Palace is in the state **southeast of** Montana and **northwest of** Iowa. __SD__
7. A life-size model of one of Columbus' ships, the *Santa Maria*, is in the state **west of** Pennsylvania and **east of** Indiana. __OH__
8. Gillette Castle is in the state **east of** New York and **south of** Massachusetts. __CT__

Page 279

The Seven Continents

Pretend you are a pilot. Your job is to land on each continent for a top-secret mission. You must learn what each continent looks like.

Write the name of each continent below its picture. Use the word bank below.

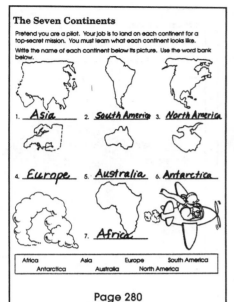

1. Asia 2. South America 3. North America

4. Europe 5. Australia 6. Antarctica

7. Africa

Africa	Asia	Europe	South America
Antarctica	Australia	North America	

Page 280

Animals Around the World

Color the animals and the continents.

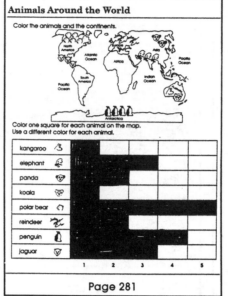

Color one square for each animal on the map.
Use a different color for each animal.

	1	2	3	4	5
kangaroo					
elephant					
panda					
koala					
polar bear					
reindeer					
penguin					
jaguar					

Page 281

The Largest Continent

Asia is the world's largest continent. It stretches for thousands of miles. More than half of all the people in the world live in Asia. Asia contains the large area that was once called the Soviet Union. China, the country with the most people living in it, is also located in Asia. India, another country in Asia, has the world's highest mountains, the Himalayas. These mountains are so high that the snow never melts. Have you ever seen a panda or an elephant? These and many other animals live in Asia.

Follow the directions below.

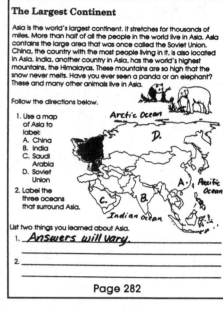

1. Use a map of Asia to label:
   A. China
   B. India
   C. Saudi Arabia
   D. Soviet Union

2. Label the three oceans that surround Asia.

List two things you learned about Asia.

1. Answers will vary.

2. _____

Page 282

Geography Crossword

Read each clue. Find an answer in the Word Bank. Write the words in the puzzle. Be sure to cross out the words you use in the Word Bank.

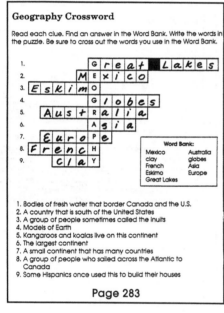

1. Great Lakes
2. Mexico
3. Eskimo
4. Globes
5. Australia
6. Asia
7. Europe
8. French
9. clay

Word Bank:
Mexico   Australia
clay   globes
French   Asia
Eskimo   Europe
Great Lakes

1. Bodies of fresh water that border Canada and the U.S.
2. A country that is south of the United States
3. A group of people sometimes called the Inuits
4. Models of Earth
5. Kangaroos and koalas live on this continent
6. The largest continent
7. A small continent that has many countries
8. A group of people who sailed across the Atlantic to Canada
9. Some Hispanics once used this to build their houses

Page 283

Speaking Strine

Australians, like Americans, have their own "language" called Strine. An Aussie might say something like this, "I'm going to take my swag and tucker down to the billabong while my jumbucks are resting." That sounds like a foreign language!

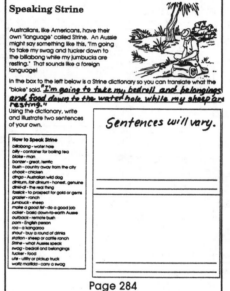

In the box to the left below is a Strine dictionary so you can translate what the "bloke" said. "I'm going to take my bedroll and belongings and food down to the water hole while my sheep are resting."

Using the dictionary, write and illustrate two sentences of your own.

Sentences will vary.

How to Speak Strine
billabong - water hole
billy - container for boiling tea
bloke - man
bonzer - great, terrific
bush - country away from the city
chook - chicken
dingo - Australian wild dog
dinkum, fair dinkum - honest, genuine
dinki-di - the real thing
fossick - to prospect for gold or gems
grazier - ranch
jumbuck - sheep
make a good fist - do a good job
ocker - basic down-to-earth Aussie
outback - remote bush
pom - English person
roo - a kangaroo
shout - buy a round of drinks
station - sheep or cattle ranch
Strine - what Aussies speak
swag - bedroll and belongings
tucker - food
ute - utility or pickup truck
waltz matilda - carry a swag

Page 284

Happy New Year!

In China, the most celebrated holiday is the New Year. The Lantern Festival is part of the celebration. That is when Chinese people welcome the first full moon of the year. The Chinese New Year is fixed according to the lunar calendar. It occurs somewhere between January 30 and February 20. Each Chinese year is represented by one of 12 animals.

Look at the chart below to see what animal represents the year you were born.

RAT	OX	TIGER	HARE (RABBIT)	DRAGON	SNAKE	HORSE	RAM	MONKEY	ROOSTER	DOG	PIG
1900	1901	1902	1903	1904	1905	1906	1907	1908	1909	1910	1911
1912	1913	1914	1915	1916	1917	1918	1919	1920	1921	1922	1923
1924	1925	1926	1927	1928	1929	1930	1931	1932	1933	1934	1935
1936	1937	1938	1939	1940	1941	1942	1943	1944	1945	1946	1947
1948	1949	1950	1951	1952	1953	1954	1955	1956	1957	1958	1959
1960	1961	1962	1963	1964	1965	1966	1967	1968	1969	1970	1971
1972	1973	1974	1975	1976	1977	1978	1979	1980	1981	1982	1983
1984	1985	1986	1987	1988	1989	1990	1991	1992	1993	1994	1995
1996	1997	1998	1999	2000	2001	2002	2003	2004	2005	2006	2007
2008	2009	2010	2011	2012	2013	2014	2015	2016	2017	2018	2019

The Festival of the Lanterns is celebrated on the third day of the New Year. Make a colorful lantern to hang in your classroom.

1. Fold a bright-colored piece of construction paper vertically.

2. Cut strips from the folded side stopping 2" from the open edge.

3. Open, bend in circle, and staple.

4. Cut out a long paper strip and staple to make a handle.

Page 285

The "Boot"

From America, Italy is across the Atlantic Ocean. It is part of a continent called Europe. Most of Italy is shaped like a boot. It also has two islands named Sicily and Sardinia. Its "boot," or mainland, extends into the Mediterranean Sea. The shape of the mainland is called a peninsula because it has water around three of its sides. Rome is Italy's capital and largest city. It has been an important city for more than 2,500 years. Italy got its name from the Romans who called its southern part Italia, meaning "land of oxen" or "grazing land."

Color Italy green.
Color the Mediterranean Sea blue.
Use the map to unscramble the names of some Italian cities below it.

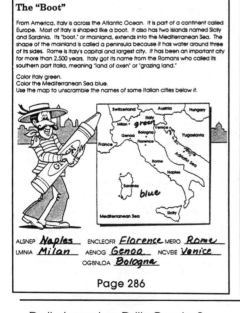

ALSNEP Naples   ENCLEOFR Florence   MERO Rome
LMNIA Milan   AENOG Genoa   NCVEIE Venice
OGBNLOA Bologna

Page 286

The American Alphabet

The United States attracts people from all over the world. We are sometimes called a nation of immigrants.

Write the alphabet in order in the boxes. Then use the Word Box and the letter in each box to write the name of each country where it belongs.

Answers for 5 and 18 may be transposed.

1. India
2. Mozambique
3. China
4. Ireland
5. France
6. Afghanistan
7. Egypt
8. Netherlands
9. Israel
10. Japan
11. Korea
12. Philippines
13. Germany
14. Canada
15. Poland
16. Puerto Rico
17. Iraq
18. Greece
19. Australia
20. Italy
21. Cuba
22. Vietnam
23. Norway
24. Mexico
25. Kenya
26. Venezuela

Word Box
Afghanistan
Australia
Canada
China
Cuba
Egypt
France
Germany
Greece
India
Iraq
Ireland
Israel
Italy
Japan
Kenya
Korea
Mexico
Mozambique
Netherlands
Norway
Philippines
Poland
Puerto Rico
Venezuela
Vietnam

Page 287

A Capital Idea

This is what Tommy's suitcase might have looked like after visiting the eight countries on his adventure. Color and cut out the travel stickers below. Paste them on the suitcase so each capital matches its country.

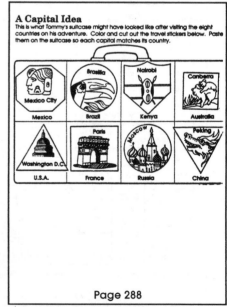

| Mexico City — Mexico | Brasília — Brazil | Nairobi — Kenya | Canberra — Australia |
| Washington D.C. — U.S.A. | Paris — France | Moscow — Russia | Peking — China |

Page 288

Name _____

Word Challenge

Write a word that matches each description below.

_____

Has one letter

_____

Has two letters

_____

Has three letters

_____

Has four letters

_____

Has five letters

_____

Has six letters

_____

Has seven letters

_____

Has eight letters

_____

Has nine letters

_____

Name _____

A Guest List

Lee is planning a party. Write the names of her guests in alphabetical order.

| Charles | Dina | Helen | Alan | Dale | Anna | Brent |

1. _____

2. _____

3. _____

4. _____

5. _____

6. _____

7. _____

Name _____

"Plane" and Simple

Help the airplane get through the clouds by following the words in ABC order.

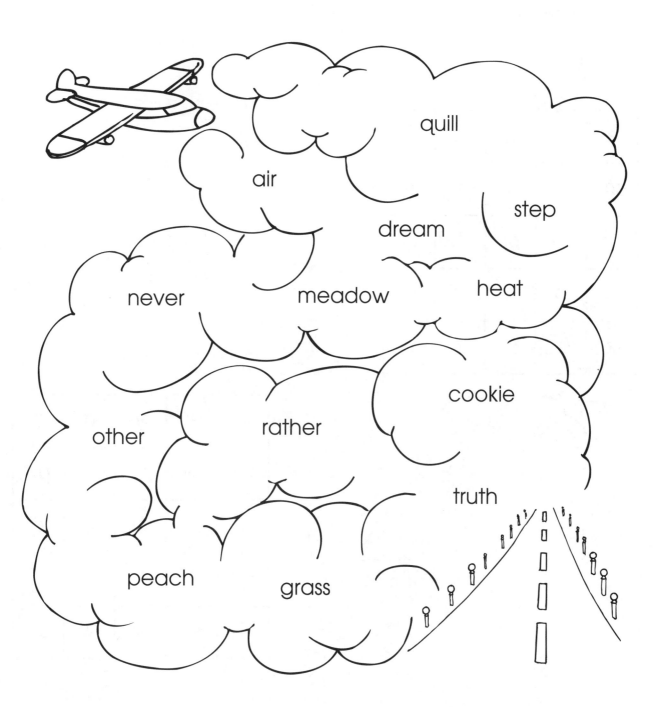

Name _____

Feed the Birds

Help each bird reach the food. Look at the letter(s) in each box. If it (or they) can be used with the two letters shown to make a word, shade the box. When you are done, the shaded boxes will make paths for the birds.

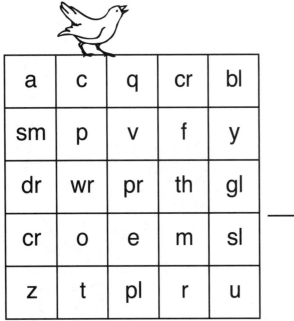

a	c	q	cr	bl
sm	p	v	f	y
dr	wr	pr	th	gl
cr	o	e	m	sl
z	t	pl	r	u

_____an

_____ed

th	r	y	d	a
wr	w	b	v	ph
i	sm	sl	tr	e
qu	f	fl	cr	il
l	sh	st	sn	sc

Name _____

Compound Hunt

What kind of soap does a skunk use to wash its hair?

Add a word from the Word Bank to each word listed below. The new word will be a compound word. Write the added word in the boxes. The answer to the riddle will be spelled in the **bold** boxes going down.

Word Bank

print	weed
snake	house
horse	mat

rattle | | | | | |

sea | | | | | |

| | a | | |

door | | | | |

finger | | | | | |

light | | | | | |

| | e | | |

sea | | | | |

It uses _____ !

Name _____

On the Farm

Help the farmer find his tractor. Follow only the compound words.

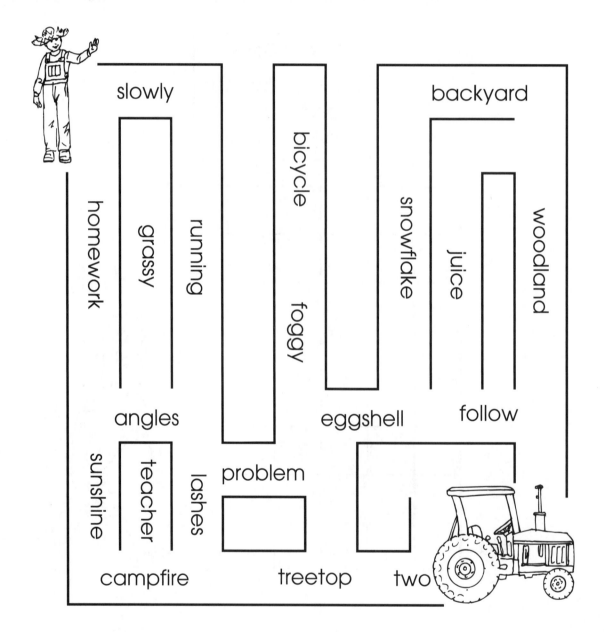

slowly

backyard

bicycle

homework   grassy   running

snowflake   juice   woodland

foggy

angles

eggshell   follow

sunshine   teacher   lashes   problem

campfire   treetop   two

Name _____

Word Circus

Read the compound words below. Then circle the two small words that make up each compound. Write the two small words on the lines. The first one is done for you.

1. (broom)(stick)   __broom__   __stick__

2. tablecloth _____   _____

3. sunshine _____   _____

4. dishpan _____   _____

5. classroom _____   _____

6. bookcase _____   _____

7. treetop _____   _____

8. playground _____   _____

9. highway _____   _____

10. suntan _____   _____

11. campfire _____   _____

12. birthday _____   _____

13. bedroom _____   _____

14. newspaper _____   _____

    Daily Learning Drills Grade 2

Name _____

Same or Different?

Read the words in each line. With a red crayon, circle the words with the same meaning.

1.	happy	soft	glad
2.	big	small	huge
3.	smiling	sick	ill
4.	evening	night	sun
5.	chore	job	chart

Read the words in each line. With a blue crayon, circle the words with opposite meanings.

6.	hot	long	cold
7.	tall	silly	short
8.	big	quiet	noisy
9.	dark	light	black
10.	merry	sad	happy

Read the words in each line. Write **S** on the line if the words have the same meaning. Write **D** on the line if the words have different meanings.

11.	give	take	_____
12.	little	tiny	_____
13.	high	low	_____
14.	ladies	women	_____
15.	push	hug	_____

Name _____

Opposite Fun

Write the opposite for each word.

1. hot _____

2. open _____

3. in _____

4. up _____

5. over _____

6. big _____

7. on _____

8. good _____

9. sad _____

10. thick _____

Name _____

Oops!

Why was the broom late?

To find out, write the past tense for each verb listed. Use the Word Bank to help you. The answer to the riddle will be spelled in the **bold** boxes going down.

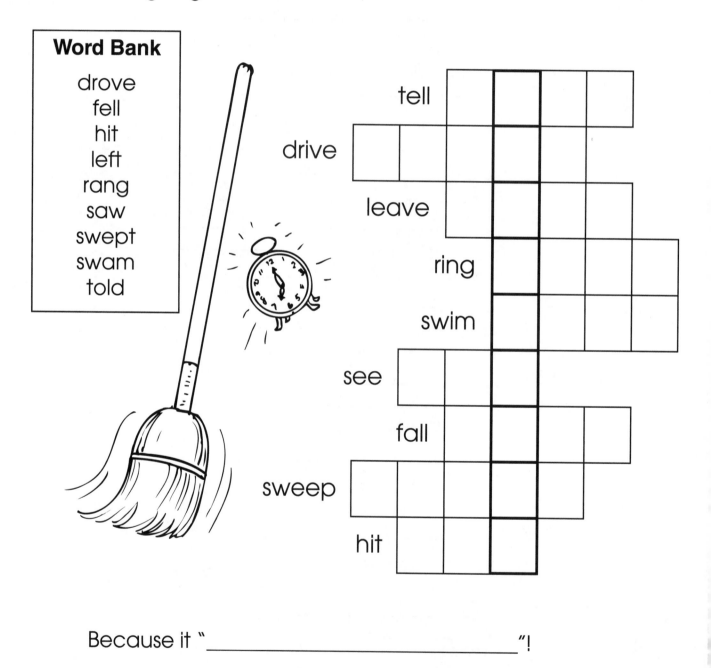

Word Bank

drove
fell
hit
left
rang
saw
swept
swam
told

tell

drive

leave

ring

swim

see

fall

sweep

hit

Because it "_____"!

Name _____

Just Do It!

Unscramble the verbs (action words). Use the Word Bank to help you. Then circle the words in the puzzle. They may go across, down, or diagonally.

glauh _____   **thosu** _____

danst _____   **klaw** _____

nikrd _____   **kolo** _____

slenti _____   **blidu** _____

Word Bank
build
stand
look
walk
laugh
shout
drink
listen

```
D  F  Z  L  A  U  G  H
B  R  P  K  W  T  S  L
S  U  I  Q  F  H  T  I
K  H  I  N  M  L  A  S
T  V  O  L  K  O  N  T
K  V  L  U  D  O  D  E
W  A  L  K  T  K  N  N
```

Name _____

Word Detective

Look carefully at the picture on this page. In the first column, list ten **nouns** you see in the picture. In the second column, write the first **adjective** you think of that describes the noun. The first one is done for you. When you are finished, color the picture.

NOUNS	ADJECTIVES
1. lion	strong
2.	
3.	
4.	
5.	
6.	
7.	
8.	
9.	
10.	

ZOO

Name _____

Crazy About Contractions

Pairs of words combined into one with an apostrophe are called **contractions**. Read the lists of words below. Combine them to make contractions and complete the puzzle. Example: did not = didn't.

Across

2. they had
4. would not
5. you are
6. he is
7. I have
8. should have
9. could not

Down

1. will not
3. do not
4. we are
5. you have
6. have not
7. it is

Daily Learning Drills Grade 2

Name _____

Straight A's

All of the words below have the long **a** sound, but it is spelled differently each time. Write the words from the Word Bank in the spaces. Then circle the words in the puzzle. They may go across, down, or backward.

Word Bank

weigh

game

obey

maid

maybe

gray

paper

great

Name _____

Road to Reading

Read the word at the top of each road. Change just one letter to make a new word beneath it. You should end up with the word at the bottom after all of the changes. Use the words from the Word Bank to help you.

Word Bank

coat	colt
camp	rule
role	lamp
came	mule

cold

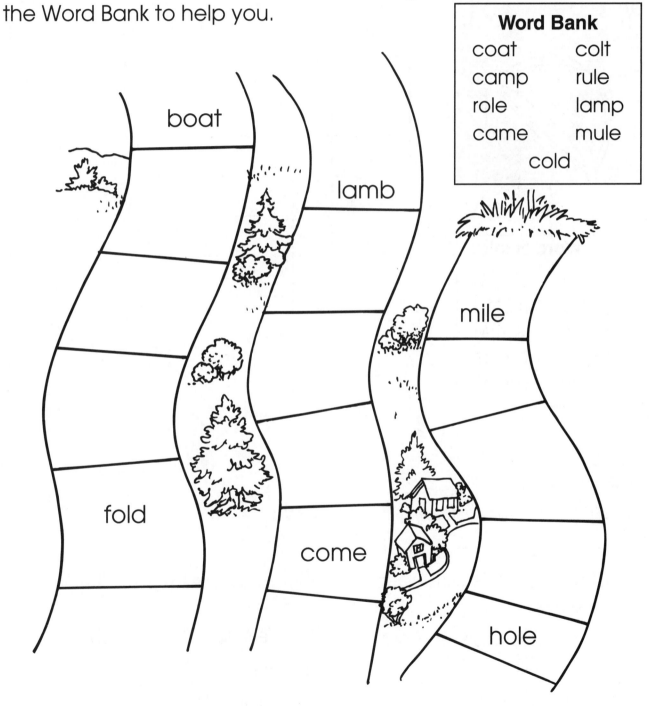

boat

lamb

mile

fold

come

hole

Name _____

Homonym Hunt

Homonyms are words that sound alike but are spelled and used differently. Read the list of homonyms in the Word Bank. Use them to answer the clues and complete the puzzle.

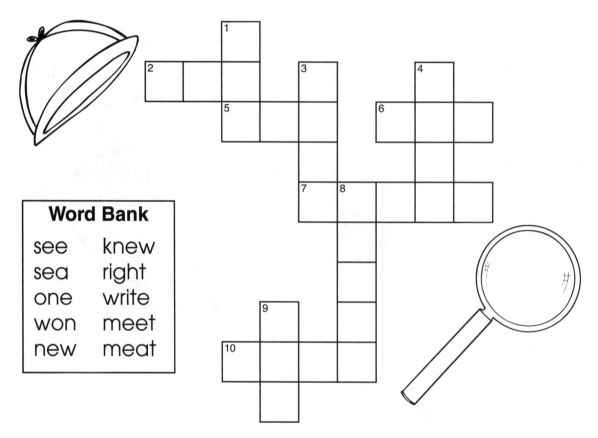

Word Bank

see	knew
sea	right
one	write
won	meet
new	meat

Across

2. _____, two, three
5. We _____ the game!
6. You do this with your eyes.
7. You do this with your pencil.
10. People eat this.

Down

1. Not old
3. I _____ you would like this.
4. We will _____ at 8:00.
8. Not left
9. Smaller than an ocean

Name _____

Color Hunt

Unscramble the color words. Use the Word Bank to help you. Then circle the words in the puzzle. They may go across or down.

ergen _____   **clkab** _____

elub _____   **prelup** _____

wornb _____   **lewloy** _____

dre _____   **theiw** _____

grenao _____   **kinp** _____

Word Bank
purple
white
pink
orange
brown
green
blue
black
red
yellow

```
R  O  R  A  N  G  E  Y
B  Q  G  R  E  E  N  E
L  T  P  R  W  R  B  L
A  W  H  I  T  E  L  L
C  P  I  N  K  D  U  O
K  P  U  R  P  L  E  W
V  Z  N  B  R  O  W  N
```

Name _____

Raindrops Are Falling

Write the missing numbers on each raindrop path.

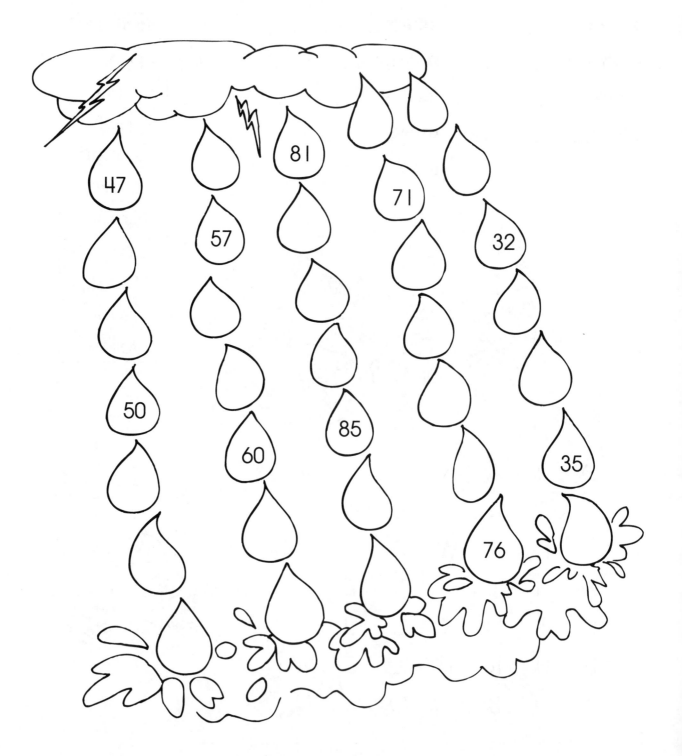

Name _____

This or That

Use the code to find the value of each pair of opposite words.
Circle the word in each pair with the higher value.

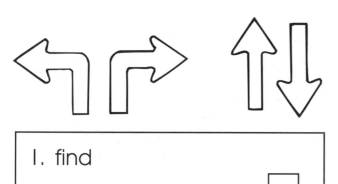

1. find	
__ + __ + __ + __ =	☐
lose	
__ + __ + __ + __ =	☐

2. fast	
__ + __ + __ + __ =	☐
slow	
__ + __ + __ + __ =	☐

3. rise	
__ + __ + __ + __ =	☐
fall	
__ + __ + __ + __ =	☐

A	1	N	4
B	2	O	5
C	3	P	1
D	4	Q	2
E	5	R	3
F	1	S	4
G	2	T	5
H	3	U	1
I	4	V	2
J	5	W	3
K	1	X	4
L	2	Y	5
M	3	Z	1

MATH REVIEW

Name _____

To the Top!

Use mental math to find the sums, working from left to right. Move the hikers up the mountain by shading a footprint for each answer. Circle the hiker who reaches the top first.

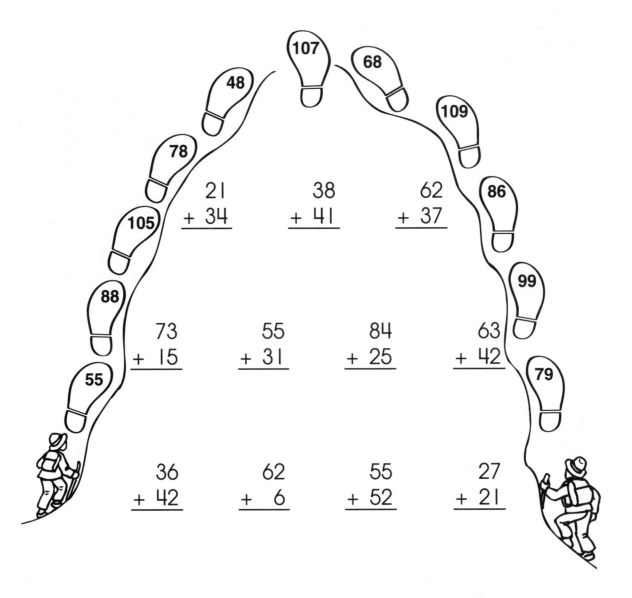

21 + 34	38 + 41	62 + 37

73 + 15	55 + 31	84 + 25	63 + 42

36 + 42	62 + 6	55 + 52	27 + 21

Fun Fact!

How high is Mount Everest in meters? Add these numbers to find out: 2,401 + 6,447 = _____ meters

Tic-Tac-Toe Addition

Solve each problem below. Then find the answer on the board and mark the box **X** or **O** as shown. Work the problems in order. Who will win, **X** or **O**? The first to get three in a row is the winner!

1. 22
   + 45

   O

2. 31
   + 34

   X

87	89	65
49	58	67
59	84	75

3. 21
   + 28

   O

4. 46
   + 12

   X

5. 46
   + 13

   O

6. 31
   + 56

   X

7. 63
   + 12

   O

8. 21
   + 68

   X

Just for Fun!

Move the numbers on the board to make the other team win.

MATH REVIEW

Name _____

Family Feud

Who will win? Find each sum working from left to right. Shade the answer in the grid on the right. The first family to completely cover their card is the winner!

81	76
49	35
74	91
98	79

```
   11        36        90
+ 24      + 33      +  8


   25        87        36
+ 51      + 12      +  3


   29        28        80
+ 50      + 21      + 11


   36        55        16
+ 11      + 31      + 13


   62        43        41
+ 35      + 31      + 15
```

69	56
47	97
99	29
86	39

Name _____

Buy Bean Bag Babies

Use the prices of the toy animals to write and solve each problem.

Anna bought a [image] and a [image]. How much did she spend in all?

Nick had 92¢. He bought a [image]. How much did he have left?

Stephen had 84¢. He bought a [image]. How much did he have left?

Rosie bought a [image] and a [image]. How much more did the [image] cost?

Mitch bought two [image]. How much did he spend in all?

Lily bought a [image] and a [image]. How much more did the [image] cost?

Name _____

Down the Slope!

Find the differences. The number in the snowflakes will answer the question.

Mount McKinley is the tallest mountain in North America. How high is it?

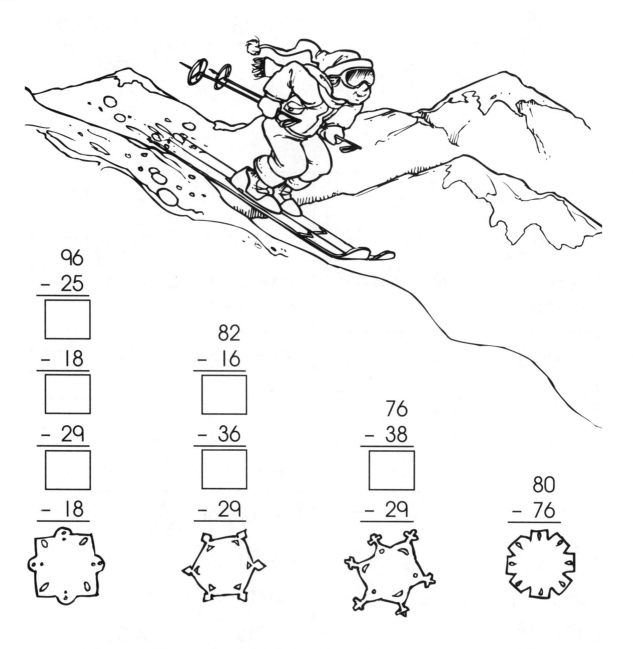

```
   96
 - 25
 [    ]

 - 18
 [    ]

 - 29
 [    ]

 - 18
```

```
   82
 - 16
 [    ]

 - 36
 [    ]

 - 29
```

```
   76
 - 38
 [    ]

 - 29
```

```
   80
 - 76
```

Mount McKinley is ___, ___ ___ ___ meters high!

Name _____

The Great Race

Use mental math to find the differences. Move the joggers along the path by shading in each answer you find. Circle the jogger that finishes the race first.

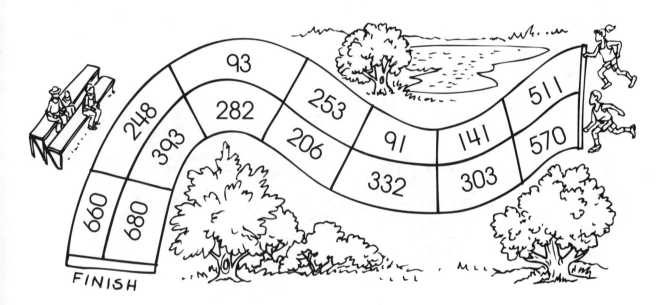

1. $\begin{array}{r} 641 \\ -\ 130 \\ \hline \end{array}$

2. $\begin{array}{r} 830 \\ -\ 260 \\ \hline \end{array}$

3. $\begin{array}{r} 324 \\ -\ 183 \\ \hline \end{array}$

4. $\begin{array}{r} 281 \\ -\ 190 \\ \hline \end{array}$

5. $\begin{array}{r} 630 \\ -\ 327 \\ \hline \end{array}$

6. $\begin{array}{r} 756 \\ -\ 424 \\ \hline \end{array}$

7. $\begin{array}{r} 945 \\ -\ 739 \\ \hline \end{array}$

8. $\begin{array}{r} 555 \\ -\ 273 \\ \hline \end{array}$

9. $\begin{array}{r} 684 \\ -\ 291 \\ \hline \end{array}$

10. $\begin{array}{r} 978 \\ -\ 725 \\ \hline \end{array}$

11. $\begin{array}{r} 374 \\ -\ 281 \\ \hline \end{array}$

12. $\begin{array}{r} 851 \\ -\ 171 \\ \hline \end{array}$

Name _____

Which Vegetable Is It?

Use the clues to answer each riddle.

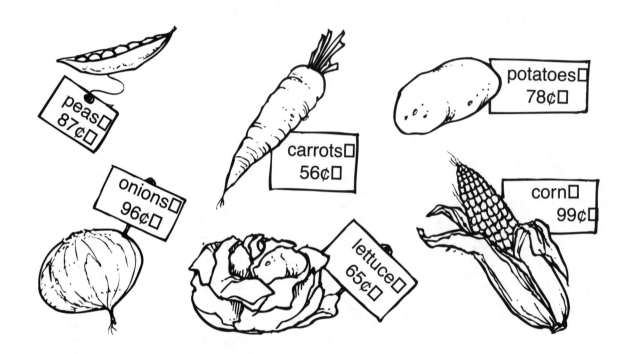

1. We cost 70¢ and 8¢. What are we? _____

2. We cost 8 tens and 7 ones. What are we? _____

3. We cost between 55¢ and 57¢. What are we? _____

4. We cost 90¢ and 6¢. What are we? _____

5. Our price is the highest two-digit number.

   What are we? _____

6. We cost 5 ones and 6 tens. What are we? _____

Name _____

Batter Up!

Rename each number by regrouping. Take from the tens place and give to the ones place as shown.

36 = 3 tens and 6 ones = __2__ tens and __16__ ones

72 = 7 tens and 2 ones = _____ tens and _____ ones

50 = 5 tens and 0 ones = _____ tens and _____ ones

23 = 2 tens and 3 ones = _____ tens and _____ ones

85 = 8 tens and 5 ones = _____ tens and _____ ones

90 = 9 tens and 0 ones = _____ tens and _____ ones

64 = 6 tens and 4 ones = _____ tens and _____ ones

MATH REVIEW

Name _____

Go Bananas!

Write <, >, or = on each tree trunk. Circle the banana with the greater number.

| < less than | > greater than | = equal to |

Name _____

Add It Up

Find the sums. Write >, <, or = in the circles to compare the sums.

221 + 425	◯ 416 + 572	344 + 523	◯ 243 + 444
671 + 304	◯ 465 + 524	206 + 133	◯ 347 + 212
417 + 341	◯ 634 + 124	142 + 153	◯ 141 + 148
281 + 612	◯ 386 + 312	623 + 311	◯ 502 + 432

Name _____

What Time Is It?

Look at each clock. Then write the time shown on the line. The first one is done for you.

1. ___8:30___   2. _____   3. _____

4. _____   5. _____   6. _____

7. _____   8. _____   9. _____

10. _____   11. _____   12. _____

Name _____

A Day at Camp

Write the time at which each camper finished his or her activity.

Harry rode a horse for 40 minutes. He started at 6:00.

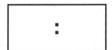

Sue swam for 20 minutes. She started at 2:00.

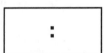

Renee climbed rocks for 30 minutes. She started at 1:15.

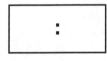

Hannah hiked for 15 minutes. She started at 7:30.

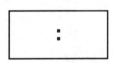

Freddy fished for 50 minutes. He started at 11:10.

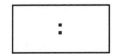

The Barry twins played ball for 25 minutes. They started at 12:00.

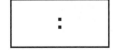

MATH REVIEW

Name _____

You Can Bank on It!

Read the words on the coins. To fill the piggy bank, find the words and circle them. They may go across, diagonally, or down.

money bank

quarter dime

dollar savings

earn count

nickel penny

coins cents

Q U A M S B R I D P L
T U D S O A M B S E C
A S A V I N G S P N O
B A S R O K E C E A I
A C E N T S I Y N T N
L O T L R E H S N O S
N I C K E L R D Y R Q
P F K E N Q U I L D U
D O L L A R Q V E I E
O M G A M R S G J M D
P E R C O U N T O E R

Name _____

The Souvenir Shop

Count the coins to find the cost of each souvenir. Write the price on the tag.

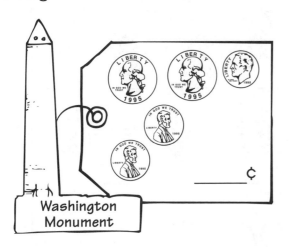

Washington Monument

_____ ¢

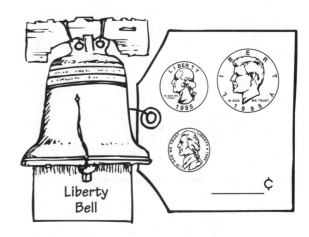

Liberty Bell

_____ ¢

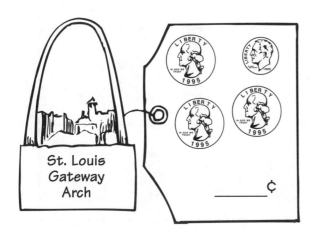

St. Louis Gateway Arch

_____ ¢

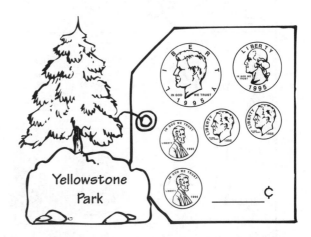

Yellowstone Park

_____ ¢

Niagara Falls

_____ ¢

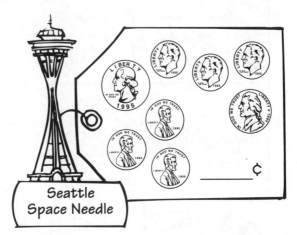

Seattle Space Needle

_____ ¢

MATH REVIEW

Name _____

Shopping for Souvenirs

Color the coins needed to make exact change for each item.

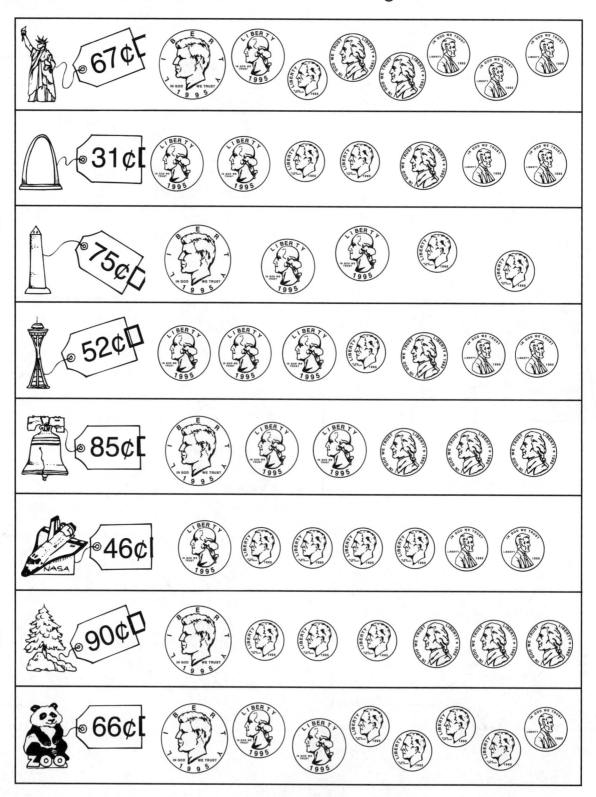

Name _____

Under the Sea

Count the money. Write the number of hundreds (h), tens (t), and ones (o). Write the three-digit number, using the dollar sign ($) and decimal point (.).

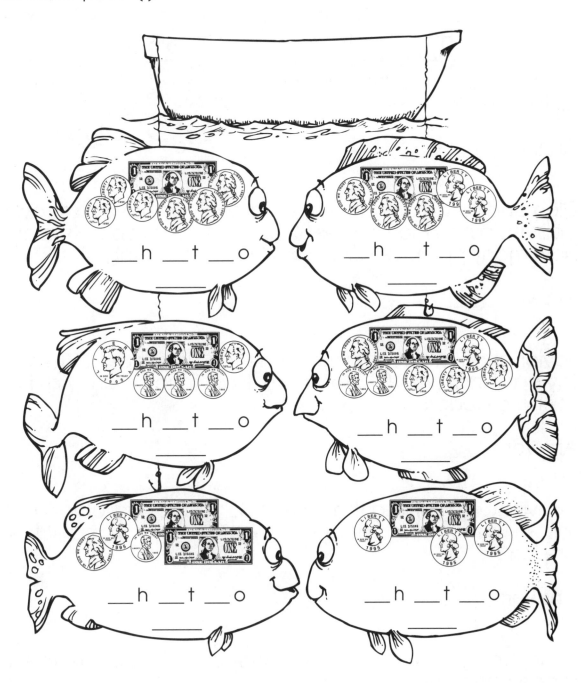

MATH REVIEW

Name _____

A Day at the Fair

Read each word problem carefully. Then add or subtract to find the answer. Show your work.

1. A clown gave away 50 balloons on Tuesday. He gave away 25 balloons on Wednesday. How many balloons did he give away all together?

    Answer: _____

2. Ellen and David are playing a game. They have to throw a ball into a net. Ellen scores 52 points. David scores 37 points. How many points did Ellen and David score together?

    Answer: _____

3. Javier and Tim bought toys at the fair. Javier paid $1.75 for a toy car. Tim paid $1.10 for a ball. How much money did they spend all together?

    Answer: _____

4. On Monday morning there were 85 tickets available for the fair. Then the ticket agent sold 34 of them. How many tickets are left?

    Answer: _____

5. Joan brought $4.50 to the fair. She spent $1.25. How much money does she have left?

    Answer: _____

Space Invasion

Measure the length of the path from each spaceship to Earth. Write the length in centimeters (cm) on each line.

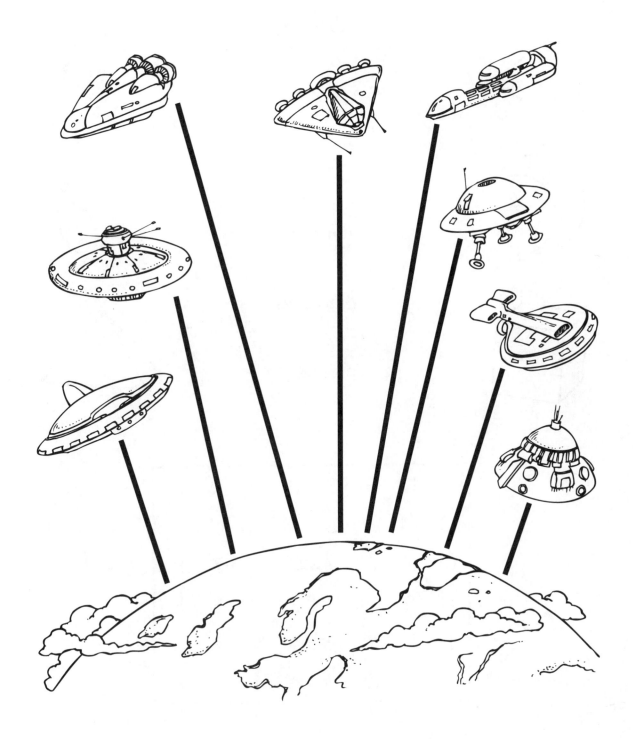

MATH REVIEW

Name _____

Shapes Are Everywhere

Draw a line to connect each shape with its name. Then circle the words in the puzzle. They may go across, down, or backward.

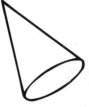

sphere

cone

cube

pyramid

diamond

crescent

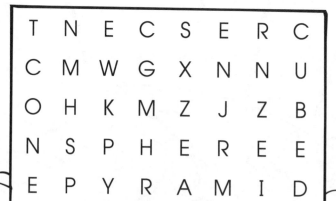

T	N	E	C	S	E	R	C
C	M	W	G	X	N	N	U
O	H	K	M	Z	J	Z	B
N	S	P	H	E	R	E	E
E	P	Y	R	A	M	I	D
D	N	O	M	A	I	D	F

Name _____

Shape Puzzles

Use the code to find the names of the shapes.

a = 1	
b = 2	
c = 3	
d = 4	
e = 5	
f = 6	
g = 7	
h = 8	
i = 9	
j = 10	
k = 11	
l = 12	
m = 13	
n = 14	
o = 15	
p = 16	
q = 17	
r = 18	
s = 19	
t = 20	
u = 21	
v = 22	
w = 23	
x = 24	
y = 25	
z = 26	

1. _____
   19   17   21   1   18   5

2. _____
   3   9   18   3   12   5

3. _____
   20   18   9   1   14   7   12   5

4. _____
   18   5   3   20   1   14   7   12   5

5. _____
   15   22   1   12

6. _____
   16   5   14   20   1   7   15   14

7. _____
   8   5   24   1   7   15   14

8. _____
   15   3   20   1   7   15   14

Daily Learning Drills Grade 2

Name _____

Fun With Fractions

Each object is divided into equal parts. Write a fraction that tells what part of each object is shaded.

Example: 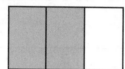 = $\frac{2}{3}$

1.

2.

3.

4.

5.

6.

7.

8.

Name _____

The Lost Treasure

Find the lost treasures. Write the letter and then the number as shown.

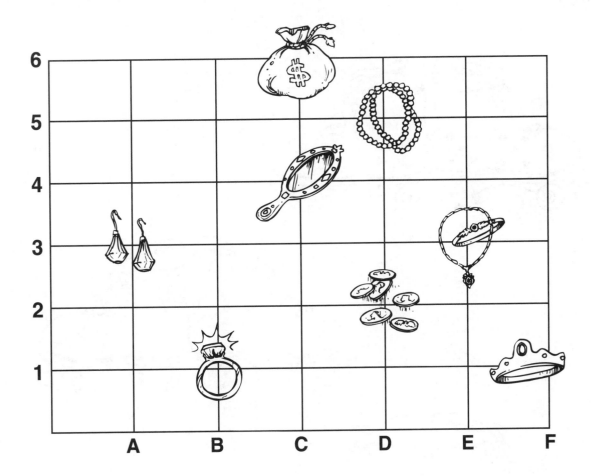

1. 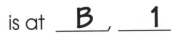 is at __B__ , __1__   5. 🦻 are at ____ , ____

2. 📿 is at ____ , ____   6. 🪙 are at ____ , ____

3. 🪐 are at ____ , ____   7. 🪞 is at ____ , ____

4. 💰 is at ____ , ____   8. 👑 is at ____ , ____

MATH REVIEW

Name _____

Roller Skates

Write a multiplication problem to match each picture. Then find the product.

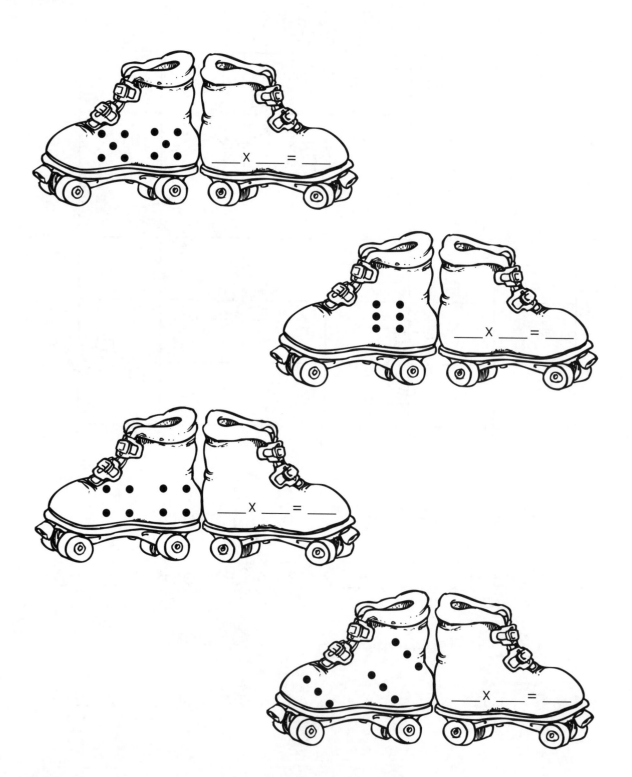

____ X ____ = ____

____ X ____ = ____

____ X ____ = ____

____ X ____ = ____

Shape Up!

Multiply to find the answers. Circle the shapes with even products.

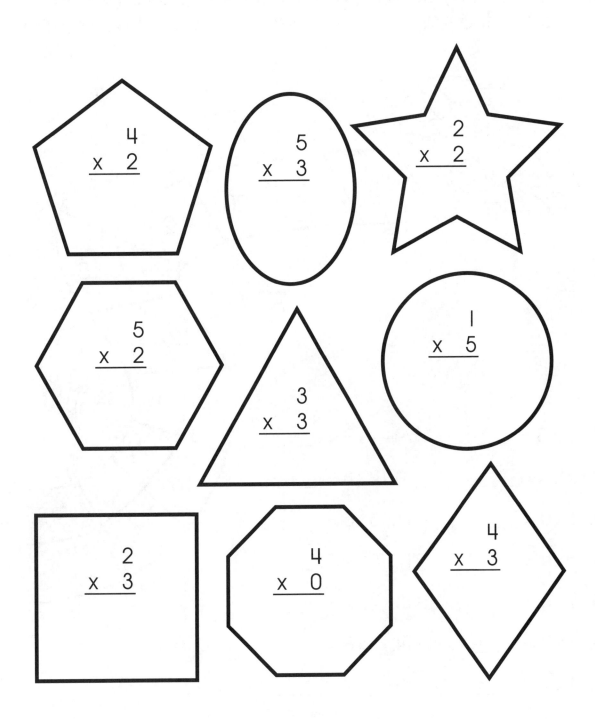

Name _____

The Race Is On!

Use mental math to find each product. Move the race cars along the track by coloring a box for each answer. Circle the car that reaches the finish line first. Be sure to complete the problems in order!

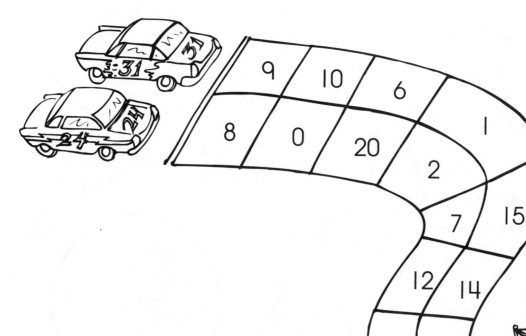

1. 3 x 3 = _____

2. 2 x 4 = _____

3. 6 x 0 = _____

4. 5 x 4 = _____

5. 2 x 5 = _____

6. 3 x 2 = _____

7. 1 x 1 = _____

8. 1 x 2 = _____

9. 1 x 7 = _____

10. 4 x 3 = _____

11. 3 x 5 = _____

12. 5 x 1 = _____

13. 7 x 2 = _____

14. 2 x 8 = _____

15. 2 x 2 = _____

16. 3 x 1 = _____

Name _____

My Body

Draw a line from each word to where it is on the body. Then circle the words in the puzzle. They may go across or down.

head   neck

chest   elbow

waist   knee

ankle   heel

T	T	E	H	E	A	D	K
N	A	L	N	E	C	K	H
F	N	B	N	R	H	R	E
K	K	O	K	N	E	E	E
Y	L	W	A	I	S	T	L
Z	E	L	D	Y	T	Q	F

Daily Learning Drills Grade 2

SCIENCE REVIEW

Name _____

A Delicious Dinner

Pretend that you get to plan a healthful dinner for your family.
Write the menu, choosing items from the lists.

Meats	**Vegetables**	**Side Dishes**
barbecue chicken	steamed broccoli	brown rice
hamburgers	creamed corn	mashed potatoes
grilled pork chops	buttered peas	baked beans

Name _____

Fruity Fun

Find and circle eight fruits in the puzzle. Write them below. Use the pictures to help you.

a	b	a	n	a	n	a	c	h	p
p	n	r	g	r	a	p	e	s	e
l	e	m	o	n	u	p	g	m	a
u	t	p	e	a	r	l	e	o	c
m	o	r	a	n	g	e	m	a	h

1. _____

2. _____

3. _____

4. _____

5. _____

6. _____

7. _____

8. _____

Name _____

Frog in Winter

Winter is coming. A little tree frog rests on a leaf in the sun. It has been hunting for food. Soon the weather will be too cold for the frog to stay warm. It will have to find cover. It may lie under some dead leaves or in a hole in a tree. There, it will go into a deep sleep. The little frog will not move until spring. The frog will breathe through its skin. When the sun melts the snow and wakes up the plants, the little tree frog will wake up, too. Color the frog.

Name _____

Frog in Winter

Use facts from the story to fill in the puzzle. The Word Bank will help you.

Word Bank

warm

move

spring

frog

breathes

winter

leaves

SCIENCE REVIEW

Across

1. A tree frog sleeps all _____.
2. The frog does not _____.
5. The frog _____ through its skin.
6. It wakes up in the _____.

Down

1. The frog must find a place to stay _____.
3. It may sleep under dead _____.
4. A little tree _____.

Name _____

We're Different

Find and circle the animal names from the Word Bank in the puzzle.
They may go across, diagonally, or down. Then group the animals.

Word Bank
frog
flounder
wasp
catfish
salamander
dragonfly
toad
beetle
cod
butterfly
perch
trout

S	C	J	A	C	P	E	R	C	H
B	A	I	T	O	A	D	N	T	K
U	T	L	H	D	W	R	J	E	F
T	F	G	A	E	F	A	A	W	L
T	I	R	F	M	D	G	S	T	O
E	S	C	O	I	A	O	V	P	U
R	H	D	Q	G	B	N	P	A	N
F	D	R	C	H	N	F	D	U	D
L	G	B	E	E	T	L	E	E	E
Y	T	R	O	U	T	Y	T	B	R

Insects

1.

2.

3.

4.

Amphibians

1.

2.

3.

Fish

1.

2.

3.

4.

5.

Name _____

What Am I?

Use the animals shown to answer the riddles below.

cow

anhinga

lion

toucan

alligator

iguana

I can be found in Africa. I have one to four babies at a time. I am a mammal with a mane. What am I? _____	I can be found in the Americas. I lay eggs. I am a reptile with stripes. What am I? _____
I can be found in South America. I lay eggs. I am a bird with a large, colorful beak. What am I? _____	I can be found in the United States. I lay 20–60 eggs at a time. I am a reptile with a long body. What am I? _____

Name _____

The Great Rain Forest

The picture shows the rain forest and some of the animals that live there. Find the eight words from the Word Bank in the puzzle. They may go across, down, diagonally, or backward.

Y	J	C	A	N	O	P	Y
F	C	A	V	C	Q	U	B
G	F	I	G	U	A	N	A
O	M	O	G	U	W	D	B
E	T	V	R	H	A	E	N
G	O	R	F	E	E	R	T
T	T	B	J	Q	S	S	M
N	N	A	C	U	O	T	Q
T	J	L	P	N	X	O	K
S	K	W	J	I	Z	R	Z
H	K	T	Q	J	R	Y	T

Word Bank

canopy

understory

forest

tapir

toucan

jaguar

iguana

tree frog

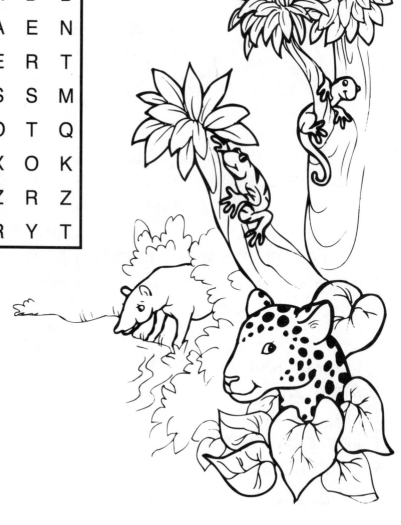

Name _____

Compare and Contrast

Look at the pictures. Write what is different and what is the same about the camels.

Dromedary camel   **Bactrian camel**

What is the same?

_____

_____

_____

What is different?

_____

_____

_____

_____

Name Maxwell

Giving Trees

Read the words in the Word Bank below. These things all come from trees! Circle these words in the puzzle. They may go across or down.

Word Bank

syrup	lumber	medicine
fruit	furniture	shelter
nuts	paper	rubber

P S H E L T E R F
A R U B B E R L R
P K N U T S L U U
E S Y R U P W M I
R N N M M V J B T
M E D I C I N E D
F U R N I T U R E

Name _____

A Funny Baby
Connect the dots.

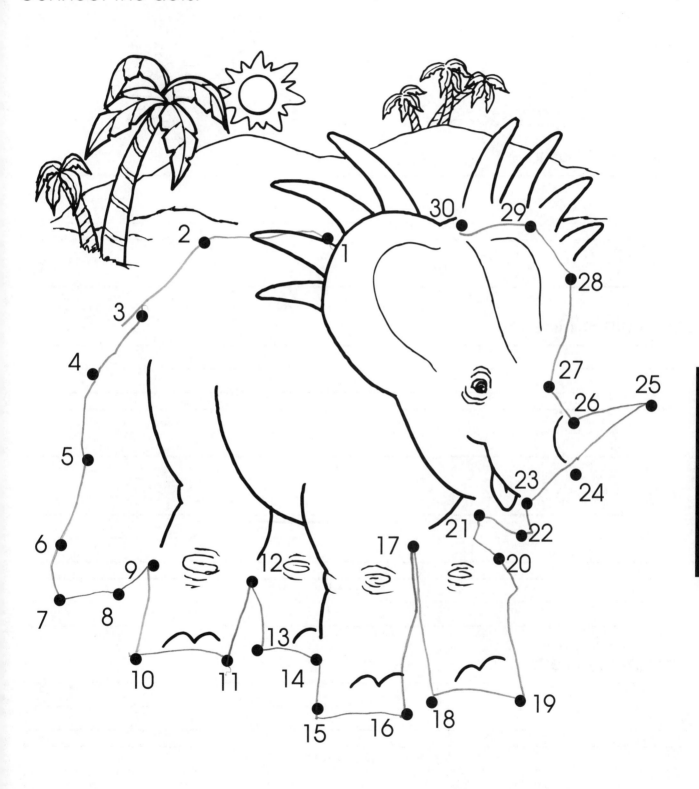

Daily Learning Drills Grade 2

SCIENCE REVIEW

Name _____

Seasonal Fun

Complete the sentences in your best handwriting.

In spring, I like to

_____

_____

_____

_____

In summer, I like to

_____

_____

_____

_____

In fall, I like to

_____

_____

_____

_____

In winter, I like to

_____

_____

_____

_____

Name _____

Wacky Weather

Unscramble the weather words. Use the Word Bank to help you. Then circle the words in the puzzle. They may go across, down, or backward.

nynus _____   **ducloy** _____

mostry _____   **inayr** _____

gogyf _____   **dinyw** _____

wosny _____   **zeyerb** _____

M	Q	T	Y	N	I	A	R	C
B	S	U	N	N	Y	J	K	L
R	T	Q	S	N	O	W	Y	O
E	O	W	I	N	D	Y	Y	U
E	R	C	B	K	J	F	T	D
Z	M	J	N	Z	F	B	M	Y
Y	Y	P	C	Y	G	G	O	F

Word Bank	
windy	foggy
cloudy	stormy
sunny	snowy
breezy	rainy

Name _____

Ounces or Pounds

Ounces are used to measure the weight of very light objects. Pounds are used to measure the weight of heavy objects. Look at each picture. Then decide if you would use ounces or pounds to measure the weight of each object. Circle your answer.

1.

ounces   pounds

2.

ounces   pounds

3.

ounces   pounds

4.

ounces   pounds

5.

ounces   pounds

6.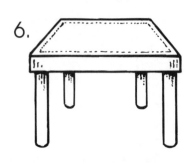

ounces   pounds

7.

ounces   pounds

8.

ounces   pounds

9.

ounces   pounds

Name _____

Dew

What is dew? Read the story below. Then find and circle the **bold** words in the puzzle. They may go across, diagonally, or down.

Have you ever felt **grass** early in the **morning**? It feels very **wet**. The water isn't rain. It's **dew**!

When the sun rises in the morning, it warms the **air**. Some of the **water** in the **warm** air **evaporates**. It changes into a gas. These "floating" water **molecules** fall to the **cool** grass. The warm molecules land on the grass and become a **liquid** again. This is called **condensation**.

R	S	A	C	O	N	W	M	O	L	G	T	M
C	O	N	D	E	N	S	A	T	I	O	N	O
A	W	L	E	S	B	O	G	R	T	G	S	L
L	A	D	W	G	A	I	R	R	M	R	W	E
I	T	R	T	C	X	W	E	T	B	A	A	C
Q	E	V	A	P	O	R	A	T	E	S	L	U
U	R	M	O	R	S	O	D	X	R	S	B	L
I	U	L	J	G	C	H	L	D	C	F	N	E
D	S	M	O	R	N	I	N	G	E	S	R	S

Name _____

Gravity: The Force Is with You

Before you drop the pairs of objects, predict which of each pair will reach the ground first. Drop the two objects at the same time from a height of 5 feet (1.5 m). Record the result after each drop.

Objects	Prediction	Result
pencil and piece of chalk		
piece of chalk and chalkboard eraser		
pencil and empty cup		
tissue box and textbook		
textbook and basketball		
encyclopedia and thick rubberband		

Name _____

Super Solar System

The names of the planets are listed below in their order from the sun. Rewrite the names in alphabetical order.

1. Mercury	2. Venus	3. Earth
4. Mars	5. Jupiter	6. Saturn
7. Uranus	8. Neptune	9. Pluto

1. Earth

2. _____

3. _____

4. _____

5. _____

6. _____

7. _____

8. _____

9. _____

Name _____

Space Case

Unscramble the planet names. Then circle the names of the planets in the puzzle. They may go across, down, diagonally, or backward.

IPtuo _____   **tahEr** _____

rnUasu _____   **arSutn** _____

esnVu _____   **uipJtre** _____

euMrrcy _____   **asrM** _____

uentNpe _____

V	J	U	P	I	T	E	R	I
N	E	U	S	R	A	M	T	H
E	E	N	R	P	L	U	T	O
P	A	A	U	A	S	A	R	I
T	R	N	G	S	N	A	Q	O
U	T	M	E	R	C	U	R	Y
N	H	U	N	C	W	T	S	R
E	N	R	U	T	A	S	T	Y

Name _____

Happy Holidays

Holidays are fun, special days. Write about three of your favorite holidays. Write why you like each one.

_____

1. I like _____

_____

because _____

_____

_____

_____

2. I like _____

_____

because _____

_____

_____

_____

3. I like _____

_____

because _____

_____

_____

_____

Name _____

One Big Family

Draw a line from each family member name to its matching picture. Then circle the names in the puzzle. They may go across or down.

mother	father	grandpa	grandma
sister	brother	baby	puppy

Name _____

You're Invited

Fill in the missing information on the party invitation.

Let's celebrate _____ 's birthday!

Please join us on _____
(day)

_____
(month, date, year)

Please be here at _____ o'clock,

R.S.V.P. _____. See you soon!
(phone number)

SOCIAL STUDIES REVIEW

Name _____

Story Puzzle

Look carefully at the pictures below. They tell a story. Then read the sentences. Each sentence tells about one picture. Put the sentences in order by writing the correct picture number on each line. Then color the pictures.

_____ José falls asleep after a busy day.

_____ José opens his birthday presents.

_____ José's parents get ready for his birthday party.

_____ José plays with his toys after the party.

_____ José wakes up on his birthday.

_____ José sees all his friends at his party.

1

2

3

4

5

6

Name _____

Fabulous Friends

Friends are the greatest! The words below describe a good friend. Circle them in the puzzle. They may go across, down, diagonally, or backward.

smart	funny	gentle	nice
helpful	honest	polite	kind

```
H  G  S  H  W  Q  J  P
K  O  E  L  P  C  N  O
M  I  N  N  Z  R  I  L
R  J  N  E  T  N  C  I
V  M  T  D  S  L  E  T
F  U  N  N  Y  T  E  E
L  U  F  P  L  E  H  F
K  S  M  A  R  T  R  K
```

Daily Learning Drills Grade 2

SOCIAL STUDIES REVIEW

Name _____

Best Friends

Lilly and Meg had been best friends since they were both in Miss Brown's class. They spent many days planting seeds, jumping rope, and painting pictures together.

But even best friends play without each other sometimes. Lilly loved to play soccer while Meg played on the monkey bars. On rainy days, Lilly liked to read books, and Meg liked to count money. Some days, Lilly rushed to karate class while Meg hurried home for piano lessons. Together or alone, the girls were still best friends.

Name _____

Best Friends

Write two sentences to describe Lilly and two to describe Meg. In the center area, write two sentences that describe both girls.

L
I
L
L
Y

1. _____
_____

2. _____
_____

1. _____
_____

2. _____
_____

1. _____
_____

2. _____
_____

M
E
G

With which girl do you have more in common? _____

What do you have in common with her? _____

_____

_____

_____

SOCIAL STUDIES REVIEW

Name _____

Graphing Fun

What are friends as good as? Read the graph. Find out which letter each number in the coded message stands for.

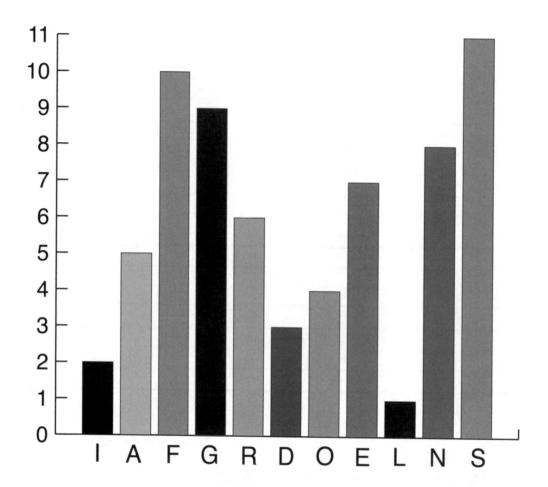

F   ___ ___ ___ ___ ___ ___ ___   ___ ___ ___   ___ ___
10 6   2   7   8   3   11   5   6   7   5   11

___ ___ ___ ___   ___ ___   ___ ___ ___ ___ !
9   4   4   3   5   11   9   4   1   3

Name _____

Dandy Directions

Look at the map and key. Name the object found in each direction from the compass rose.

Map Key

forest

fountain

lake

bridge

village

river

tower

castle

1. north _____

2. south _____

3. west _____

4. east _____

5. northwest _____

6. southeast _____

7. southwest _____

8. northeast _____

SOCIAL STUDIES REVIEW

Name _____

A Busy Day

What a day! Max and Gina spent the day cleaning up their park. They began by picking up the trash. Then they painted the park benches. Last, they planted new trees. What a change they made!

Name _____

A Busy Day

Read each sentence. If the sentence tells about something you learned in the story, color the picture by it. Then go back to the previous page and color the same object on that page.

Max and Gina planted trees.

Gina helped pick up trash.

They played on the swings.

They painted the benches.

Max helped clean the park.

They planted flowers.

Max and Gina are brother and sister.

SOCIAL STUDIES REVIEW

Name _____

A Long Race

Every year, sled drivers meet in Alaska to race their teams of dogs. The race is over one thousand miles long. It lasts for more than a week. The drivers and dogs face dangers on the trail. Sometimes there are snowstorms, wild animals, and deep snow.

The trail has been there for many years. Long ago, it was used to carry goods to people working in the gold mines. Later, a terrible sickness broke out. Many people were saved when medicine was carried to them over the trail. Now, every March, the same trail is used for the big race.

Name _____

A Long Race

Read each sentence. Color the sled red if it is true. Color the sled blue if it is not true.

Sometimes there are dangers in the race.

The race lasts for a day and a half.

The trail was built for the railroad.

The big race is in June.

Long ago, the trail led to gold mines.

The race covers more than a thousand miles.

SOCIAL STUDIES REVIEW

Name _____

Whose House?

Use the pictures of the Native American houses to answer the riddles.

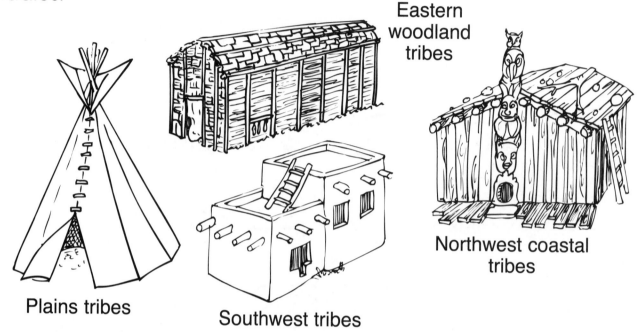

Eastern
woodland
tribes

Northwest coastal
tribes

Plains tribes

Southwest tribes

This house has no beds. Many families live in it. It is made of adobe brick. It has no doors, only windows. Whose house is it? _____	This is called a plank house. Many families live in it. It is made of large beams and trees. It has a totem pole in front. Whose house is it? _____
This is called a long house. It has bunk beds. It is made of branches and bark. Fire burns in the center of it. Whose house is it? _____	This house can be set up in 10 minutes. One family lives in it. It is made of poles and animal skins. A fire burns inside. Whose house is it? _____

Name _____

Picture Clues

Look carefully at each picture. Write who the person is in the picture. Then write clues from the picture that helped you figure it out. Finally, write a sentence describing what is happening in the picture.

1. Person: _____

   Clues: _____

   Description: _____

2. Person: _____

   Clues: _____

   Description: _____

        Daily Learning Drills Grade 2

Name _____

A Great State

Write the answers.

1. In what state do you live?

   _____
   -
   _____

2. What is your state's capital?

   _____
   -
   _____

3. In what city do you live?

   _____
   -
   _____

4. Why is your city nice?

   _____
   -
   _____
   -
   _____
   -
   _____

THANK YOU FOR VISITING OUR GREAT STATE!

Name _____

A Special Trip

Draw a picture of a special trip you took, then write about it.

SOCIAL STUDIES REVIEW

Name _____

Buffalo Bill

Have you ever heard of Buffalo Bill? His real name was William Frederick Cody. Buffalo Bill was born in 1846. When he was fourteen years old, he became a rider for the Pony Express. He helped carry mail across the American West. Later, he worked as an army scout.

Some railroad men hired Buffalo Bill to hunt for buffalo. They needed buffalo meat to feed the workers who were laying railroad tracks through Kansas. Buffalo Bill Cody got his name for his skill at hunting buffalo.

Name _____

Buffalo Bill

Use facts from the story to fill in the puzzle.
The Word Bank will help you.

Word Bank

buffalo
Kansas
Pony
railroad
Cody
Bill

Across

2. These animals were hunted.

4. Men built a _____ through Kansas.

5. William Frederick _____ was Buffalo Bill's real name.

Down

1. The railroad workers in _____ needed food.

2. Cody became known as Buffalo _____ .

3. When he was young, Buffalo Bill worked as a _____ Express rider.

SOCIAL STUDIES REVIEW

Daily Learning Drills Grade 2

Name _____

Hawaii

Hawaii was the last state to become part of the United States. It is the 50th state. Hawaii is made up of eight large islands and many small islands. The islands are mountains that were made long ago under the ocean. Some mountains in Hawaii still shoot out steam and melted rock. Sugar cane and pineapples grow in Hawaii. People in Hawaii enjoy warm weather and colorful flowers.

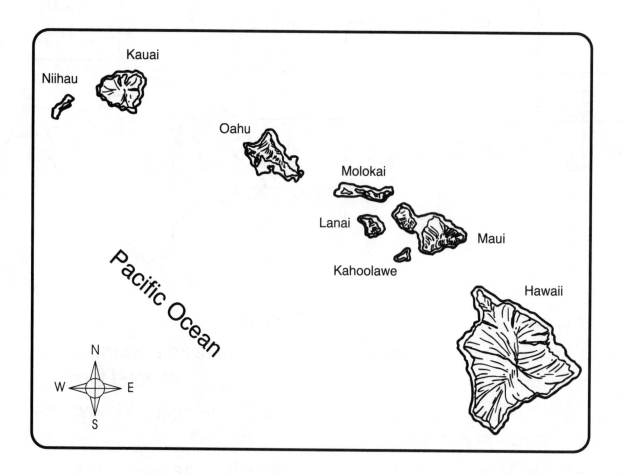

Name _____

Hawaii

Use facts from the story to fill in the crossword puzzle. The Word Bank will help you.

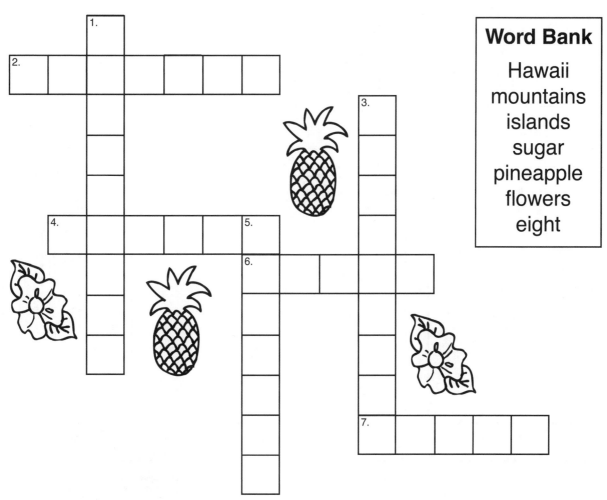

Word Bank

Hawaii
mountains
islands
sugar
pineapple
flowers
eight

Across

2. Colorful _____ grow in Hawaii.

4. The 50th state

6. _____ cane grows on the islands.

7. Hawaii has _____ large islands.

Down

1. The islands are _____.

3. _____ grows in Hawaii.

5. Hawaii is made up of many _____.

Review Answer Key

Word Challenge
Write a word that matches each description below.

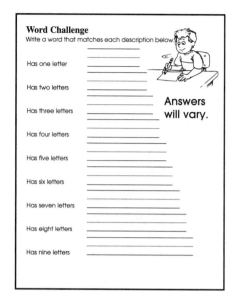

Has one letter _____

Has two letters _____

Has three letters _____

Has four letters _____

Has five letters _____

Has six letters _____

Has seven letters _____

Has eight letters _____

Has nine letters _____

Answers will vary.

321

A Guest List
Lee is planning a party. Write the names of her guests in alphabetical order.

| Charles | Dina | Helen | Alan | Dale | Anna | Brent |

1. Alan
2. Anna
3. Brent
4. Charles
5. Dale
6. Dina
7. Helen

322

"Plane" and Simple
Help the airplane get through the clouds by following the words in ABC order.

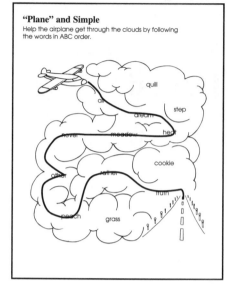

323

Feed the Birds
Help each bird reach the food. Look at the letter(s) in each box. If it (or they) can be used with the two letters shown to make a word, shade the box. When you are done, the shaded boxes will make paths for the birds.

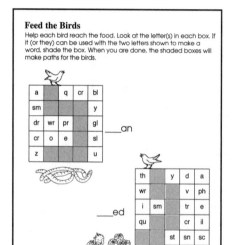

a	q	cr	bl
sm			y
dr	wr	pr	gl
cr	o	e	sl
z			u

___an

th		y	d	a
wr			v	ph
i	sm		tr	e
qu			cr	il
		st	sn	sc

___ed

324

Compound Hunt
What kind of soap does a skunk use to wash its hair?

Add a word from the box to each word listed below. The new word will be a compound word. Write the added word in the boxes. The answer to the riddle will be spelled in the **bold** boxes going down.

Word Box
print   weed
snake   house
horse   mat

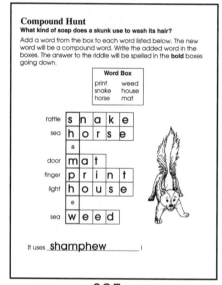

rattle | s n a k e
sea | h o r s e
| a
door | m a t
finger | p r i n t
light | h o u s e
| e
sea | w e e d

It uses __shamphew__ !

325

On the Farm
Help the farmer find his tractor. Follow only the compound words. A **compound word** is made by joining two words.

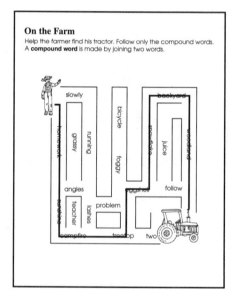

326

Word Circus
Read the compound words below. Then circle the two small words that make up each compound. Write the two small words on the lines. The first one is done for you.

1. broom stick — broom — stick
2. tablecloth — table — cloth
3. sunshine — sun — shine
4. dishpan — dish — pan
5. classroom — class — room
6. bookcase — book — case
7. treetop — tree — top
8. playground — play — ground
9. highway — high — way
10. suntan — sun — tan
11. campfire — camp — fire
12. birthday — birth — day
13. bedroom — bed — room
14. newspaper — news — paper

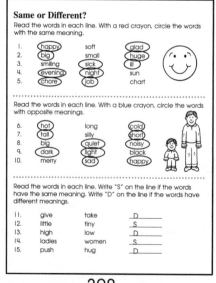

327

Same or Different?
Read the words in each line. With a red crayon, circle the words with the same meaning.

1. (happy)   soft   (glad)
2. (big)   small   (huge)
3. smiling   (sick)   (ill)
4. (evening)   (night)   sun
5. (chore)   (job)   chart

Read the words in each line. With a blue crayon, circle the words with opposite meanings.

6. (hot)   long   (cold)
7. (tall)   silly   (short)
8. big   (quiet)   (noisy)
9. (dark)   (light)   black
10. merry   (sad)   (happy)

Read the words in each line. Write "S" on the line if the words have the same meaning. Write "D" on the line if the words have different meanings.

11. give   take   D
12. little   tiny   S
13. high   low   D
14. ladies   women   S
15. push   hug   D

328

Opposite Fun
Write the opposite for each word.

1. hot — cold
2. open — closed
3. in — out
4. up — down
5. over — under
6. big — small
7. on — off
8. good — bad
9. sad — happy
10. thick — thin

329

Oops!

Why was the broom late?

To find out, write the past tense for each verb listed. Use the Word Box to help you. The answer to the riddle will be spelled in the **bold** boxes going down.

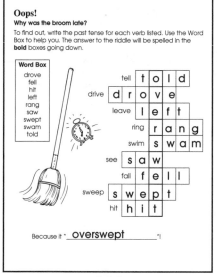

Word Box
drove
fell
hit
left
rang
saw
swept
swam
told

tell | t o l d
drive | d r o v e
leave | l e f t
ring | r a n g
swim | s w a m
see | s a w
fall | f e l l
sweep | s w e p t
hit | h i t

Because it "**overswept**"!

330

Just Do It!

Unscramble the verbs (action words). Use the Word Box to help you. Then circle the words in the puzzle. They may go across, down, or diagonally.

glauh __laugh__   thosu __shout__
danst __stand__   klaw __walk__
nikrd __drink__   kolo __look__
slenti __listen__   blidu __build__

Word Box
build
stand
look
walk
laugh
shout
drink
listen

D F Z L A U G H
B R P K W T S L
S U I Q F H T I
K H I N V L O S
T V O K U D N T
K V L U D K D N
W A L K T

331

Word Detective

Look carefully at the picture on this page. In the first column, list ten nouns you see in the picture. In the second column, write the first adjective you think of that describes the noun. The first one is done for you. When you are finished, color the picture.

	NOUNS	ADJECTIVES
1.	lion	strong
2.		
3.		
4.	Answers will vary.	
5.		
6.		
7.		
8.		
9.		
10.		

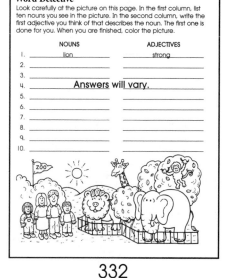

332

Crazy About Contractions

Pairs of words combined into one with an apostrophe are called contractions. Read the lists of words below. Combine them to make contractions and complete the puzzle. Example: did not = didn't.

Across
2. they had
4. would not
5. you are
6. he is
7. I have
8. should have
9. could not

Down
1. will not
3. do not
4. we are
5. you have
6. have not
7. it is

w o n '
t h e y ' d
o
w o u l d n ' t
t
y o u ' r e
o
u '
h e ' s
I ' v e
t
s h o u l d ' v e
c o u l d n ' t

333

Straight "A"s

All of the words below have the long **a** sound, but it is spelled differently each time. Write the words from the Word Box in the spaces. Then circle the words in the puzzle. They may go across, down, or backward.

w e i g h   p a p e r   g r e a t

g r a y   m a i d   m a y b e

g a m e   o b e y

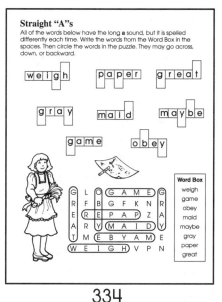

Word Box
weigh
game
obey
maid
maybe
gray
paper
great

G L O G A M E G
F B G F K N R
R E P A P Z A
A R Y M A I D Y
T M E B Y A M E
W E I G H V P N

334

Road to Reading

Read the word at the top of each road. Change just one letter to make a new word beneath it. You should end up with the word at the bottom after all of the changes. Use the words on the sign to help you.

coat	colt
camp	rule
role	lamp
came	mule
cold	

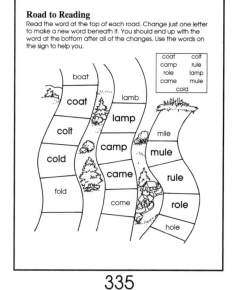

boat → coat → colt → cold → fold

lamb → lamp → camp → came → come

mile → mule → rule → role → hole

335

Homonym Hunt

Homonyms are words that sound alike but are spelled and used differently. Read the list of homonyms below. Use them to answer the clues and complete the puzzle.

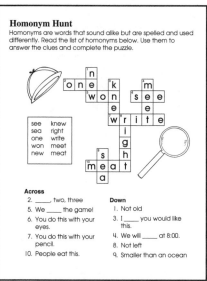

n
o n e   k   m
w o n   s e e
w r i t e
i
g
s   h
m e a t
a

see | knew
sea | right
one | write
won | meet
new | meat

Across
2. _____, two, three
5. We _____ the game!
6. You do this with your eyes.
7. You do this with your pencil.
10. People eat this.

Down
1. Not old
3. I _____ you would like this.
4. We will _____ at 8:00.
8. Not left
9. Smaller than an ocean

336

Color Hunt

Unscramble the color words. Use the Word Box to help you. Then circle the words in the puzzle. They may go across or down.

ergen __green__   clkab __black__
elub __blue__   prelup __purple__
wornb __brown__   lewloy __yellow__
dre __red__   theiw __white__
grenao __orange__   kinp __pink__

Word Box
purple
white
pink
orange
brown
green
blue
black
red
yellow

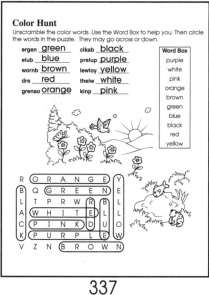

R O R A N G E Y
B Q G R E E N E
L T P R W R L
A W H I T E L L
C P I N K U O
K P U R P L E W
V Z N B R O W N

337

Raindrops Are Falling

Write the missing numbers on each raindrop path.

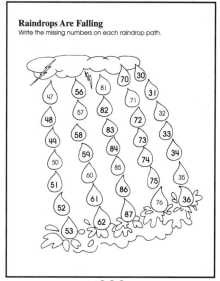

338

This or That

Use the code to find the value of each pair of opposite words. Circle the word in each pair with the higher value.

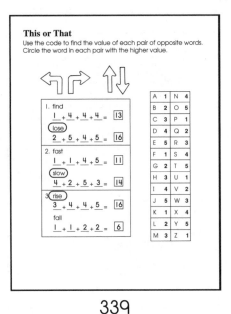

A	1	N	4
B	2	O	5
C	3	P	1
D	4	Q	2
E	5	R	3
F	1	S	4
G	2	T	5
H	3	U	1
I	4	V	2
J	5	W	3
K	1	X	4
L	2	Y	5
M	3	Z	1

1. find
$4 + 4 + 4 + 4 = $ 13
(lose)
$2 + 5 + 4 + 5 = $ 16

2. fast
$1 + 1 + 4 + 5 = $ 11
(slow)
$4 + 2 + 5 + 3 = $ 14

3. (rise)
$3 + 4 + 4 + 5 = $ 16
fall
$1 + 1 + 2 + 2 = $ 6

To the Top!

Use mental math to find the sums, working from left to right. Move the hikers up the mountain by shading a footprint for each answer. Circle the hiker who reaches the top first.

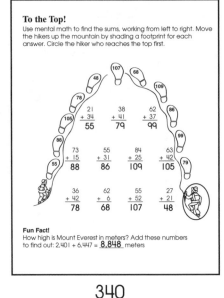

21 + 34 55	38 + 41 79	62 + 37 99	
73 + 15 88	55 + 31 86	84 + 25 109	63 + 42 105
36 + 42 78	62 + 6 68	55 + 52 107	27 + 21 48

Fun Fact!
How high is Mount Everest in meters? Add these numbers to find out: 2,401 + 6,447 = __8,848__ meters

---

Tic-Tac-Toe Addition

Solve each problem below. Then find the answer on the board and mark the box **X** or **O** as shown. Work the problems in order. Who will win, **X** or **O**? The first to get three in a row is the winner!

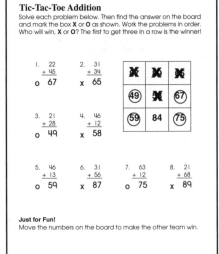

1. 22
+ 45
o 67

2. 31
+ 34
x 65

3. 21
+ 28
o 49

4. 46
+ 12
x 58

5. 46
+ 13
o 59

6. 31
+ 56
x 87

7. 63
+ 12
o 75

8. 21
+ 68
x 89

Just for Fun!
Move the numbers on the board to make the other team win.

---

339   340   341

Family Feud

Who will win? Find each sum working from left to right. Shade the answer in the grid on the right. The first family to completely cover their card is the winner!

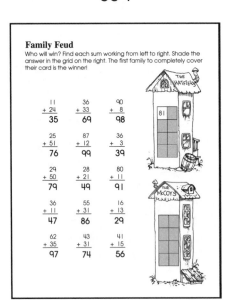

11 + 24 35	36 + 33 69	90 + 8 98
25 + 51 76	87 + 12 99	36 + 3 39
29 + 50 79	28 + 21 49	80 + 11 91
36 + 11 47	55 + 31 86	16 + 13 29
62 + 35 97	43 + 31 74	41 + 15 56

Buy Bean Bag Babies

Use the prices of the toy animals to write and solve each problem.

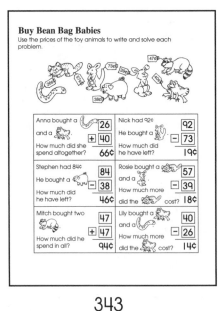

Anna bought a and a
How much did she spend altogether?
26 + 40 = 66¢

Nick had 92¢
He bought a
How much did he have left?
92 − 73 = 19¢

Stephen had 84¢
He bought a
How much did he have left?
84 − 38 = 46¢

Rosie bought a and a
How much more did the cost?
57 − 39 = 18¢

Mitch bought two
How much did he spend in all?
47 + 47 = 94¢

Lily bought a and a
How much more did the cost?
40 − 26 = 14¢

Down the Slope!

Find the differences. The number in the snowflakes will answer the question.

Mount McKinley is the tallest mountain in North America. How high is it?

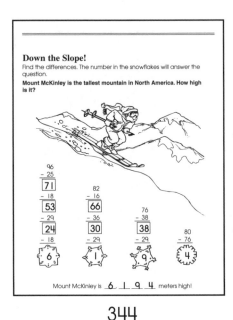

96
− 25
71

− 18
53

82
− 16
66

− 29
24

− 36
30

76
− 38
38

− 29
9

80
− 76
4

6   1   9   4

Mount McKinley is __6 1 9 4__ meters high!

---

342   343   344

The Great Race

Use mental math to find the differences. Move the joggers along the path by shading in each answer you find. Circle the jogger that finishes the race first.

1. 641
− 130
511

2. 830
− 260
570

3. 324
− 183
141

4. 281
− 190
91

5. 630
− 327
303

6. 756
− 424
332

7. 945
− 739
206

8. 555
− 273
282

9. 684
− 291
393

10. 978
− 725
253

11. 374
− 281
93

12. 851
− 171
680

Which Vegetable Is It?

Use the clues to answer each riddle.

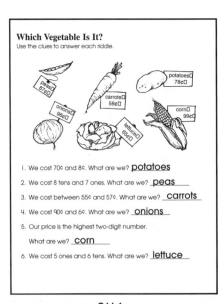

peas 87¢   potatoes 78¢   carrots 56¢   onions 96¢   corn 99¢   lettuce 65¢

1. We cost 70¢ and 8¢. What are we? __potatoes__

2. We cost 8 tens and 7 ones. What are we? __peas__

3. We cost between 55¢ and 57¢. What are we? __carrots__

4. We cost 90¢ and 6¢. What are we? __onions__

5. Our price is the highest two-digit number.
What are we? __corn__

6. We cost 5 ones and 6 tens. What are we? __lettuce__

Batter Up!

Rename each number by regrouping. Take from the tens place and give to the ones place as shown.

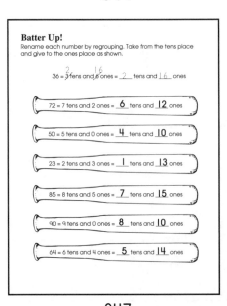

36 = 3 tens and 6 ones = __2__ tens and __16__ ones

72 = 7 tens and 2 ones = __6__ tens and __12__ ones

50 = 5 tens and 0 ones = __4__ tens and __10__ ones

23 = 2 tens and 3 ones = __1__ tens and __13__ ones

85 = 8 tens and 5 ones = __7__ tens and __15__ ones

90 = 9 tens and 0 ones = __8__ tens and __10__ ones

64 = 6 tens and 4 ones = __5__ tens and __14__ ones

---

345   346   347

Go Bananas!

Write <, >, or = on each tree trunk. Circle the banana with the greater number.

| < less than | > greater than | = equal to |

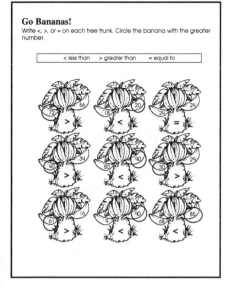

Add It Up

Find the sums. Write >, <, or = in the circles to compare the sums.

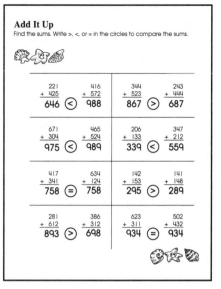

221 + 425 **646**	416 + 572 **988**	344 + 523 **867**	243 + 444 **687**
646 (<) 988		867 (>) 687	
671 + 304 **975**	465 + 524 **989**	206 + 133 **339**	347 + 212 **559**
975 (<) 989		339 (<) 559	
417 + 341 **758**	634 + 124 **758**	142 + 153 **295**	141 + 148 **289**
758 (=) 758		295 (>) 289	
281 + 612 **893**	386 + 312 **698**	623 + 311 **934**	502 + 432 **934**
893 (>) 698		934 (=) 934	

348

349

What Time Is It?

Look at each clock. Then write the time shown on the line. The first one is done for you.

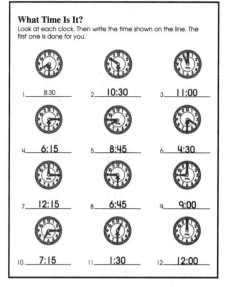

1. 8:30 2. 10:30 3. 11:00
4. 6:15 5. 8:45 6. 4:30
7. 12:15 8. 6:45 9. 9:00
10. 7:15 11. 1:30 12. 12:00

350

A Day at Camp

Write the time at which each camper finished his or her activity.

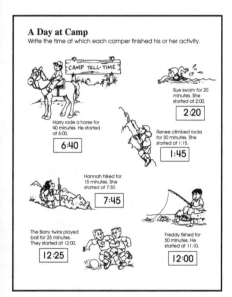

Sue swam for 20 minutes. She started at 2:00. **2:20**

Harry rode a horse for 40 minutes. He started at 6:00. **6:40**

Renee climbed rocks for 30 minutes. She started at 1:15. **1:45**

Hannah hiked for 15 minutes. She started at 7:30. **7:45**

The Barry twins played ball for 25 minutes. They started at 12:00. **12:25**

Freddy fished for 50 minutes. He started at 11:10. **12:00**

351

You Can Bank on It!

Read the words on the coins. To fill the piggy bank, find the words and circle them. They may go across, diagonally, or down.

money bank, quarter, dollar savings, earn count, dime, nickel penny, coins cents

352

The Souvenir Shop

Count the coins to find the cost of each souvenir. Write the price on the tag.

Washington Monument **62¢**

Liberty Bell **80¢**

St. Louis Gateway Arch **85¢**

Yellowstone Park **97¢**

Niagara Falls **78¢**

Seattle Space Needle **63¢**

353

Shopping for Souvenirs

Color the coins needed to make exact change for each item.

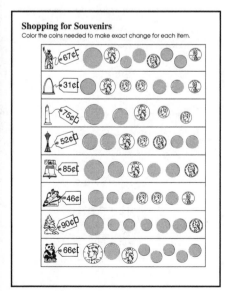

67¢
31¢
75¢
52¢
85¢
46¢
90¢
66¢

354

Under the Sea

Count the money. Write the number of hundreds (h), tens (t), and ones (o). Write the three-digit number, using the dollar sign ($) and decimal point (.).

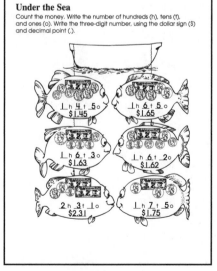

1 h 4 t 5 o $1.45

1 h 6 t 5 o $1.65

1 h 6 t 3 o $1.63

1 h 6 t 2 o $1.62

2 h 3 t 1 o $2.31

1 h 7 t 5 o $1.75

355

A Day at the Fair

Read each word problem carefully. Then add or subtract to find the answer. Show your work.

1. A clown gave away 50 balloons on Tuesday. He gave away 25 balloons on Wednesday. How many balloons did he give away all together?

   Answer: **75**

2. Ellen and David are playing a game. They have to throw a ball into a net. Ellen scores 52 points. David scores 37 points. How many points did Ellen and David score together?

   Answer: **89**

3. Javier and Tim bought toys at the fair. Javier paid $1.75 for a toy car. Tim paid $1.10 for a ball. How much money did they spend all together?

   Answer: **$2.85**

4. On Monday morning there were 85 tickets available for the fair. Then the ticket agent sold 34 of them. How many tickets are left?

   Answer: **51**

5. Joan brought $4.50 to the fair. She spent $1.25. How much money does she have left?

   Answer: **$3.25**

356

Daily Learning Drills Grade 2

Space Invasion

Measure the length of the path from each spaceship to Earth. Write the length in centimeters (cm) on each line.

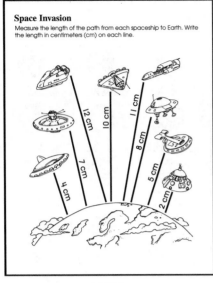

12 cm
10 cm
11 cm
8 cm
7 cm
5 cm
4 cm
2 cm

357

Shapes Are Everywhere

Draw a line to connect each shape with its name. Then circle the words in the puzzle. They may go across, down, or backward.

sphere
cone
cube
pyramid
diamond
crescent

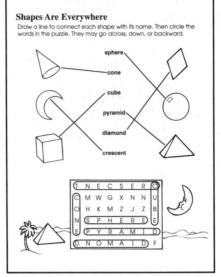

T	N	E	C	S	E	R	C
C	M	W	G	X	N	N	U
O	H	K	M	Z	J	Z	B
N	S	P	H	E	R	E	E
E	P	Y	R	A	M	I	D
D	N	O	M	A	I	D	F

358

Shape Puzzles

Use the code to find the names of the shapes.

a = 1	n = 14
b = 2	o = 15
c = 3	p = 16
d = 4	q = 17
e = 5	r = 18
f = 6	s = 19
g = 7	t = 20
h = 8	u = 21
i = 9	v = 22
j = 10	w = 23
k = 11	x = 24
l = 12	y = 25
m = 13	z = 26

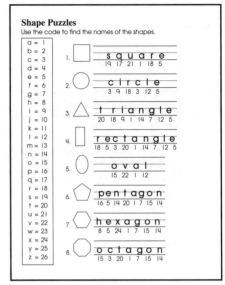

1. s q u a r e
   19 17 21 1 18 5

2. c i r c l e
   3 9 18 3 12 5

3. t r i a n g l e
   20 18 9 1 14 7 12 5

4. r e c t a n g l e
   18 5 3 20 1 14 7 12 5

5. o v a l
   15 22 1 12

6. p e n t a g o n
   16 5 14 20 1 7 15 14

7. h e x a g o n
   8 5 24 1 7 15 14

8. o c t a g o n
   15 3 20 1 7 15 14

359

Fun With Fractions

Each object is divided into equal parts. Write a fraction that tells what part of each object is shaded.

Example: = 2/3

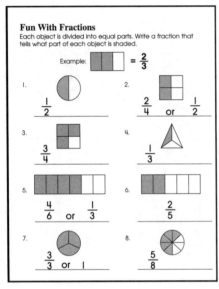

1. 1/2

2. 2/4 or 1/2

3. 3/4

4. 1/3

5. 4/6 or 1/3

6. 2/5

7. 3/3 or 1

8. 5/8

360

The Lost Treasure

Find the lost treasures. Write the letter and then the number as shown.

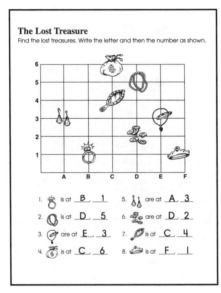

1. is at B 1   5. are at A 3
2. is at D 5   6. are at D 2
3. are at E 3   7. is at C 4
4. is at C 6   8. is at F 1

361

Roller Skates

Write a multiplication problem to match each picture. Then find the product.

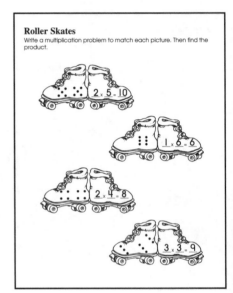

2 x 5 = 10

1 x 6 = 6

2 x 4 = 8

3 x 3 = 9

362

Shape Up!

Multiply to find the answers. Circle the shapes with even products.

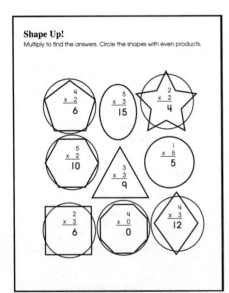

4 x 2 = 6
5 x 3 = 15
x 2 / 4
5 x 2 = 10
3 x 3 = 9
1 x 5 = 5
2 x 3 = 6
4 x 0 = 0
4 x 3 = 12

363

The Race Is On!

Use mental math to find each product. Move the race cars along the track by coloring a box for each answer. Circle the car that reaches the finish line first. Be sure to complete the problems in order!

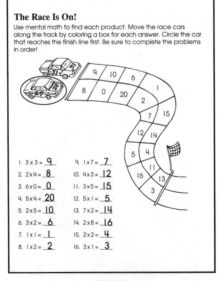

1. 3 x 3 = 9
2. 2 x 4 = 8
3. 6 x 0 = 0
4. 5 x 4 = 20
5. 2 x 5 = 10
6. 3 x 2 = 6
7. 1 x 1 = 1
8. 1 x 2 = 2
9. 1 x 7 = 7
10. 4 x 3 = 12
11. 3 x 5 = 15
12. 5 x 1 = 5
13. 7 x 2 = 14
14. 2 x 8 = 16
15. 2 x 2 = 4
16. 3 x 1 = 3

364

My Body

Draw a line from each word to where it is on the body. Then circle the words in the puzzle. They may go across or down.

head   neck
chest   elbow
waist   knee
ankle   heel

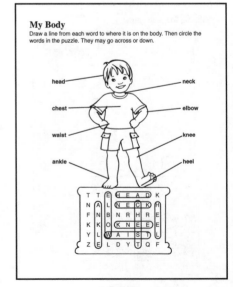

T	T	E	H	E	A	D	K
N	A	L	N	E	C	K	A
F	N	B	N	R	H	R	E
K	K	O	K	N	E	E	E
Y	E	I	W	A	I	S	U
Z	E	L	D	Y	T	Q	F

365

A Delicious Dinner

Pretend that you get to plan a healthful dinner for your family. Write the menu, choosing items from the lists.

Meats	Vegetables	Side Dishes
barbecue chicken	steamed broccoli	brown rice
hamburgers	creamed corn	mashed potatoes
grilled pork chops	buttered peas	baked beans

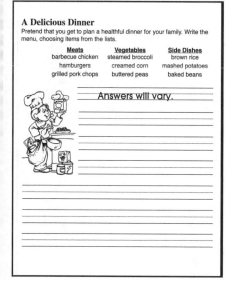

Answers will vary.

366

Fruity Fun

Find and circle eight fruits in the puzzle. Write them below. Use the pictures to help you.

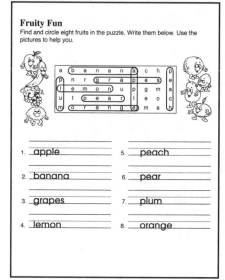

1. apple
2. banana
3. grapes
4. lemon
5. peach
6. pear
7. plum
8. orange

367

Frog In Winter (continued)

Use facts from the story to fill in the puzzle. The Word Box will help you.

Word Box
warm
move
spring
frog
breathes
winter
leaves

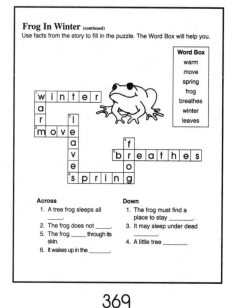

Across
1. A tree frog sleeps all ____.
2. The frog does not ____.
5. The frog ____ through its skin.
6. It wakes up in the ____.

Down
1. The frog must find a place to stay ____.
3. It may sleep under dead ____.
4. A little tree ____.

369

We're Different

Find and circle the animal names in the puzzle. They may go across, diagonally, or down. Then group the animals.

frog
flounder
wasp
catfish
salamander
dragonfly
toad
beetle
cod
butterfly
perch
trout

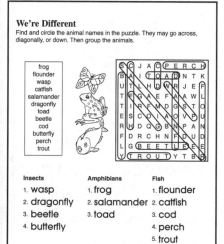

Insects
1. wasp
2. dragonfly
3. beetle
4. butterfly

Amphibians
1. frog
2. salamander
3. toad

Fish
1. flounder
2. catfish
3. cod
4. perch
5. trout

370

What Am I?

Use the animals shown to answer the riddles below.

I can be found in Africa. I have one to four babies at a time. I am a mammal with a mane. What am I? **lion**	I can be found in the Americas. I lay eggs. I am a reptile with stripes. What am I? **iguana**
I can be found in South America. I lay eggs. I am a bird with a large, colorful beak. What am I? **toucan**	I can be found in the United States. I lay 20–60 eggs at a time. I am a reptile with a long body. What am I? **alligator**

371

The Great Rain Forest

The picture shows the rain forest and some of the animals that live there. Find the eight words in the puzzle. They may go across, down, diagonally, or backward.

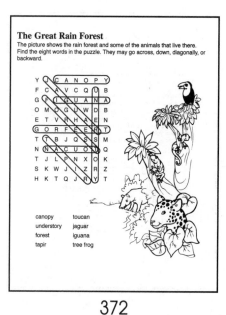

canopy
understory
forest
tapir
toucan
jaguar
iguana
tree frog

372

Compare and Contrast

Look at the pictures. Write what is different and what is the same about the camels.

Dromedary camel   **Bactrian camel**

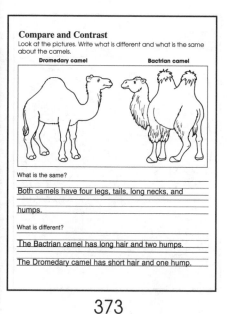

What is the same?

Both camels have four legs, tails, long necks, and humps.

What is different?

The Bactrian camel has long hair and two humps.

The Dromedary camel has short hair and one hump.

373

Giving Trees

Read the words below. These things all come from trees! Circle these words in the puzzle. They may go across or down.

syrup   lumber   medicine
fruit   furniture   shelter
nuts   paper   rubber

374

A Funny Baby

Connect the dots.

375

Seasonal Fun
Complete the sentences in your best handwriting.

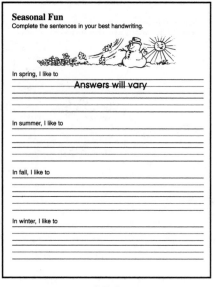

In spring, I like to
___Answers will vary___
_____
_____

In summer, I like to
_____
_____
_____

In fall, I like to
_____
_____
_____

In winter, I like to
_____
_____
_____

376

Wacky Weather
Unscramble the weather words. Use the Word Box to help you. Then circle the words in the puzzle. They may be going across, down, or backward.

nynus __sunny__   ducloy __cloudy__
mostry __stormy__   inayr __rainy__
gogyf __foggy__   dinyw __windy__
wosny __snowy__   zeyerb __breezy__

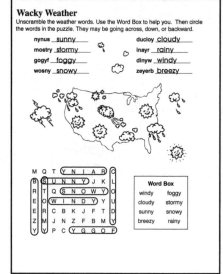

M Q T Y N I A R C
B S U N N Y J K L
R T Q S N O W Y O
E O W I N D Y Y U
E R C B K J F T D
Z M J N Z F B M V
Y P C Y G G O F

Word Box
windy   foggy
cloudy   stormy
sunny   snowy
breezy   rainy

377

Ounces or Pounds
Ounces are used to measure the weight of very light objects. Pounds are used to measure the weight of heavy objects. Look at each picture. Then decide if you would use ounces or pounds to measure the weight of each object. Circle your answer.

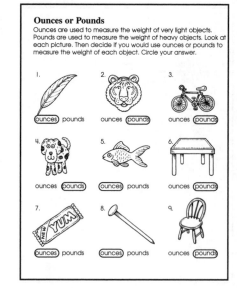

1. (ounces) pounds   2. ounces (pounds)   3. ounces (pounds)

4. ounces (pounds)   5. (ounces) pounds   6. ounces (pounds)

7. (ounces) pounds   8. (ounces) pounds   9. ounces (pounds)

378

Dew
What is dew? Read the story below. Then find and circle the **bold** words in the puzzle. They may go across, diagonally, or down.

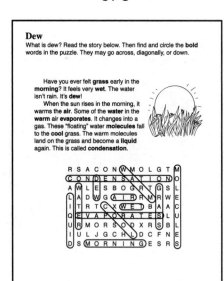

Have you ever felt **grass** early in the **morning**? It feels very **wet**. The water isn't rain. It's **dew**!

When the sun rises in the morning, it warms the **air**. Some of the **water** in the **warm** air **evaporates**. It changes into a gas. These "floating" water **molecules** fall to the **cool** grass. The warm molecules land on the grass and become a **liquid** again. This is called **condensation**.

R S A C O N W M O L G T M
C O N D E N S A T I O N O
A W L E S B O G R T G S L
L A D W G A I R M R W E C
I T R T C X W E B A A L U
Q E V A P O R A T E S L L
U R M O R S O D X R S B L
I U L J G C H L D C F N E
D S M O R N I N G E S R S

379

Gravity: The Force Is With You
Before you drop the pairs of objects, predict which of each pair will reach the ground first. Drop the two objects at the same time from a height of 5 feet (1.5 m). Record the result after each drop.

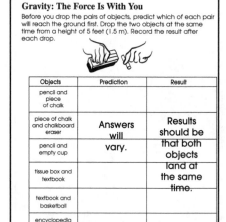

Objects	Prediction	Result
pencil and piece of chalk		
piece of chalk and chalkboard eraser	Answers will vary.	Results should be that both objects land at the same time.
pencil and empty cup		
tissue box and textbook		
textbook and basketball		
encyclopedia and thick rubberband		

380

Super Solar System
The names of the planets are listed below in their order from the sun. Rewrite the names in alphabetical order.

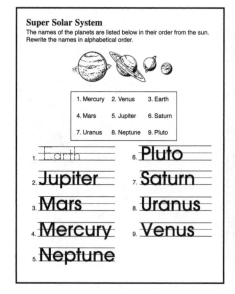

1. Mercury	2. Venus	3. Earth
4. Mars	5. Jupiter	6. Saturn
7. Uranus	8. Neptune	9. Pluto

1. Earth   6. Pluto
2. Jupiter   7. Saturn
3. Mars   8. Uranus
4. Mercury   9. Venus
5. Neptune

381

Space Case
Unscramble the planet names. Then circle the names of the planets in the puzzle. They may go across, down, diagonally, or backward.

IPtuo __Pluto__   tahEr __Earth__
rnUasu __Uranus__   arSutn __Saturn__
esnVu __Venus__   uipJtre __Jupiter__
euMrrcy __Mercury__   asrM __Mars__
uentNpe __Neptune__

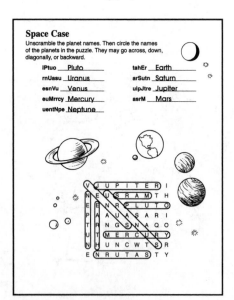

V J U P I T E R I
N E U S R A M T H
E E N R P L U T O
P A A U A S A R I
T R N G S N A Q O
U I M E R C U R Y
N H U N C W T S R
E N R U T A S T Y

382

Happy Holidays
Holidays are fun, special days. Write about three of your favorite holidays. Write why you like each one.

1. I like _____

because _____
___Answers will vary.___

2. I like _____

because _____
_____

3. I like _____

because _____
_____

383

One Big Family
Draw a line from each family name to its matching picture. Then circle the names in the puzzle. They may go across or down.

mother   father   grandpa   grandma
sister   brother baby   puppy

G L S I S T E R K
R Y T B P N X F
A G R A N D P A
N Q L B H B G T
D N T Y Z M Y
M P U P P Y G E
A N M O T H E R
B R O T H E R X

384

You're Invited
Fill in the missing information on the party invitation.

Answers will vary.

Let's celebrate _____'s birthday!

Please join us on _____
(day)

_____
(month, date, year)

Please be here at _____ o'clock.

R.S.V.P. _____, See you soon!
(phone number)

385

Story Puzzle
Look carefully at the pictures below. They tell a story. Then read the sentences. Each sentence tells about one picture. Put the sentences in order by writing the correct picture number on each line. Then color the pictures.

6 ____ José falls asleep after a busy day.
4 ____ José opens his birthday presents.
2 ____ José's parents get ready for his birthday party.
5 ____ José plays with his toys after the party.
1 ____ José wakes up on his birthday.
3 ____ José sees all his friends at his party.

386

Fabulous Friends
Friends are the greatest! The words below describe a good friend. Circle them in the puzzle. They may go across, down, diagonally, or backward.

smart   funny   gentle   nice

helpful   honest   polite   kind

387

Best Friends (continued)
Write two sentences to describe Lilly and two to describe Meg. In the center area, write two sentences that describe both girls.

L I L L Y

1. Lilly played soccer,
Lilly read books, or
2. Lilly took karate class.

1. Lilly and Meg planted seeds
Lilly and Meg jumped rope, or
2. Lilly and Meg painted pictures.

M E G

1. Meg liked the monkey bars,
Meg counted money, or
2. Meg took piano lessons.

With which girl do you have more in common? _____

What do you have in common with her? _____

Answers will vary

389

Graphing Fun
What are friends as good as? Read the graph. Find out which letter each number in the coded message stands for.

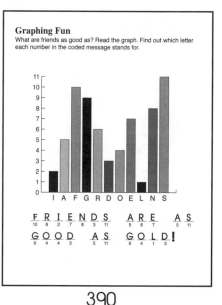

I A F G R D O E L N S

F R I E N D S   A R E   A S
10 6 2 7 8 3 11   5 6 7   5 11

G O O D   A S   G O L D !
9 4 4 3   5 11   9 4 1 3

390

Dandy Directions
Look at the map and key. Name the object found in each direction from the compass rose.

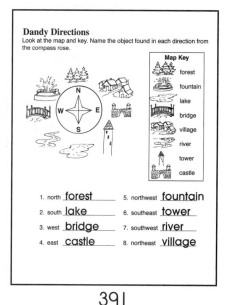

Map Key
- forest
- fountain
- lake
- bridge
- village
- river
- tower
- castle

1. north **forest**   5. northwest **fountain**
2. south **lake**   6. southeast **tower**
3. west **bridge**   7. southwest **river**
4. east **castle**   8. northeast **village**

391

A Busy Day (continued)
Read each sentence. If the sentence tells about something you learned in the story, color the picture by it. Then go back to page 10 and color the same object on that page.

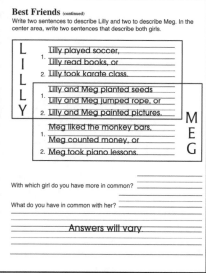

Max and Gina planted trees.

Gina helped pick up trash.

They played on the swings.

They painted the benches.

Max helped clean the park.

They planted flowers.

Max and Gina are brother and sister.

393

A Long Race (continued)
Read each sentence. Color the sled red if it is true. Color the sled blue if it is not true.

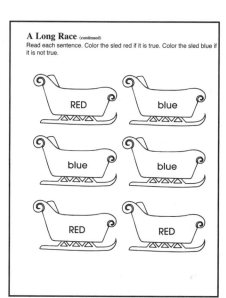

RED   blue

blue   blue

RED   RED

395

Whose House?
Use the pictures of the Native American houses to answer the riddles.

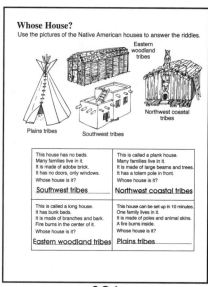

Eastern woodland tribes
Northwest coastal tribes
Plains tribes
Southwest tribes

This house has no beds.
Many families live in it.
It is made of adobe brick.
It has no doors, only windows.
Whose house is it?
Southwest tribes

This is called a plank house.
Many families live in it.
It is made of large beams and trees.
It has a totem pole in front.
Whose house is it?
Northwest coastal tribes

This is called a long house.
It has bunk beds.
It is made of branches and bark.
Fire burns in the center of it.
Whose house is it?
Eastern woodland tribes

This house can be set up in 10 minutes.
One family lives in it.
It is made of poles and animal skins.
A fire burns inside.
Whose house is it?
Plains tribes

396

Picture Clues

Look carefully at each picture. Write who the person is in the picture. Then write clues from the picture that helped you figure it out. Finally, write a sentence describing what is happening in the picture.

1. Person: __Teacher__
   Clues: __Answers will vary__
   Description: _____

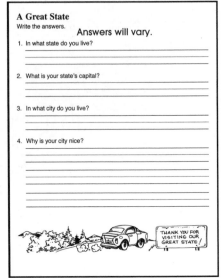

2. Person: __Pilot__
   Clues: _____
   Description: __Answers will vary__

397

A Great State

Write the answers.   Answers will vary.

1. In what state do you live?
   _____
   _____

2. What is your state's capital?
   _____
   _____

3. In what city do you live?
   _____
   _____

4. Why is your city nice?
   _____
   _____
   _____
   _____
   _____
   _____
   _____

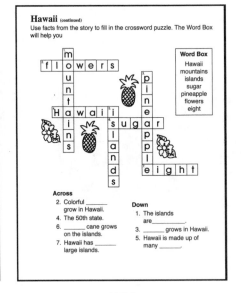

398

A Special Trip

Draw a picture of a special trip you took. Write three sentences about it.

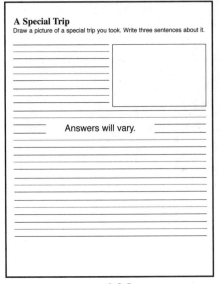

Answers will vary.

399

Buffalo Bill (continued)

Use facts from the story to fill in the puzzle. The Word Box will help you.

Word Box
buffalo
Kansas
Pony
railroad
Cody
Bill

Crossword answers:
K a n s a s (down), b u f f a l o (across), P o n y (down), r a i l r o a d (across), C o d y (across), B i l l (down)

Across
2. These animals were hunted.
4. Men built a _____ through Kansas.
5. William Frederick _____ was Buffalo Bill's real name.

Down
1. The railroad workers in _____ needed food.
2. Cody became known as Buffalo _____ .
3. When he was young, Buffalo Bill worked as a _____ Express rider.

401

Hawaii (continued)

Use facts from the story to fill in the crossword puzzle. The Word Box will help you

Word Box
Hawaii
mountains
islands
sugar
pineapple
flowers
eight

Crossword answers:
f l o w e r s (across), m o u n t a i n s (down), p i n e a p p l e (down), H a w a i i (across), s u g a r (across), i s l a n d s (down), e i g h t (across)

Across
2. Colorful _____ grow in Hawaii.
4. The 50th state.
6. _____ cane grows on the islands.
7. Hawaii has _____ large islands.

Down
1. The islands are_____.
3. _____ grows in Hawaii.
5. Hawaii is made up of many _____.

403